Books by Donald Day

Backwoods to Border
   (*Edited with Mody C. Boatright: a Texas Folklore Society Publication*)

From Hell to Breakfast
   (*Edited with Mody C. Boatright: a Texas Folklore Society Publication*)

Big Country: Texas
   (*American Folkways Series*)

The Autobiography of Will Rogers
   (*Editor*)

Franklin D. Roosevelt's Own Story
   (*Editor*)

How We Elect Our Presidents (by Will Rogers)
   (*Editor*)

Woodrow Wilson's Own Story
   (*Editor*)

Woodrow Wilson's
OWN STORY

Woodrow Wilson's
OWN STORY

SELECTED AND EDITED BY

Donald Day

Little, Brown and Company · *Boston*

History Bk. Club.
Dividend.

Quotations from articles, addresses, public statements and letters
by Woodrow Wilson are used by kind permission of Edith Bolling
Wilson.

Published simultaneously
in Canada by McClelland and Stewart Limited

PRINTED IN THE UNITED STATES OF AMERICA

52–9078
1–53

To
Edith Bolling Wilson

Contents

Prologue   3

PART I
"When a Man Comes to Himself"

I   "The Mind Is Not a Prolix Gut"   7
II   "The Profession I Chose Was Politics"   12
III He Comes to Himself Emotionally   20
IV   He Comes to Himself as a Teacher   32
V   He Comes to Himself as a "Literary Politician"   43
VI   What It Will Take for the Country to Come to Itself   51
VII "When a Man Comes to Himself"   60

PART II
When a University Comes to Itself

VIII "Princeton for the Nation's Service"   71
IX   Education and Democracy   76

PART III
When a "State" Comes to Itself

X   "The Profession I Chose"   101
XI   "We Are Put into This World to Act"   109
XII "The New Freedom"   118

CONTENTS

PART IV

When a Nation Comes to Itself

XIII Full Realization of His Powers 137

XIV The World Comes Apart 165

XV "Too Proud to Fight" 179

XVI "Preparedness Must Be Both Physical and Spiritual" 194

XVII The Difference between a Republican and a Democrat 220

PART V

When a World Comes to Itself

XVIII "The World Must Be Made Safe for Democracy" 235

XIX Making the World Safe for Democracy 249

XX Over the Heads of the Rulers 284

XXI Making Democracy Safe for the World 298

XXII The Machinery for Making the World Safe 313

XXIII The People or the "Rulers" in the United States 325

XXIV Making Democracy Unsafe for the World 349

Epilogue — How the World May Come to Itself 353

Thank You 357

Sources and Acknowledgments 359

Index 361

Woodrow Wilson's
OWN STORY

Prologue

This is not Woodrow Wilson's life story. That has been written in many places and with numerous interpretations. It is rather an attempt to discover the meaning of his life, the significance of his singular and unique career.

"The best autobiographies are confessions," said George Bernard Shaw, "but if a man is a deep writer all his words are confessions."

It is from his own words, in chronological order against the background of their utterance or composition, that Woodrow Wilson's Own Story *comes.*

"Democracy," Wilson said, "is always a-making." It is never finished, never completed. This is its fundamental — its dynamic — difference from totalitarianism. Thus it is an ever-searching, an ever-building process. And its great figures like Jefferson and Lincoln and Wilson need to be studied for pathways — *not for* specific *ways.*

Each figure needs to be approached in a manner that shows the pathways *down which we came, where we are, and where we are headed. For Wilson this can be best done by illustrations.*

One of Wilson's favorite passages in the Bible is from II Corinthians IV.18:

> *While we look not at the things which are seen, but at the things which are not seen: for the things which are seen are temporal; but the things which are not seen are eternal.*

The clue to an understanding of Wilson's thinking is in this passage. The "seen" things are of the materialistic world and are "tem-

poral"; the unseen things are eternal. In Wilson the two terms most often used are "expediency" and "principles."

On the expediency level compromise, shifting of viewpoint, yielding ground, even giving up a struggle, are permissible; on the principle level fundamentals are dealt with and no compromise is permitted.

Thus it was that on the expediency level Wilson accepted the Treaty of Versailles because it was the best that he could get in the circumstances. But before doing so he saw to it that the League of Nations was included in the treaty, which left the way open for correcting the inequities.

In selecting the material for this book the one criterion has been to get, as nearly as possible, "expediency" and "principles" in their proper perspective in dealing with Wilson as an individual, as a student, as a family man, as a teacher, as a college president, as governor of a state, as President of the United States, as a world leader, and, over all, as a source for pathways so that democracy may be made safe for the world.

DONALD DAY

Chappaqua, New York

PART I

"When a Man Comes to Himself"

"The Mind Is Not a Prolix Gut"

Woodrow Wilson was born at Staunton, Virginia, on December 28, 1856. The following November the family moved to Augusta, Georgia, where his father, the Reverend Joseph R. Wilson, had a call to become pastor of the Presbyterian Church. Wilson later wrote:

My earliest recollection is of standing at my father's gateway in Augusta, Georgia, when I was four years old, and hearing someone pass and say that Mr. Lincoln was elected and there was to be war. Catching the intense tones of his excited voice, I remember running in to ask my father what it meant.

The war that followed left an indelible impression on the boy. Augusta became a center of manufacturing for the Confederate government particularly in the production of munitions. His father's church was used as a hospital in which to house the sick and wounded. Hardly a family missed having a member, or several members, killed or maimed. Then the region knew the bitter gall of defeat and Reconstruction — a victor's peace, the marks of which have not yet been erased.

In his own home, however, young Wilson had security and love. Of the training that he got there, he later wrote:

A boy never gets over his boyhood, and never can change those subtle influences which have become a part of him, that were bred in him as a child.

The knowledge you supply to the little fellow in the home is not merely conveyed to him in order that he may be full; the knowledge that is supplied to him in school is not put in him as if he were merely a little vessel to be filled to the top.

My father, who was a very plain-spoken man, used to use a phrase which was rough, but it expressed the meaning exactly. He said, "My son, the mind is not a prolix gut to be stuffed." That is not the object of it. It is not a vessel made to contain something; it is a vessel made to transmute something. The process of digestion is of the essence, and the only part of the food that is of any consequence is the part that is turned into blood and fructifies the whole frame. He used to say to me:

"When you frame a sentence don't do it as if you were loading a shotgun, but as if you were loading a rifle. Don't fire in such a way and with such a load that while you hit the thing you aim at you will hit a lot of things in the neighborhood besides; but shoot with a single bullet and hit that one thing alone."

"What do you mean by that?" he would ask when I fumbled a sentence.

I would explain.

"Then why don't you say so?"

I remember hearing a very wise man say once, a man grown old in the service of a great church, that he had never taught his son religion dogmatically at any time; that he and the boy's mother had agreed that if the atmosphere of that home did not make a Christian of the boy, nothing that they could say would make a Christian of him. They knew that Christianity was catching, and if they did not have it, it would not be communicated. If they did have it, it would penetrate while the boy slept, almost; while he was unconscious of the sweet influences that were about him, while he reckoned nothing of instruction, but merely breathed into his lungs the wholesome air of a Christian home.

Religion is communicable (as other things) only by example. No amount of didactic teaching in a home whose life is not Christian will ever get into the consciousness and life of the children. If you wish your children to be Christians, you must really take the trouble to be Christians yourselves. Those are the only terms upon which the home will work the gracious miracle.

If the children do not get this into their blood atmospherically, they are not going to get it into their blood at all until, it may be, they come to a period of life where the influences of Christian lives outside of the home may profoundly affect them and govern their consciences. We must realize that the first and most intimate and most important organization for the indoctrinating of the next generation is the home, is the family.

The things that impress the young person and the old are convictions and earnestness in action that look like business, and a certain dignity and simplicity that go along with being in earnest.

The only thing that governs any of us is authority. And the reason that it is harder to govern us when we are grown up than when we are young is that we question the authority, and you have to convince our minds of the reasonableness of the authority.

But the young mind yields to the authority that believes in itself. That is the reason that consistency of conduct is indispensable to the maintenance of authority.

You cannot make the young person do what you do not do yourself. You cannot make him believe what you do not believe yourself. You must believe the things you tell the children.

It is conviction, authority, simplicity, the directness of one who is going about his business, and goes about it with genuineness, which governs young people.

The mind must be trained as an instrument for use, not as a storehouse; religion was life, not doctrine; reading was for definite instruction as well as for relaxation and amusement (Wilson's father read to the children, pointing out the meaning of what he had read, then asking questions, before they were allowed to learn to read themselves); education was to train for a rounder, fuller, more complete life, not just for veneering.

By the time Wilson entered Princeton in September, 1875, he

*was ready to "command his own development." He almost imme-
diately began digging into books to find out things for himself,
instead of relying on what the professors said. He later wrote:*

In order to know institutions, you must know men; you must be
able to imagine histories, to appreciate characters radically unlike
your own, to see into the heart of society and assess its notions,
great and small. Your average critic, it must be acknowledged,
would be the worst possible commentator on affairs. He has all the
movements of intelligence without any of its reality. But a man
who sees authors with a Chaucerian insight into them as men, who
knows literature as a realm of vital thought conceived by real men,
of actual motives felt by concrete persons, this is a man whose opinions you may confidently ask, if not on current politics, at any rate
on all that concerns the permanent relations of men in society.

In an essay in the Gentleman's Magazine *Wilson found an article
which contended that John Bright and William E. Gladstone were
the only real orators in the English Parliament because the others
lacked "earnestness and simple conviction." To an orator, "this
atmosphere of sincerity and honest conviction is a mighty power."
But to have conviction, and to have it honestly, meant basing it on
principles and not mere expediency. Yet even that was not enough.
It must be put into operation.*

*So Wilson's search did not stop merely at seeking for principles so
that he, as he had made up his mind at sixteen to be, could become
a statesman in a democracy. He even studied the career of Bismarck
and found that his extraordinary leadership was based on the ability
"to act with boldness and energy combined with foresight and prudence." It was Bismarck's "cool judgment, quick determination, and
masterly execution," together with the "singleness of his aim that
concentrated his powers," which made him a leader of men.*

*In going to such a man for methods, in a totally different type of
governmental organization, Wilson was early showing that objec-
tivity which would later make him advise the United States to look*

to every source, monarchial or otherwise, for methods in order to improve administration in a democracy.

But it was chiefly to men and institutions in English parliamentary procedure and in the development of representative government in the United States that he went — to Green's Short History of the English People; to Edmund Burke, John Bright, William E. Gladstone, Walter Bagehot; to the Federalist Papers, de Tocqueville, Daniel Webster, and many more.

He early made a study of the troubles besetting the growth of democracy in the United States and published an article on his findings in the International Review (on which Henry Cabot Lodge was an editor), in which he concluded that the weakness of both political parties in the country came out of assumption by Congress of most of the powers of the Federal government. Because of this, leadership was divided, hidden and confused. His summary was in eight words: "No leaders, no principles; no principles, no parties."

In his senior year at Princeton, following what he had learned as the criterion for becoming a real orator, Wilson refused to defend protective tariff in a debate because he was opposed to protective tariff and could not argue his case with "conviction and sincerity." In his book on Wilson, William Allen White states that Wilson "refused to take pot luck with his fellows. The feeling of his [debating] society, left unprotected by his withdrawal, he did not understand. If only the gang at Augusta [Georgia] could have larruped the habit of teamwork into him, the 'Happy Warrior' might not have had so many melancholy hours."

Perhaps the basic trouble with the United States today is that in college and otherwise too many people go with the gang, the corporation, the company, the party — or what have you? — instead of the way of right and truth. The Organization seems to have grown more important than right or truth. If the college debate is a farce, then why not the Congressional debate? And so on ad infinitum.

CHAPTER TWO

"The Profession I Chose Was Politics"

❯❯❮❮❮❯❯❮❮❮❯❯❮❮❮❯❯❮❮❮❯❯❮❮❮❯❯❮❮❮❯❯❮❮❮❯❯❮❮❮❯❯❮❮❮❯❯❮❮❮❯❯❮❮❮

In September, 1879, Wilson entered the law school of the University of Virginia to prepare himself for law as a steppingstone to entering politics.

He and Charles Talcott, a fellow student at Princeton, had entered into a compact to communicate with each other on the progress made toward their mutual goal of becoming statesmen. Wilson wrote him:

JULY 7, 1879

I have not yet hit upon any definite plans for the work we promise ourselves, except that we should, I think, lose no opportunity offered us by leisure moments to improve ourselves in *style* and *knowledge*, should leave nothing undone to keep ourselves fresh from the prejudices and free from foolish inaccuracies of those with whom we will constantly be thrown by the necessities of our law practice, in order that when the time comes for us to write and work for a cause we may be able to command a hearing, and may be strong for the struggle which, it is to be hoped, will raise us above the *pettiness* of our profession.

In my daily efforts at composition, and the preparation of my voice for public speaking, I try to keep these things in view. I am thus able to give such exercises more dignity and a thousand times more interest.

Without some such definite aim I could not endure them.

While at the University of Virginia, Wilson published articles on both John Bright and William E. Gladstone which contained items indicating points he had learned from these two statesmen.

MARCH, 1880 ["JOHN BRIGHT," *University of Virginia Magazine*]

If we could study the character of some one man, though that man be our nearest neighbor or our closest friend, we are in constant danger of separating him from his surroundings, holding him responsible for what circumstances have made him, reckoning him debased by frailties not his own, or exalted by greatness which was not born with him but thrust upon him.

Fortunately, however, when we seek to familiarize ourselves with the characters of those men whom it is our habit to call great — such men as have led thought or conceived philosophies or framed policies — we are relieved from embarrassment by one saving circumstance: we find every truly great man identified with some special cause. His purposes are steadfastly set in some definite direction. The career which he works out for himself constitutes so intimate a part of the history of his times that to dissociate him from his surroundings were as impossible as it would be undesirable.

Tolerance is an admirable intellectual gift: but it is of little worth in politics. Politics is a war of *causes;* a joust of principles. Government is too serious a matter to admit of meaningless courtesies.

In this grand contestation of warring principles he who doubts is a laggard and an impotent.

Shall we condemn the statesman because in this intense strife, in which he fights, not for empty formulas or unpractical speculations, but for the triumph of those principles which are in his eyes vitally essential to the welfare of the State in whose service he is spending and being spent — because in the very heat of this battle he does not stop to weigh out careful justice to his foe?

He grants him all the privileges, he extends to him all the courtesies, of war. He acknowledges, it may be, his integrity of character and his uprightness of purpose. But is he to stultify himself by prais-

ing that against which he vehemently protests and strenuously
fights?

Absolute identity with one's cause is the first and great condition
of successful leadership. It is that which makes the statesman's plans
clear-cut and decisive, his purposes unhesitating — it is that which
makes him a leader of States and a maker of history.

I would not for a moment be understood as seeking to lend any
color of justification to that most humiliating and degrading precept,
"Party, right or wrong."

This is the maxim of knaves, or of fools. The idea I would press
upon you is as far separated from this as is the east from the west.
I would urge that entire identity with the cause — with the principle — you espouse wherein alone abide strength and the possibility of success.

Party?

What is it? It is only a convenient — it may be accidental — union
of those who hold certain great leading principles in common. It is
a mere outward sign of agreement.

Is it the *party*, then, to which men of thought owe and pay allegiance? No. It is to the *principles*, of which party is the embodiment.

The man, therefore, who adheres to any party after it has ceased
to avow the principles which to him are dear and in his eyes are
vital; the man who follows the leadings of a party which seems to
him to be going wrong, is acting a lie, and has lost either his wit or
his virtue.

The lesson of John Bright's life is that duty lies wheresoever truth
directs us; that statesmanship consists, not in the cultivation and
practice of the arts of intrigue, nor in the pursuit of all the crooked
intricacies of the paths of party management, but in the lifelong
endeavor to lead first the attention and then the will of the people
to the acceptance of truth in its application to the problems of government; that not the adornments of rhetoric, but an absorbing love
for justice and truth and a consuming passionate devotion to principle are the body and soul of eloquence; that complete identifica-

tion with some worthy cause is the first and great prerequisite of abiding success.

APRIL, 1880 [ON GLADSTONE IN THE *University of Virginia Magazine*]
Perhaps the most vital characteristic of Mr. Gladstone's nature is his keen poetical sensibility.

By poetical sensibility I do not mean an imaginativeness which clothes all the common concerns of life with poetical forms or weds the mind to those things which are picturesque rather than the matters of practical business, to fancies rather than to the interests of ordinary everyday life, to images rather than to fertile purposes.

I mean, rather, breadth of sympathy such as enables its possessor to take in the broader as well as the pettier concerns of life, with unconscious ease of apprehension and unfailing precision of judgment; to identify himself with interests far removed from the walks of his own life; to throw himself, as if by instinct, on that side of every public question which, in the face of present doubts, is in the long run to prove the side of wisdom and of clear-sighted policy; such a sympathy as makes a knowledge of men in him an *intuition* instead of an experience.

Such a faculty is preëminently poetical, raising men above experience, as it seems to do, and enabling them to guide the policy of a government, almost before they can be truly said to have learned to manage the affairs of their own households.

And yet it is quite as evidently an intensely practical faculty. Great statesmen seem to direct and rule by a sort of power to put themselves in the place of the nation over whom they are set, and may thus be said to possess the souls of poets at the same time that they display the coarser sense and the more vulgar sagacity of practical men of business.

Many persons would be inclined to reckon Gladstone's an inconsistent course. I cannot so regard it.

The question of consistency is not a question of absolute fixedness of opinion. One can hardly help pitying one who is incapable of changing his opinions; though, of course, it is scarcely less difficult to withhold one's admiration from that man who has all along adopted the conclusions of truth.

It seems to me that right and truth are the proper standards in this matter.

He who proves his mind so free from the shackles of prejudice and the blinds of bigotry as to be ready at every turn to abandon its former positions of error or mistake for the new positions of truth and right, and who, moreover, follows the leadings of his progressing convictions without thought of turning back, is no less consistent — consistent with the true standards of consistency — than is he who has from the first occupied the advanced posts of inquiry whither the other has just arrived.

If immutability of belief be the criterion of consistency, then let us taunt scientists with fickleness because their investigations have brought them far beyond where they were, even within the short memory of men. Let us sneer at all governments which are not despotisms. Let us laugh at civilization because it did not stop in the darkness of the middle ages.

Few men stand in their old age where they stood in their youth. The untested opinions of the early life do not always or often stand the trial of experience. In public life especially, so varied and varying are the conditions of government, their purposes must be trimmed to possibilities.

In this is found the answer to critics who condemn Wilson because he changed from a Hamiltonian to a Jeffersonian — with experience.

MAY 20, 1880 [TO CHARLES TALCOTT]

Those indistinct plans of which we used to talk grow on me daily, until a sort of calm confidence of great things to be accomplished has come over me which I am puzzled to analyse the nature of. I can't tell whether it is a mere figment of my own inordinate vanity, or a deep-rooted determination which it will be within my power to act up to.

In December, 1880, Wilson had to withdraw from the University of Virginia on account of his health. He went to Wilmington, North

Carolina, where his family now lived, to continue the study by himself. Here he continued to practice "elocution hard and systematically every day." "I intend," he wrote, "to spare no trouble in gaining complete command of my voice in reading and speaking."

By the end of the summer, 1881, he considered himself ready to begin the practice of law.

SEPTEMBER 22, 1881 [TO CHARLES TALCOTT]

After innumerable hesitatings as to a place of settlement, I have at length fixed upon Atlanta, Ga. It, more than almost every other Southern City, offers all the advantages of business activity and enterprise. Its growth has during late years been wonderful. After standing still, under slavery, for half a century, she is now becoming roused to a new work and waking to a new life. There appear to be no limits to the possibilities of her development; and I think that to grow up with a new section is no small advantage to one who seeks to gain position and influence.

OCTOBER 28, 1882 [TO A FORMER PRINCETON CLASSMATE, ROBERT BRIDGES]

I keep myself in good humour by indulging in my favourite recreation, composition. I allow myself my afternoons for writing — and for reading on my old and loved topics, history and political science; devouring the *American Statesman* series and *English Citizen* series — both altogether to my taste.

JANUARY 4, 1883 [TO ROBERT BRIDGES]

I am still following the young lawyer's occupation of *waiting*. One or two minute fees I have earned — nothing more — though I have had business enough of a certain kind, the collection — or the effort to collect — numberless desperate claims.

JANUARY 11, 1883

R. Heath Dabney, a fellow student at the University of Virginia, had gone to Germany to work for his doctorate. Wilson wrote him:

History and Political Science! why they are of all studies my favourites; and to be allowed to fill all my time with them, instead

of, as now, stealing only a chance opportunity or two for hasty
perusal of those things which are most delightful to me, would be
of all privileges the most valued by yours humbly. I have to be
content with a very precarious allowance of such good things.

However I am much interested in even the names of your courses
and am impelled to beg that you will give me some particular account of them; that you will tell me just what line the German students pursue — especially in Political Science. To know what they
think the best methods of study would be of much advantage to me.
I should like, as far as possible, to go along with you in your work.

*While practicing law in Atlanta, Wilson went to watch the Georgia
state senate in action. From the gallery he saw a poorly trained
bunch — country lawyers, merchants, farmers, mere politicians —
densely ignorant of politics and parliamentary procedure, running
the politics of the state. He had envisioned himself as a great leader
on the floor of a parliamentary body, but what a different kind of
body!*

*Someone introduced a resolution to ask the Federal government
for aid. Wilson wrote to Robert Bridges:*

I heard but one speech made in opposition to this begging resolution. It was a sturdy appeal to the self-respect and independence of
the majority in view of what the speaker treated as the unquestioned
ability of the State to support a school system of any dimensions.
No one seemed to regard it worth while answering this speech — and
the resolution was carried. The whole proceeding impressed me as a
shameless declaration of the determination on the part of a well-
to-do community, to enjoy the easy position of a beneficiary of the
national govt. to the fullest possible extent.

*Wilson later wrote, "The profession I chose was politics; the
profession I entered was law." When he realized that the practice
of law would not lead him into the profession that he had chosen,
he quit. That was in line with his principles; otherwise he would
have let expediency rule.*

MAY 11, 1883 [TO R. HEATH DABNEY]

I have about made up my mind to study at Johns Hopkins University the very subjects which you are now studying in Germany under the great masters with unpronounceable names.

In doing this I am following the natural bent of my mind. I can never be happy unless I am enabled to lead an intellectual life.

The practice of law, when conducted for purposes of gain, is antagonistic to the best interests of the intellectual life. The philosophical *study* of the law — which must be a pleasure to any thoughtful man — is a very different matter from its scheming and haggling practice.

You know my passion for original work, you know my love for composition, my keen desire to become a master of philosophical discourse, to become capable and apt in instructing as great a number of persons as possible.

What better can I be, therefore, than a professor, a lecturer upon subjects whose study most delights me? Therefore it is that I have prayed to be made a fellow of Johns Hopkins; and therefore it is that I am determined, if I fail of that appointment (as I probably shall, since it is not won but given) to go next winter anyhow to Baltimore to attend the University lectures and bury myself for a season in the grand libraries of that beautiful city.

CHAPTER THREE

He Comes to Himself Emotionally

>>>((((->>>((((->>>((((->>>((((->>>((((->>>((((->>>((((->>>((((->>>((((->>>((((->>>((((->>>(((

Wilson had come to himself spiritually when he joined the church; intellectually at Princeton when he began to use his mind as an "instrument" to try to ferret out from books and men and institutions the secrets that would guide him toward his selected goal; now he was to come to himself emotionally in the love for a woman that would give him, as a man, the ballast that his mother had given him as a child. To her for many years he would write his innermost thoughts.

OCTOBER 11, 1883 [TO ELLEN AXSON]

The first time I saw your face to note it was in church one morning during the first of my last spring's visits to Rome [*Georgia*] in April, wasn't it? You wore a heavy crepe veil, and I remember thinking "what a bright, pretty face; what splendid, mischievous, laughing eyes! I'll lay a wager that this demure little lady has lots of life and fun in her!"

When I learned that this was Miss "Ellie Lou" Axson, of whom I had heard so often, quite a flood of light was let in on my understanding and I was conscious of having formed a small resolution. I took an early opportunity of calling on the Rev. Mr. Axson. That dear gentleman received me with unsuspecting cordiality and sat down to entertain me under the impression that I had come to see only him.

I *had* gone to see him, but I had not gone to see him *alone.* I had not forgotten that face, and I wanted much to see it again: so I asked rather pointedly after his daughter's health, and he, in some apparent surprise, summoned you to the parlour.

Do you remember? and do you remember the topic of conversation? how your father made me "tackle" that question that was much too big for me, "Why have night congregations grown so small?"

OCTOBER 16, 1883 [TO ELLEN AXSON, AFTER GOING TO JOHNS HOPKINS]

When I got within range of these professors here I found that they wanted to set everybody under their authority to working on what they called "institutional history," to digging, that is, into the dusty records of old settlements and colonial cities, to rehabilitating in authentic form the stories, now almost mythical, of the struggles, the ups and downs, of the first colonists here, there and everywhere on this then interesting continent — and other rummaging work of a like dry kind, which seemed very tiresome in comparison with the grand excursions amongst imperial policies which I had planned for myself.

After tea this evening I went to see Dr. Adams, my chief, and made a clean breast of it: told him that I had a hobby which I had been riding for some years with great entertainment and from which I was loath to dismount. He received my confidences with sympathy, readily freed me from his "institutional" work, and bade me go on with my "constitutional" studies, promising me all the aid and encouragement he could give me, and saying that the work I proposed was just such as he wanted to see done!

Do you wonder that I feel elated and encouraged?

OCTOBER 18, 1883 [TO ELLEN AXSON, AFTER THEIR ENGAGEMENT]

I am proud and wilful beyond all measure and I used to think, like other young men I suppose, that I should never pay any but entirely voluntary homage to any woman.

What an absurd price of intellect. I thought it might be possible to get along with a wife as a leisure-moment companion, dispensing with intellectual sympathy. Not that I did not *want* such sympathy — I knew that there would be a dreary side to life without it — nor because I thought women as a rule incapable of giving it; but principally, I believe, because I thought it would be unreasonable to expect my wife to go with me, even in spirit, into all the so-esteemed dry paths into which my studies were naturally leading me.

I made a discovery that thrilled me; that you knew what sort of wife *I* needed — no man who isn't merely a student, simply a thinking machine, could wish to marry a woman such as John Stuart Mill married and doted on, who expels sentiment from life, knows as much as her husband of the matters of his special study, and furnishes him with opinions, ministering not to his love but to his logical faculty. But, on the other hand, a man with any of the keen sensibilities of the student must be miserable if he have a study into which his wife cannot come as a close companion.

OCTOBER 30, 1883 [TO ELLEN AXSON]

I want to contribute to our literature what no American has ever contributed, studies in the philosophy of our institutions, not the abstract and occult, *but the practical and suggestive,* philosophy which is at the core of our governmental methods; their use, their meaning, "the spirit that makes them workable." I want to divest them of the theory that obscures them and present their weakness and their strength without disguise, and with such skill and such plenitude of proof that it shall be seen that I have succeeded and that I have added something to the resources of knowledge upon which statecraft must depend.

My ambition could not be fulfilled at the bar; the studies for which I was best fitted were not legitimate in a law office, and I was compelled in very justice to myself to seek some profession in which they would be legitimate. A professorship was the only feasible place for me, the only place that would afford leisure for reading and for original work, the only strictly literary berth with an income attached.

True, professors could not participate actively in public affairs; but the occupancy of office had never been an essential part of my political programme. Indeed, I knew very well that a man without independent fortune must in any event content himself with becoming an *outside* force in politics, and I was well enough satisfied with the prospect of having whatever influence I might be able to exercise make itself felt through literary and non-partisan agencies.

A man must know the times into which he has been born; and this I did *not* know when I left college and chose my profession.

It is plain to see why lawyers used to be the only politicians. In a new country, in communities where every man had his bread to earn, they were the only men (except the minister and the physician) who stopped amidst the general hurry of life to get learning; and they were the only men, without exception, who were skilled in those arts of forensic contest that were calculated to fit men for entering the lists at political tilts, or for holding their own in legislative debate. They could hope too, when a turn of parties might have come, or their own popularity might have waned, to return to their places at the bar to find a place still open for them, to find themselves not altogether and hopelessly crowded out; they could even, like Webster and Jeremiah Mason and many others of less genius, make law and state craft live and thrive together, pleading causes in the courts even while holding seats in the Senate or leading parties in the House.

But those times are passing away. A man who has to earn a livelihood cannot nowadays turn aside from his trade for intervals of office-holding and political activity. He is constrained by a minute division of labour to bend all his energies to the one thing that is nearest at hand. Even in the law men are becoming specialists.

Whoever thinks, as I thought, that he can practise law successfully and study history and politics at the same time is woefully mistaken. If he is to make a living at the bar he must be a lawyer *and nothing else*.

The profession I chose was politics; the profession I entered was law. I entered the one because I thought it would lead to the other.

OCTOBER 30, 1883 [TO ELLEN AXSON, ON HIS TEACHERS]

It [*oratory*] does not generally come into the lectures of college professors; but it should. Oratory is not declamation, not swelling tones and an excited delivery, but the art of persuasion, the art of putting things so as to appeal irresistibly to an audience.

And how can a teacher stimulate young men to study, how can he fill them with great ideas and worthy purposes, how can he draw them out of themselves and make them to become forces in the world without oratory? Perfunctory lecturing is of no service in the world. It's a nuisance.

Style is not much studied here; *ideas* are supposed to be everything — their vehicle comparatively nothing. But you and I know that there can be no greater mistake; that, both in its amount and in its length of life, an author's influence depends upon the power and the beauty of his style; upon the flawless perfection of the mirror he holds up to nature; upon his facility in catching and holding, because he pleases, the attention: and style shall be, as under my father's guidance, it has been, one of my chief studies. A writer must be artful as well as strong.

JANUARY 1, 1884 [TO ELLEN AXSON]

I've planned a set of four or five essays on "The Government of the Union" in which it is my purpose to show our constitutional system as it looks in operation. My desire and ambition are to treat the American constitution as Mr. Bagehot has treated the English Constitution.

His book has inspired my whole study of our government. He brings to the work a fresh and original method which has made the British system much more intelligible to ordinary men than it ever was before, and which, if it could be successfully applied to the exposition of our Federal constitution, would result in something like a revelation to those who are still reading the *Federalist* as an authoritative constitutional manual.

An immense literature has already accumulated upon this subject; but I venture to think that the greater part of it is either irrelevant or already antiquated.

An observer who looks at the living reality will wonder at the contrast to the paper description.

He will see in the life much which is not in the books; and he will find in the rough practice many refinements of the literary theory.

JANUARY 8, 1884 [TO ELLEN AXSON]

I have imagined a style clear, bold, fresh, and facile; a style flexible but always strong, capable of light touches or of heavy blows; a style that could be driven at high speed — a brilliant, dashing, coursing speed — or constrained to the slow and stately progress of grave argument, as the case required; a style full of life, of colour and vivacity, of soul and energy, of inexhaustible power — of a thousand qualities of beauty and grace and strength that would make it immortal.

Is it any wonder that I am disgusted with the stiff, dry, mechanical, monotonous sentences in which my meagre thoughts are compelled to masquerade, as in garments which are too mean even for *them!*

APRIL 22, 1884 [TO ELLEN AXSON]

The man who reads everything is like the man who eats everything: he can digest nothing; and the penalty for cramming one's mind with other men's thoughts is to have no thoughts of one's own. Only that which enables one to do his own thinking is of real value: which is my explanation of the fact that there are to be found in history so many great thinkers and great leaders who did little reading of books — if you reckon reading by volumes — but much reading of men and of their own times.

OCTOBER 7, 1884 [TO ELLEN AXSON, ABOUT *Congressional Government*]

I have just finished preparing my *ms.* to be sent to Boston and am about to start out for the express office. Then I shall be free to turn to my University work, until the *ms.* is returned and has to be sent to some other publishing house.

NOVEMBER 2 AND 5, 1884 [TO ELLEN AXSON]

Only my profound trust in an over-ruling Providence will keep me from the deepest despondency if Cleveland should be defeated.

God only knows what will be our political destiny if the Republican machine should triumph again!

Cleveland was elected.

NOVEMBER 8, 1884 [TO ELLEN AXSON]

As for the [*Ph.D.*] degree father advises me not to try for it; and, since his advice coincides with my own coolest judgment in the matter, I have concluded to make no special effort in reading for it.

I am quite sure that I shall profit much more substantially from a line of reading of my own choosing, in the lines of my own original work, than I should from much of the reading necessary in the Ph.D. course — though my *inclinations* will take me through the most important topics of that course.

The difference will be that I will read, *outside* of the proscribed lines, a great deal that will be of infinitely more service to me than the volumes of another sort which I should perfunctorily peruse, to the mortification of my own tastes and desires, were I to goad myself to the tasks heaped upon the degree candidate.

It is probable that I would fetch a bigger price with a Ph.D. label on me than I can fetch without it. It's a choice, apparently, between pecuniary profit and mental advancement.

NOVEMBER 25, 1884 [TO ELLEN AXSON]

I enjoy speaking because it sets my mind — all my faculties — aglow: and I suppose that this very excitement gives my manner an appearance of confidence and self-command which arrests the attention. However that may be, I *feel* a sort of transformation — and it's hard to go to sleep afterwards.

There is absolute joy in facing and conquering a hostile audience or thawing out a cold one.

I talked about *oratory*, its aims and the difficulties surrounding its cultivation in a University, where exact knowledge overcrowds everything else and the art of persuasion is neglected on principle.

Oratory must be full of the spirit of the world; that spirit is excluded from University life.

NOVEMBER 27, 1884 [TO ELLEN AXSON, ON HIS GOING TO BRYN MAWR TO TEACH]

Just before the lecture, Dr. Adams came to me and asked me if I wouldn't come into his office a moment and "meet some persons who were interested in me and in historical work."

I went; and was introduced to Miss Carey Thomas and Dr. Rhoads. Miss Thomas is a daughter of one of the Hopkins trustees, is a graduate (a Ph.D.), I understand, of a German University, and is head, or "dean," of the faculty of Bryn Mawr college, of which Dr. Rhoads, a prominent *"Friend"* of Philadelphia, is a trustee.

NOVEMBER 28, 1884 [TO ELLEN AXSON, ON ACCEPTANCE OF HIS BOOK]

They have actually offered me as good terms as if I were already a well-known writer! The success is of such proportions as almost to take my breath away — it has distanced my biggest hopes.

Wilson's Congressional Government *marked a real milestone in the study of politics in the United States. Instead of figuring how to fit our government, in its operation, into the constitution, it tried to present the real article — the government as it functioned, as it lived.*

He tried to get at, not the letter of the law but the spirit. He was not concerned with the question of whether it worked as the constitution set forth but, does it work at all? Can it make a policy and adhere to it? Can responsibility, both legislative and executive, be fixed?

NOVEMBER 30, 1884 [TO ELLEN AXSON]

I shall agree with you, that you are a "little goose," if you bemoan the fact that you don't know as much as the Bryn Mawr girls are expected to know!

What do you think of *my* case?

I am to be one of their instructors, and yet I not only could not pass the entrance examinations without special preparation, but could not even be an advanced student, much less a Fellow, in my own department — because I can't read German at sight!

But that by no means indicates that I am not infinitely better educated than my pupils will be. Both you and I have what is immeasurably better than the *information* which is all that would be needed for passing Bryn Mawr, or any other college, examination!

For my part I want to have to carry as little *information* in my head as possible — just as (to use someone's illustration) I want to forget the figures in the column whose *sum* and *result* I have ascertained and want to keep. I must *scan* information, must question it closely as to every essential detail, in order that I may extract its meaning; but, the meaning once mastered, the information is lumber.

It is enough to know where to find it, for corroboration, for illustration, etc. Of course one *can't* make himself familiar with facts for such a purpose without remembering some of the more essential of them; but it is sheer, barren, ignorant waste of energy to try to remember a fact for *its own sake.*

DECEMBER 2, 1884 [TO ELLEN AXSON]

It was unreasonable, I confess, to be low-spirited so soon after hearing Houghton and Mifflin's decision about my *mss.;* but then you must remember that I am constituted, as regards such things, on a very peculiar pattern.

Success does not flush or elate me, except for the moment. I could almost wish it did. I need a large infusion of the devil-may-care element.

The acceptance of my book has of course given me the deepest satisfaction and has cleared away a whole storm of anxieties: it is an immense gain every way.

But it has sobered me a good deal too. The question is, What next?

I must be prompt to follow up the advantage gained: and I must follow it up in the direction in which I have been preparing to do effectual political service. I feel as I suppose a general does who has gained a first foothold in the enemy's country. I must push on: to linger would be fatal. There is now a responsibility resting upon me where before there was none.

My rejoicing, therefore, has in it a great deal that is stern and sober, like that of the strong man to run a race.

DECEMBER 7, 1884 [TO ELLEN AXSON]

It isn't pleasant or convenient to have strong passions. I have the uncomfortable feeling that I am carrying a volcano about with me.

My salvation is in being loved. You are the only person in the world — except the dear ones at home — with whom I do *not* have to act a part, to whom I do *not* have to deal out confidences cautiously; and you are the only person in the world — without *any* exception — to whom I can tell *all* that my heart contains. There surely never lived a man with whom love was a more critical matter than it is with me.

DECEMBER 18, 1884 [TO ELLEN AXSON]

I have a sense of power in dealing with men collectively which I do not feel always in dealing with them singly. In the former case the pride of reserve does not stand so much in my way as it does in the latter. One feels no sacrifice of pride necessary in courting the favour of an assembly of men such as he would have to make in seeking to please one man.

FEBRUARY 15, 1885 [TO ELLEN AXSON]

The Constitution is not honoured by blind worship. The more open-eyed we become, as a nation, to its defects, and the prompter we grow in applying with the unhesitating courage of conviction all thoroughly-tested or well-considered expedients necessary to make self-government among us a straightforward thing of simple method, single, unstinted power, and clear responsibility, the nearer will we approach the sound sense and practical genius of the great and honourable statesmen of 1787.

FEBRUARY 24, 1885 [TO ELLEN AXSON]

I feel a very real regret that I have been shut out from my heart's *first* — primary — ambition and purpose, which was, to take an active, if possible a leading part in public life, and strike out for myself, if I had the ability, a *statesman's* career. That is my heart's — or rather, my *mind's* — deepest secret.

But don't mistake the feeling for more than it is. It is nothing *more* than a regret; and the more I study the conditions of public service in this country the less *personal* does the regret become.

My disappointment is in the fact that there is no room for such a career in this country for *anybody*, rather than in the fact that there is no chance for *me*.

Had I had independent means of support, even of the most modest proportions, I should doubtless have sought an entrance into politics *anyhow*, and have tried to fight my way to predominant influence even amidst the hurly-burly and helter-skelter of Congress.

I have a strong instinct of leadership, an unmistakably oratorical temperament, and the keenest possible delight in affairs; and it has required very constant and stringent schooling to content me with the sober methods of the scholar and the man of letters. I have no patience for the tedious toil of what is known as "research"; I have a passion for interpreting great thoughts to the world; I should be complete if I could inspire a great movement of opinion, if I could read the experiences of the past into the practical life of men of to-day and so communicate the thought to the minds of the great mass of the people as to impel them to great political achievement.

My feeling has been that such literary talents as I have are *secondary* to my equipment for other things: that my power to write was meant to be a handmaiden to my power to speak and to organize action.

MARCH 25, 1885 [TO CHARLES TALCOTT]

But, my dear fellow, my having put "Woodrow," without introduction of "T," on a title page, *Congressional Government*, or anywhere else, gives you no good excuse for dropping "Tommy" in converse with your chum, who values the nickname as a badge of that old fellowship which is amongst the treasures of his memory, and which it is his ambition to perpetuate in spite of separation and the thousand other ills that college friendship is heir to. You would not call me "Woodrow" to my face with impunity: and you should pay me the delicate compliment of seeming not to notice my modest efforts to compact my name and avoid the awkward device (so happily characterized by one Ridgeway Wright) of "parting my name in the middle."

APRIL 5, 1885 [TO ELLEN AXSON]

It may shock you — it ought to — but I'm afraid it will not, to learn that I have a reputation (?) amongst most of my kin and certain of my friends for being irrepressible, in select circles, as a maker of grotesque addresses from the precarious elevation of chair seats, as a wearer of all varieties of comic grimaces, as a simulator of sundry unnatural, burlesque styles of voice and speech, as a lover of farces — even as a dancer of the "*can-can!*"

Woodrow Wilson married Ellen Axson on June 24, 1885, at Savannah, Georgia. The following September they went to Bryn Mawr, where he began his teaching career.

CHAPTER FOUR

He Comes to Himself as a Teacher

❯❯❯❮❮❮❯❯❯❮❮❮❯❯❯❮❮❮❯❯❯❮❮❮❯❯❯❮❮❮❯❯❯❮❮❮❯❯❯❮❮❮❯❯❯❮❮❮❯❯❯❮❮❮❯❯❯

NOVEMBER 14, 1886 [TO CHARLES TALCOTT]

In the thinking and writing I am trying to do, I constantly feel the disadvantages of the closet. I want to keep close to the practical and practicable in politics; my ambition is to add something to the statesmanship of the country, if that something be only thought, and not the old achievement of which I used to dream when I hoped that I might enter practical politics.

I seek, therefore, in the acquaintances I make, not other "professors," not other *book*-politicians, but men who have direct touch of the world; in order that I may study *affairs*, rather than doctrine. But the "practical men" I meet have not broad horizons; *they* are *not* students of affairs: they learn what they know rather by friction than by rational observation; they are at the opposite extreme from the men of books, who are all horizon — and the one extreme is as fatal to balanced thought as the other.

Now you, Charlie, are both *in* affairs and studious of them; if ever I met a fellow with whose ways of thinking I could sympathize, and from whom, consequently, I could receive aid and comfort, thou art the man — *and I need you.*

I believe, Charlie, that if a band of young fellows (say ten or twelve) could get together (and by "getting together" I mean getting their *opinions* together, whether by circular correspondence or other means) upon a common platform, and, having gotten together on good solid planks with reference to the questions of the immediate future, should raise a united voice in such periodicals, great or small, as they could gain access to, gradually working their way out, by means of a real understanding of the questions they handled, to a position of prominence and acknowledged authority in the public prints, and so in the public mind, a long step would have been taken towards the formation of such a new political sentiment and party as the country stands in such pressing need of — and I am ambitious that we should have a hand in forming such a group.

All the country needs is a new and sincere body of thought in politics, coherently, distinctly, and boldly uttered by men who are sure of their ground.

MARCH, 1887 ["OF THE STUDY OF POLITICS" IN THE *New Princeton Review*]

The success of great popular preachers contains a lesson for students of politics who would themselves convert men to a saving doctrine.

The great preacher reaches the heart of his hearers not by knowledge, but by sympathy — by showing himself a brother man to his fellow men.

And this is just the principle which the student of politics must heed.

He must frequent the street, the counting house, the drawing room, the club house, the administrative offices, the halls — yes, and the lobbies — of legislature. He must cross-examine the experience of government officials; he must hear the din of conventions, and see their intrigues; he must witness the scenes of election day.

Government is meant for the good of ordinary people, and it is for ordinary people that the student should elucidate its problems. This is not to commend the writer on politics to narrow "practical" views and petty comment; it is not to ask him to find a philosophy of government which will fit the understanding and please the taste of the "ward politician"; it is only to ask him to keep his generalizations firmly bottomed on fact and experience.

His philosophy will not overshoot the hearts of men because it is feathered with high thought unless it be deliberately shot in air.

Thoughts do not fail of acceptance because they are not common-place enough, but because they are not true enough; and, in the sort of writing about which we are here speaking, truth is a thing which can be detected better by the man who knows life than by the man who knows only logic.

You cannot lift truth so high that men cannot reach it; the only caution to be observed is, that you do not ask them to climb where they cannot go without leaving *terra firma*.

Nor is the student to leave books and sit all his time in wiseacre observation amidst busy men.

His books are his ballast.

And of course the men of his day are not the only men from whom he can learn politics. Government is as old as man; men have always been politicians; the men of today are only politicians of a particular school; the past furnishes examples of politicians of every other school, and there is as much to be learned about government from them as from their successors.

Do not expect to find the life of constitutions painted in the great "standard authorities," but, following with becoming patience their legal anatomy of institutions, watch their slightest movement toward an illustrative footnote, and try to find under that the scent you are in quest of.

If your text mention names of consequence, seek them out in biographies, and scan there the personal relations of men with affairs, for hints of the methods by which governments are operated from day to day. Interview judges off the bench, courtiers away from court, officers off duty.

Such excursions will often get quite out of sight of the starting point, the "standard authority."

The fact is that all literature teems with suggestions on this topic of politics. Approach the life of States by such avenues, and you will be convinced of the organic nature of political society.

View society from what point you will, you always catch sight of some part of government; man is so truly a "political animal" that you cannot examine him at all without seeing the points — points of his very structure — whereat he touches and depends upon, or upholds, the State.

Politics is the life of the State, and nothing which illustrates that life, nothing which reveals any habit contracted by man as a political animal, comes amiss in the study of politics.

The writer on politics must expound his subject by means of the highest literary methods. Only master workers in language and in the grouping and interpretation of heterogeneous materials can achieve the highest success in making real in word the complex life of states.

Obviously, Wilson intended his "teaching" to go beyond the students in front of him. In an article published in the Political Science Quarterly *he outlined some needs of government which he felt were vitally needed in the field of administration.*

JUNE, 1887

It is the object of administrative study to discover, first, what government can properly and successfully do, and, secondly, how it can do these proper things with the utmost possible efficiency and at the least possible cost either of money or of energy.

Whoever would effect a change in a modern constitutional government must first educate his fellow citizens to want *some* change. That done, he must persuade them to want the particular change he wants. He must first make public opinion willing to listen and then see to it that it listens to the right thing. He must stir it up to search for an opinion, and then manage to put the right opinion in its way.

Administration lies outside the proper sphere of *politics*. Administrative questions are not political questions. Although politics sets the tasks for administration, it should not be suffered to manipulate its offices. Politics is the special province of the statesman, administration of the technical official.

The broad plans of governmental action are not administrative; the detailed execution of such plans is administrative. Constitutions, therefore, properly concern themselves only with those instrumentalities of government which are to control general law.

Administration, to be efficient, must discover the simplest arrangement by which responsibility can be unmistakably fixed upon officials; the best way of dividing authority without hampering it, and responsibility without obscuring it.

Large powers and unhampered discretion seem to me the indispensable conditions of responsibility. Public attention must be easily directed to just the man deserving of praise or blame. There is no danger in power, *if only it be not irresponsible.*

If it be divided, dealt out in shares to many, it is obscured; and if it be obscured, it is made irresponsible. But if it be centered in heads of the service and in heads of branches of the service, it is easily watched and brought to book.

What part shall public opinion take in the conduct of administration? Public opinion shall play the part of authoritative critic.

Our peculiar American difficulty in organizing administration is not the danger of losing liberty, but the danger of not being able or willing to separate its essentials from its accidents. Our success is made doubtful by that besetting error of ours, the error of trying to do too much by vote. Self-government does not consist in having a hand in everything, any more than housekeeping consists necessarily in cooking dinner with one's hands.

The problem is to make public opinion efficient without suffering it to be meddlesome. Directly exercised in the oversight of the daily details, public criticism is a clumsy nuisance, a rustic handling delicate machinery. But as superintending the greater forces of formative policy alike in politics and administration, public criticism is altogether safe and beneficent, altogether indispensable.

JUNE, 1887

The first germ of the League of Nations appears in an article on "The Study of Administration."

There is a tendency — is there not? — a tendency as yet dim, but already steadily impulsive and clearly destined to prevail, towards, first the confederation of parts of empires like the British, and finally of great states themselves. Instead of centralization of power, there is to be wide union with tolerated divisions of prerogative. This is a tendency towards the American type — of governments joined with governments for the pursuit of common purposes, in honorary equality and honourable subordination.

In the fall of 1888 Wilson went to Wesleyan University, Middletown, Connecticut, to teach. While there, in an article entitled "An Old Master," in the New Princeton Review, *he set forth his ideas on a good teacher.*

SEPTEMBER, 1888

Are not our college classrooms, in being robbed of the old-time lecture, and getting instead a science-brief of *data* and bibliography, being deprived also of that literary atmosphere which once pervaded them?

We are unquestionably gaining in thoroughness; but are we gaining in thoughtfulness? We are giving to many youths an insight, it may be profound, into specialties; but are we giving any of them a broad outlook?

Some of the subtlest and most lasting effects of genuine oratory have gone forth from secluded lecture desks into the hearts of quiet groups of students; and it would seem to be good policy to endure much indifferent lecturing for the sake of leaving places open for the men who have in them the inestimable force of chastened eloquence.

For one man who can impart an undying impulse there are several score, presupposing the requisite training, who can impart a method; and here is the well understood ground for the cumulating disfavor of college lecturing and the rapid substitution of "laboratory drill."

But will not higher education be cut off from communion with the highest of all forces, the force of personal inspiration in the field of great themes of thought, if you interdict the literary method in the classroom?

Adam Smith knew that wit was of no avail, without wit's proper words; sagacity mean, without sagacity's mellow measure of phrase. He bestowed the most painstaking care, therefore, not only upon what he was to say, but also upon the way in which he was to say it.

The charm of his discourses consisted in the power of statement which gave them life, in the clear and facile processes of proof which gave them speed, and in the vigorous, but chastened, imagination which lent them illumination.

He constantly refreshed and rewarded his hearers by bringing them to those clear streams of practical wisdom and happy illustration which everywhere irrigate his expositions.

He was a great thinker — and that was much; but he also made men recognize him as a great thinker, because he was a master of style — which was more.

He did not put his candle under a bushel, but in a candlestick.

There are two distinct kinds of observation: that which makes a man alert and shrewd, cognizant of every trifle and quick with every trick of speech; and that which makes a man a philosopher, conscious of the steady set of affairs and ready in the use of all the substantial resources of wise thought.

Commend me to the former for a chat; commend me to the latter for a book. The first will sparkle; the other burns a steady flame.

The things that strike us most about Adam Smith are, his boldness of conception and wideness of outlook, his breadth and comprehensiveness of treatment, and his carefully clarified and beautified style.

He was no specialist except *in the relation of things*.

He took most of his materials at second hand. But no matter who mined the gold, he coined it; the image and superscription are his. Certain separate, isolated truths which served under him may have been doing individual, guerilla warfare elsewhere for the advancement of science; but it was he who marshalled them into drilled hosts for the conquering of the nations.

Adam Smith was doubtless indebted to the Physiocrats, but all the world is indebted to Adam Smith.

Education and the world of thought need men who, like this man, will dare to know a multitude of things. Without them and their bold synthetic methods, all knowledge and all thought would fall apart into a weak analysis. Their minds do not lack in thoroughness; their thoroughness simply lacks in minuteness.

In this day of narrow specialties, our thinking needs such men to fuse its parts, correlate its forces, and centre its results; and our thinking needs them in its college stage, in order that we may command horizons from our study windows in after days.

MARCH 9, 1889 [TO ELLEN AXSON WILSON]
Wilson was lecturing on politics at Johns Hopkins.

Have I told you that latterly — since I have been here, a distinct *feeling* of maturity — or rather of maturing — has come over me?

The *boyish* feeling that I have so long had and cherished is giving place, consciously, to another feeling — the feeling that I am no longer young (though not old quite!) and that I need no longer hesitate (as I have so long and sensitively done) to assert myself and my opinions in the presence of and against the selves and opinions of old men, "my elders."

APRIL 30, 1889
In a speech on the one-hundredth anniversary of the inauguration of President Washington, Wilson stated his fundamental "democratic" creed — that democracy is "always a-making."

I fear that we are becoming a little prone as a nation to mistake the real nature of our success. It does not lie in the forms but in the essence of our institution. We are not great in popular government because we invented written constitutions: for we did not invent them. We are great because of what we perfected and fulfilled, not because of anything that we discovered: and it is only by extending such lines of development as can be clearly traced backwards through the normal evolutions of politics in the past that we can make further permanent advance. We did not break with the past: we understood and obeyed it, rather.

It is no light thing to have such traditions behind us: liberty is not something that can be laid away in a document, a completed work. It is an organic principle, a principle of life, renewing and being renewed. Democratic institutions are never done — they are, like the living tissue, always a-making.

It is a strenuous thing this of living the life of a free people; and we cannot escape the burden of our inheritance.

JUNE 3, 1889

Wilson wrote to Professor Albert Bushnell Hart, who had asked him to write one of the histories in Hart's "Epochs in American History" series.

Though born in the South and bred in its sympathies, I am not of Southern-born parents. My father was born in Ohio, my mother in England. Ever since I have had independent judgments of my own I have been a Federalist (!) It is this mixture of elements in me — full identification with the South, non-Southern blood, and Federalist principles — that makes me hope that a detachment of my affectionate, reminiscent sympathies from my historical judgments is not beyond hoping for.

In the fall of 1890 Wilson went from Wesleyan University to Princeton to teach. This move gave him ampler scope for growth and development.

In his teaching Wilson's practice was to read slowly four or five general statements so that they could be taken down by the students. Then he would develop, embroider, and elaborate the subjects at great length in a lecture full of wit, vivid bits of description, graphic characterization.

He often commented upon current politics and political leaders — with the understanding that he was not to be reported in the press.

Always he was trying to make his students visualize for themselves — and keep on visualizing — the organic life of society, of political institutions.

JULY 1, 1891 [TO R. HEATH DABNEY]

My work here is proving very stimulating indeed: it is like lecturing constantly to cultivated audiences, for my electives number about 160 men each; and it stimulates me immensely to have to interest so many minds in the more abstruse topics of jurisprudence.

FEBRUARY, 1894 ["A CALENDAR OF GREAT AMERICANS" IN *Forum*]

The American spirit is something more than the old, the immemorial Saxon spirit of liberty from which it sprung. It has been bred by the conditions attending the great task which we have all the century been carrying forward: the task, at once material and ideal, of subduing a wilderness and covering all the wide stretches of a vast continent with a single free and stable policy. It is, accordingly, above all things, a hopeful and confident spirit. It is progressive, optimistically progressive, and ambitious of objects of national scope and advantage. It is unpedantic, unprovincial, unspeculative, unfastidious; regardful of law, but as using it, not as being used by it or dominated by any formalism whatever; in a sense unrefined, because full of rude force; but prompted by large and generous motives, and often as tolerant as it is resolute.

To meet this test Wilson found no one except Lincoln "big or various enough to embody this active and full-hearted spirit in its qualities," although Benjamin Franklin would come close. Of Franklin he said, "He will stand the final and characteristic test of Americanism; he would unquestionably have made a successful frontiersman, capable at once of wielding the axe and of administering justice from the fallen trunk." Of Lincoln, as the "first American," Wilson wrote:

He would be a rash man who should say he understood Abraham Lincoln. No doubt natures deep as his, and various almost to the point of self-contradiction, can be sounded only by the judgment of men of a like sort — if any such there be. But some things we all may see and judge concerning him.

Lincoln owed nothing to his birth, everything to his growth: had no training save what he gave himself; no nurture, but only a wild and native strength. His life was his schooling, and every day of it gave to his character a new touch of development. His manhood not only, but his perception also, expanded with his life. His eyes, as they looked more and more abroad, beheld the national life, and comprehended it: and the lad who had been so rough-cut a provincial became, when grown to manhood, the one leader in all the nation who held the whole people singly in his heart: held even the Southern people there, and would have won them back.

And so we have in him what we must call the perfect development of native strength, the rounding out and nationalization of the provincial.

He never ceased to stand, in his bony angles, the express image of the ungainly frontiersman. His mind never lost the vein of coarseness that had marked him grossly when a youth.

And yet how he grew and strengthened in the real stuff of dignity and greatness: how nobly he could bear himself without the aid of grace!

He kept always the shrewd and seeing eye of the woodsman and the hunter, and the flavor of wild life never left him: and yet how easily his view widened to great affairs; how surely he perceived the value and the significance of whatever touched him and made him neighbor to itself!

Lincoln's marvelous capacity to extend his comprehension to the measure of what he had in hand is the one distinguishing mark of the man: and to study the development of that capacity in him is little less than to study, where it is as it were perfectly registered, the national life itself.

CHAPTER FIVE

He Comes to Himself as a "Literary Politician"

In a letter to Horace Scudder of the Atlantic Monthly, *May 19, 1891, Wilson had written: "I am afraid to keep constantly intent upon my special topics of study. It is my creed that literary training and method are as essential to the production of good political science as to the production of good poetry or valid criticism. It is my practice, consequently, to try my hand, whenever I can, at various sorts of writing as unlike my professional tasks as possible."*

In the next decade Wilson did every type of writing: from a biography of George Washington, through literary criticism and essays on education and politics, to his History of the American People.

At the same time he began traveling over the United States and made several trips to England.

SEPTEMBER, 1894 ["UNIVERSITY TRAINING AND CITIZENSHIP," IN *Forum*]

Wilson made a plea for university training that would school the student's "spirits for their common life as citizens."

Nations, as well as individuals, must seek wisdom: the truth that will make them free. There is a learning of purpose as well as a learning of science; for there is a truth of spirit as well as a truth of fact. And scholarship, though it must everywhere seek the truth, may select the truths it shall search for and emphasize. It is this selection that should be national. A wise man will choose what to learn; and so also will a wise nation.

A university should be an organ of memory for the State for the transmission of its best traditions. Every man sent out from a university should be a man of his nation, as well as a man of his time.

It would not be necessary to erect a new university to try the experiment of such a synthesis of university courses. Anybody can establish the modern sort of university, anywhere. It has no necessary nationality or character. Such a university would be a National Academy — the only sort worth having. It can be done by only a comparatively slight readjustment of subjects and instructors in the greater of the universities we already have.

A considerable number of young tutors, serving their novitiate for full university appointments, might easily enough effect an organization of the men that would secure the reading. Taking them in groups of manageable numbers, suggesting the reading of each group, and by frequent interviews and quizzes seeing that it was actually done, explaining and stimulating as best they might by the way, they could not only get the required tasks performed, but relieve them of the hateful appearance of being tasks, and cheer and enrich the whole life of the university.

The idea of a balance between general and special training has been temporarily lost sight of by the necessity to make room for the modern scientific studies.

Of all things that a university should do for a man, the most important is to put him in possession of the materials for a systematic criticism of life.

The reasoning of the scientific method, for all but a few constructive minds, is analytical reasoning. It picks things to pieces and examines them in their ultimate elements. It is jealous, if not quite intolerant, of all traditional views; will receive nothing, but test everything; and its influence is very marked and pervasive. It produces, for one thing, an overweening confidence in the pure reasoning faculty. Now, it happens that the pure reasoning faculty, whose only standard is logic and whose only data are put in terms of determinable force, is the worst possible instrument for reforming society.

The only thing that makes modern socialism more dangerous than like doctrine has ever been is, that its methods are scientific and that the age also is scientific. Two-thirds of our college graduates are not taught anything that would predispose them against accepting its logic or its purpose to put all things into a laboratory of experiment and arbitrarily recombine the elements of society.

The "humane" spirit of our time is a very different thing from the *human* spirit. The humanity which we nowadays affect is scientific and pathological. It treats men as specimens, and seeks to subject them to experiment. It cuts cross-sections through the human spirit and calls its description of what is thereby disclosed moral essays and sociological novels. It is self-conscious and without modesty or humour.

The human spirit is a very different thing. It has a memory and a sense of humour. It cannot read Ibsen after having read Shakespeare, any more than it can prefer sugar and butter and flour and sweets separately, in their individual intensity, to their toothsome and satisfying combination in pudding.

Its literature is that which has the one flavour for every generation, and the same broad and valid sagacity.

It regards the scientific method of investigation as one, but only one, method of finding out the truth; and as a method for finding only one kind of truth.

The worst possible enemy to society is the man who, with a strong faculty for reasoning and for action, is cut loose in his standards of judgment from the past; and universities which train men to use their minds without carefully establishing the connection of their thought with that of the past, are instruments of social destruction.

Of course no man's thought is entirely severed from the past, or ever can be. But it is worth while to remember that science is no older than the present century, and is apt to despise old thought. At least its young votaries are: not because they are "scientists," but because they are only scientists. They are as much pedants, in their narrowness, as the men trained exclusively in the classics, whose thought is all in the past.

FEBRUARY 19, 1895 [TO ELLEN AXSON WILSON]

That I am an idealist, with the heart of a poet, I do not hesitate to avow: but that fact is not reassuring. On the contrary it is tragical.

If I could only write prose that was delicate, imaginative, full at once of grace, force, and distinction, that would be something: my thoughts would at least go clad like aristocrats. But I shall but wear my soul out trying.

JULY 26, 1896

From London, he wrote to Ellen Axson Wilson on the nomination of William J. Bryan by the Democratic Party.

Really, you know, you are having a most extraordinary presidential campaign in that odd country of yours! I shall have to be told where I am when I get back.

It looks as if *I* would have to vote for McKinley!

Oh Lord, how long!

OCTOBER 21, 1896 [ON RELIGION]

There is nothing that gives such pith to public service as religion. A God of truth is no mean prompter to the enlightened service of mankind; and character formed as if in His eyes has always a fibre and sanction such as you shall not obtain for the ordinary man from the mild promptings of philosophy.

It is noteworthy how *often* God-fearing men have been forward in those revolutions which vindicated rights, and how *seldom* in those which have wrought a work of destruction.

In an address delivered at the Princeton Sesquicentennial, October 21, 1896, Wilson summed up what he considered to be the functions of a university in a democracy, together with the prime dangers facing a democracy because of the changing emphasis in university teaching. His subject was "Princeton in the Nation's Service" (Forum, December, 1896).

This speech started him on to the presidency of the university. In his inauguration address he took the subject, "Princeton for the Nation's Service."

The difference in the prepositions is highly important. In 1896
he could tell theoretically what should be done; in 1902 as president
of the university he could announce what he was going to try to do.

In 1896, above all, he warned that universities must train their
students to become citizens of the world. The chief threat to this
that he saw creeping in was the adoption in all phases of instruction
by the scientific method. He warned:

The college in our day lies very near indeed to the affairs of the
world. It is a place of the latest experiments; its laboratories are
brisk with the spirit of discovery; its lecture rooms resound with the
discussion of new theories of life and novel programmes of reform.
There is no radical like your learned radical, bred in the schools;
and thoughts of revolution have in our time been harbored in universities as naturally as they were once nourished among the Encyclopedists. It is the scientific spirit of the age which has wrought
the change. No man more heartily admires the gain and the enlightenment that have come to the world through the extraordinary
advances in physical science which this great age has witnessed.
But I am a student of society and should deem myself unworthy of
the comradeship of great men of science should I not speak the plain
truth with regard to what I see happening under my own eyes.

I have no laboratory but the world of books and men in which I
live; but I am much mistaken if the scientific spirit of the age is not
doing us a great disservice, working in us a certain great degeneracy.
Science has bred in us a spirit of experiment and a contempt for
the past. It made us credulous of quick improvement, hopeful of
discovering panaceas, confident of success in every new thing.

I have no indictment against what science has done: I have only
a warning to utter against the atmosphere which has stolen from
laboratories into lecture rooms and into the general air of the world
at large. Science — our science — is new. It is a child of the nineteenth century. It has transformed the world and owes little debt of
obligation to any past age. It has driven mystery out of the Universe;
it has made malleable stuff of the hard world, and laid it out in its

elements upon the table of every class-room. Its own masters have known its limitations: they have stopped short at the confines of the physical universe; they have declined to reckon with spirit or with the stuffs of the mind, have eschewed sense and confined themselves to sensation. But their work has been so stupendous that all other men of all other studies have been set staring at their methods, imitating their ways of thought, ogling their results.

We look in our study of the classics nowadays more at the phenomena of language than at the movement of spirit; we suppose the world which is invisible to be unreal; we doubt the efficacy of feeling and exaggerate the efficacy of knowledge; we speak of society as an organism and believe that we can contrive for it a new environment which will change the very nature of its constituent parts; worst of all, we believe in the present and in the future more than in the past, and deem the newest theory of society the likeliest.

This is the disservice scientific study has done us: it has given us agnosticism in the realm of philosophy, scientific anarchism in the field of politics.

It has made the legislator confident that he can create, and the philosopher sure that God cannot.

Past experience is discredited and the laws of matter are supposed to apply to spirit and the make-up of society.

Let me say once more, this is not the fault of the scientist; he has done his work with an intelligence and success which cannot be too much admired. It is the work of the noxious, intoxicating gas which has somehow got into the lungs of the rest of us from out the crevices of his workshop — a gas, it would seem, which forms only in the outer air, and where men do not know the right use of their lungs.

I should tremble to see social reform led by men who had breathed it; I should fear nothing better than utter destruction from a revolution conceived and led in the scientific spirit.

Science has not changed the laws of social growth or betterment. Science has not changed the nature of society, has not made history a whit easier to understand, human nature a whit easier to reform.

It has won for us a great liberty in the physical world, a liberty from superstitious fear and from disease, a freedom to use nature as a familiar servant; but it has not freed us from ourselves. It has not purged us of passion or disposed us to virtue. It has not made us less covetous or less ambitious or less self-indulgent.

On the contrary, it may be suspected of having enhanced our passions, by making wealth so quick to come, so fickle to stay.

It has wrought such instant, incredible improvement in all the physical setting of our life, that we have grown the more impatient of the unreformed condition of the part it has not touched or bettered, and we want to get at our spirits and reconstruct them in like radical fashion by like processes of experiment.

We have broken with the past and have come into a new world.

Can any one wonder, then, that I ask for the old drill, the old memory of times gone by, the old schooling in precedent and tradition, the old keeping of faith with the past, as a preparation for leadership in days of social change?

We have not given science too big a place in our education; but we have made a perilous mistake in giving it too great a preponderance in method in every other branch of study. We must make the humanities human again; must recall what manner of men we are; must turn back once more to the region of practicable ideals.

It is indispensable, it seems to me, if it is to do its right service, that the air of affairs should be admitted to all its class-rooms. I do not mean the air of party politics, but the air of the world's transactions, the consciousness of the solidarity of the race, the sense of the duty of man toward man, of the presence of men in every problem, of the significance of truth for guidance as well as for knowledge, of the potency of ideas, of the promise and the hope that shine in the face of all knowledge.

There is laid upon us the compulsion of the national life. We dare not keep aloof and closet ourselves while a nation comes to its maturity. The days of glad expansion are gone, our life grows tense and difficult; our resource for the future lies in careful thought, providence, and a wise economy; and the school must be of the nation.

I have had sight of the perfect place of learning in my thought: a free place, and a various, where no man could be and not know with how great a destiny knowledge had come into the world — itself a little world; but not perplexed, living with a singleness of aim not known without; the home of sagacious men, hard-headed and with a will to know, debaters of the ways of democracy; and yet a place removed — calm Science seated there, recluse, ascetic, like a nun; not knowing that the world passes, not caring, if the truth but come in answer to her prayer; and Literature, walking within her open doors, in quiet chambers, with men of olden time, storied walls about her, and calm voices infinitely sweet; here "magic casements, opening on the foam of perilous seas, in fairy lands forlorn," to which you may withdraw and use your youth for pleasure; there windows open straight upon the street, where many stand and talk, intent upon the world of men and business. A place where ideals are kept in heart in an air they can breathe; but no fool's paradise. A place where to hear the truth about the past and hold debate about the affairs of the present, with knowledge and without passion; like the world in having all men's life at heart, a place for men and all that concerns them; but unlike the world in its self-possession, its thorough way of talk; its care to know more than the moment brings to light; slow to take excitement, its air pure and wholesome with a breath of faith; every eye within it bright in the clear day and quick to look toward heaven for the confirmation of its hope.

Who shall show us the way to this place?

CHAPTER SIX

What It Will Take for the Country to Come to Itself

➤➤➤《《➤➤➤《《➤➤➤《《➤➤➤《《➤➤➤《《➤➤➤《《➤➤➤《《➤➤➤《《➤➤➤《《➤➤➤《《➤➤➤《《

The Spanish–American War threw the United States squarely back into the stream of the world's affairs from which she had imagined, for a short period, that she was isolated. Wilson was one of the first to realize the import of this.

DECEMBER 22, 1900 [A SPEECH ON "THE PURITAN"]

When you reflect that Washington wrote his Farewell Address to something over three million people, to whom he was, if his letters are to be believed, very willing to say good-bye, and if you will understand that Address to have meant, as it would seem to have meant: "I want you to discipline yourselves and stay still and be good boys until you grow up, until you are big enough to stand the competition of foreign countries, until you are big enough to go abroad in the world," I think you will have put the proper interpretation on it. "Wait," he said, "until you need not be afraid of foreign influence, and then you shall be ready to take your part in the field of the world." I do not accept the interpretation of Washington's Farewell Address that those people who have but seen the curtain go down accept.

MARCH, 1901 ["DEMOCRACY AND EFFICIENCY" IN THE *Atlantic Monthly*]

In this article Wilson set forth his ideas on what it was going to take for Democracy to come to itself:

It is no longer possible to mistake the reaction against democracy. The nineteenth century was above all others a century of democracy;

and yet the world is no more convinced of the benefits of democracy as a form of government at its end than it was at its beginning.

Many excellent suggestions, valid and applicable everywhere, we have given the world, with regard to the spirit in which government should be conducted.

No doubt class privilege has been forever discredited because of our example. We have taught the world the principle of the general welfare as the object and end of government, rather than the prosperity of any class or section of the nation, or the preferment of any private or petty interest. We have made the law appear to all men an instrument wherewith to secure equality of rights and a protection which shall be without respect of persons. There can be no misgivings about the currency or the permanency of the *principles* of right which we have exalted.

But we have not equally commended the forms or the organizations of the government under which we live.

A federal union of diverse commonwealths we have indeed made to seem both practicable and efficient as a means of organizing government on a great scale, while preserving at the same time the utmost possible latitude and independence in local self-government. It would be hard to exaggerate the shock which has been given to hopeful experiment, in the field of political action, by our conspicuous successes as constitution-makers and reformers.

Democracy is merely the most radical form of "constitutional" government.

A "constitutional" government is one in which there is a definite understanding as to the sphere and power of government; one in which individual liberty is defined and guaranteed by specific safeguards, in which the authority and the functions of those who rule are limited and determined by unmistakable custom or explicit fundamental law.

It is a government in which these understandings are kept up, alike in the making and in the execution of laws, by frequent conferences between those who govern and those who are governed;

those intrusted with government being present in person, the people by deputy.

Representative government has had its long life and excellent development, not in order that common opinion, the opinion of the street, might prevail, but in order that some sober and best opinion might be created, by thoughtful and responsible discussion conducted by men intimately informed concerning the public weal, and officially commissioned to look to its safeguarding and advancement.

This is the central object to which we have devoted our acknowledged genius for practical politics. During the first half century of our national life we seemed to have succeeded in an extraordinary degree in approaching our ideal, in organizing a nation for counsel and cooperation, and in moving forward with cordial unison and with confident and buoyant step toward the accomplishment of tasks and duties upon which all were agreed.

Our later life has disclosed serious flaws, has even seemed ominous of pitiful failure, in some of the things we most prided ourselves upon having managed well: notably, in pure and efficient local government, in the successful organization of great cities, and in well-considered schemes of administration.

The boss — a man elected by no votes, preferred by no open process of choice, occupying no office of responsibility — makes himself a veritable tyrant amongst us, and seems to cheat us of self-government; parties appear to hamper the movements of opinion rather than to give them form and means of expression; multitudinous voices of agitation, an infinite play of forces at cross-purpose, confuse us; and there seems to be no common counsel or definite union for action, after all.

We keep heart the while because still sure of our principles and of our ideals: the common weal, a common and cordial understanding in matters of government, secure private rights and yet concerted public action, a strong government and yet liberty also. We know what we have to do; what we have missed and mean to find; what we have lost and mean to recover; what we still strive after and mean to achieve.

Democracy is a principle with us, not a mere form of government.

What we have blundered at is its new applications and details, its successful combination with efficiency and purity in government action. We tell ourselves that our partial failure in these things has been due to our absorption in the tasks of material growth, that our practical genius has spent itself upon wealth and the organization of industry. But it is to be suspected that there are other elements in the singular fact.

We have supposed that there could be one way of efficiency for democratic governments and another for monarchial. We have declined to provide ourselves with a professional civil service, because we deemed it undemocratic; we have made shift to do without a trained diplomatic and consular service, because we thought the training given by other governments to their foreign agents unnecessary in the case of affairs so simple and unsophisticated as the foreign relations of a democracy in politics and trade — transactions so frank, so open, so straightforward, interests so free from all touch of chicane or indirection; we have hesitated to put our presidents or governors or mayors into direct and responsible relations of leadership with our legislatures and councils in the making of laws and ordinances, because such a connection between lawmakers and executive officers seemed inconsistent with the theory of checks and balances.

Our theory has paid as little heed to efficiency as our practice. It has been a theory of non-professionalism in public affairs; and in many great matters of public action non-professionalism is non-efficiency.

"If only we had our old leisure for domestic affairs, we should devise a way of our own to be efficient, consonant with our principles, characteristic of our genius for organization," we have heard men say. "How fatal it may prove to us that our attention has been called off from a task but half done to the tasks of the world, for which we have neither inclination nor proper training nor suitable organization — from which, until now, we were so happily free! We shall now be forever barred from perfection, our own perfection, at home!"

But may it not be that the future will put another face upon the matter, and show us our advantage where least we thought it to lie? May it not be that the way to perfection lies along these new paths of struggle, of discipline, and of achievement? What will the re-action of new duty be? What self-revelations will it afford; what lessons of unified will, of simplified method, of clarified purpose; what disclosures of the fundamental principles of right action, the efficient means of just achievement, if we but keep our ideals and our character?

The affairs of the world stand in such a case, the principles for which we have battled the long decades through are now put in such jeopardy amidst the contests of nations, the future of mankind faces so great a peril of reactionary revolution, that our own private business must take its chances along with the greater business of the world at large.

We dare not stand neutral.

All mankind deem us the representatives of the moderate and sensible discipline which makes free men good citizens, of enlightened systems of law and a temperate justice, of the best experience in the reasonable methods and principles of self-government, of public force made consistent with individual liberty; and we shall not realize these ideals at home, if we suffer them to be hopelessly discredited amongst the peoples who have yet to see liberty and the peaceable days of order and comfortable progress.

We should lose heart ourselves, did we suffer the world to lose faith in us as the champions of these things.

There is no masking or concealing the new order of the world. It is not the world of the eighteenth century, nor yet of the nineteenth.

A new era has come upon us like a sudden vision of things unprophesied, and for which no polity has been prepared.

Here is straightway a new frontage for the nations — this frontage toward the Orient. Our almost accidental possession of the Philippines has put us in the very presence of the forces which must make the politics of the twentieth century radically unlike the politics of the nineteenth; but we must have taken cognizance of them and dealt with them in any event.

They concern us as nearly as they concern any other nation in the world. They concern all nations, for they shall determine the future of the race.

Fortunately, they have not disclosed themselves before we were ready. I do not mean that our thought was prepared for them; I do not mean that our domestic affairs were in such shape as to seem fairly well ordered, so that we might in good conscience turn from them as from things finished and complete, and divert our energies to tasks beyond our borders. I mean that this change in the order of the world came, so far as we are concerned, at the natural point in our national development.

There has been a certain singular unity in our national task, hitherto; and these new duties now thrust upon us will not break that unity. They will perpetuate it, rather, and make it complete, if we keep but our integrity and our old-time purpose true.

Until 1890 the United States had always a frontier; looked always to a region beyond, unoccupied, unappropriated, an outlet for its energy, a new place of settlement and of achievement for its people. For nearly three hundred years their growth had followed a single law — the law of expansion into new territory.

England sought colonies at the ends of the earth to set her energy free and give vent to her enterprise; we, a like people in every impulse of mastery and achievement, had our own vast continent and were satisfied. There was always space and adventure enough and to spare, to satisfy the feet of our young men.

The great process put us to the making of states; kept the wholesome blood of sober and strenuous and systematic work warm within us; perpetuated in us the spirit of initiative and of practical expediency which had made of the colonies vigorous and heady states; created in us that national feeling which finally put sectionalism from the field and altered the very character of the government;

gave us the question of the extension of slavery, brought on the civil war, and decided it by the weight of the West.

No other modern nation has been schooled as we have been in big undertakings and the mastery of novel difficulties. We have become confirmed in energy, in resourcefulness, in practical proficiency, in self-confidence.

We have become confirmed, also, so far as our character is concerned, in the habit of acting under an odd mixture of selfish and altruistic motives. Having ourselves a population fit to be free, making good its freedom in every sort of unhampered enterprise, determining its own destiny unguided and unbidden, moving as it pleased within wide boundaries, using institutions, not dominated by them, we have sympathized with freedom everywhere; have deemed it niggardly to deny an equal degree of freedom to any race or community that desired it; have pressed handsome principles of equity in international dealings; have rejoiced to believe that our principles might some day make every government a servant, not a master, of its people.

Ease and prosperity have made us wish the whole world to be as happy and well-to-do as ourselves; and we have supposed that institutions and principles like our own were the simple prescription for making them so.

And yet, when issues of our own interest arose, we have not been unselfish. We have shown ourselves kin to all the world, when it came to pushing an advantage.

Even Mr. Jefferson, philanthropist and champion of peaceable and modest government though he was, exemplified this double temper of the people he ruled. "Peace is our passion," he had declared; but the passion abated when he saw the mouth of the Mississippi about to pass into the hands of France. Though he had loved France and hated England, he did not hesitate then what language to hold.

It is only just now, however, that we have awakened to our real relationship to the rest of mankind. Absorbed in our own development, we had fallen into a singular ignorance of the rest of the

world. The isolation in which we lived was quite without parallel
in modern history. Our only near neighbor of any consequence
was like ourselves in every essential particular.

And so we have looked upon nothing but our own ways of living, and have been formed in isolation. This has made us — not
provincial, exactly: upon so big and various a continent there
could not be the single pattern of thought and manners and purpose to be found cloistered in a secluded province. But if *provincial* be not the proper word, it suggests the actual fact. We have,
like provincials, too habitually confined our view to the range of
our own experiences. We have acquired a false self-confidence, a
false self-sufficiency, because we have heeded no successes or
failures but our own.

Democracy is unquestionably the most wholesome and livable
kind of government the world has yet tried. It supplies as no other
system could the frank and universal criticism, the free play of
individual thought, the open conduct of public affairs, the spirit
and pride of community and of cooperation, which make governments just and public-spirited. But the question of efficiency is the
same for it as for any other kind of polity; and if only it have the
principle of representation at the centre of its arrangements, where
counsel is held and policy determined and law made, it can afford
to put into its administrative organization any kind of discipline
as if of a profession that it may think most likely to serve it. This
we shall see, and this we shall do.

Every man now knows that the world is to be changed. The
whole world has already become a single vicinage; each part has
become neighbor to all the rest. No nation can live any longer to
itself, the tasks and the duties of neighborhood being what they are.

The East is to be opened and transformed, whether we will or no;
nations and peoples which have stood still the centuries through
are to be quickened, and made part of the universal world of commerce and of ideas which has so steadily been a-making by the
advance of European power from age to age. It is our peculiar
duty, as it is also England's, to moderate the process in the inter-

ests of liberty: to impart to the peoples thus driven out upon the road of change, so far as we have opportunity or can make it, our own principles of self-help; teach them order and self-control in the midst of change; impart to them, if it be possible by contact and sympathy and example, the drill and habit of law and obedience which we long ago got out of the strenuous processes of English history; secure for them, when we may, the free intercourse and the natural development which shall make them at least equal members of the family of nations.

This we shall do, not by giving them out of hand our codes of political morality or our methods of political action, the generous gifts of complete individual liberty or the full-fangled institutions of American self-government — a purple garment for their nakedness — for these things are not blessings, but a curse, to undeveloped peoples, still in the childhood of their political growth; but by giving them, in the spirit of service, a government and rule which shall moralize them by being itself moral, elevate and steady them by being itself pure and steadfast, inducting them into the rudiments of justice and freedom.

In other words, it is the aid of our character they need, and not the premature aid of our institutions.

Our institutions must come after the ground of character and habit has been made ready for them; as effect, not cause, in the order of political growth. It is thus that we shall ourselves recognize the fact, at last patent to all the world, that the service of democracy has been the development of ideals rather than the origination of practical methods of administration of universal validity, or any absolute qualification of the ultimate conceptions of sovereignty and the indispensable disciplinary operation of law. We must aid their character and elevate their ideals, and then see what these will bring forth, generating after their kind.

CHAPTER SEVEN

"When a Man Comes to Himself"

⊰⊱⊰⊱⊰⊱⊰⊱⊰⊱⊰⊱⊰⊱⊰⊱⊰⊱⊰⊱⊰⊱⊰⊱⊰⊱

JUNE, 1901 [IN *Century Magazine*]

It is a very wholesome and regenerating change which a man undergoes when he "comes to himself." It is not only after periods of recklessness or infatuation, when he has played the spendthrift or the fool, that a man comes to himself.

He comes to himself after experiences of which he alone may be aware: when he has left off being wholly preoccupied with his own powers and interests and with every petty plan that centers in himself; when he has cleared his eyes to see the world as it is, and his own true place and function in it.

It is a process of disillusionment. The scales have fallen away. He sees himself soberly, and knows under what conditions his powers must act, as well as what his powers are. He has got rid of earlier prepossessions about the world of men and affairs, both those which were too favorable and those which were too unfavorable — both those of the nursery and those of a young man's reading. He has learned his own paces, or at any rate, is in a fair way to learn them; has found his footing and the true nature of the "going" he must look for in the world; over what sorts of roads he must expect to make his running, and at what expenditure of effort; whither his goal lies, and what cheer he may expect by the way. It is a process of disillusionment, but it disheartens no soundly made man. It brings him into a light which guides instead of deceiving him; a light which does not make the way look cold to any man whose eyes are fit for use in the open, but which shines wholesomely, rather, upon the obvious path, like the honest rays of the frank sun, and makes traveling both safe and cheerful.

There is no fixed time in a man's life at which he comes to himself, and some men never come to themselves at all. It is a change reserved for the thoroughly sane and healthy, and for those who can detach themselves from the tasks and drudgery long and often enough to get, at any rate once and again, a view of the proportions of life and of the stage and plot of its action.

We speak often with amusement, sometimes with distaste and uneasiness, of men who "have no sense of humor," who take themselves too seriously, who are intense, self-absorbed, over-confident in matters of opinion, or else go plumed with conceit, proud of we cannot tell what, enjoying, appreciating, thinking of nothing so much as themselves.

These are men who have not suffered that wholesome change. They have not come to themselves. If they be serious men, and real forces in the world, we may conclude that they have been too much and too long absorbed; that their tasks and responsibilities long ago rose about them like a flood, and have kept them swimming with sturdy strokes the years through, their eyes level with the troubled surface — no horizon in sight, no passing fleets, no comrades but those who struggled in the flood themselves. If they be frivolous, light-headed, men without purpose or achievement, we may conjecture, if we do not know, that they were born so, or spoiled by fortune, or befuddled by self-indulgence. It is no great matter what we think of them.

It is enough to know that there are some laws which govern a man's awakening to know himself and the right part to play.

A man *is* the part he plays among his fellows.

He is not isolated; he cannot be. His life is made up of the relations he bears to others — is made or marred by those relations, guided by them, judged by them, expressed in them. There is nothing else upon which he can spend his spirit — nothing else that we can see. It is by these he gets his spiritual growth; it is by these we see his character revealed, his purpose, and his gifts.

Adjustment is exactly what a man gains when he comes to himself. Some men gain it late, some early; some get it all at once, as if by one distinct act of deliberate accommodation; others get it by degrees and quite imperceptibly. No doubt to most men it comes by the slow process of experience — at each stage of life a little.

A man who lives only for himself has not begun to live — has yet to learn his use, and his real pleasure, too, in the world. It is unselfish action, growing slowly into the high habit of devotion, and at last, it may be, into a sort of consecration, that teaches a man the wide meaning of his life, and makes him a steady professional in living, if the motive be not necessity, but love. Necessity may make a mere drudge of a man, and no mere drudge ever made a professional of himself; that demands a higher spirit and a finer incentive than his.

Surely a man has come to himself only when he has found the best that is in him, and has satisfied his heart with the highest achievement he is fit for. It is only then that he knows of what he is capable and what his heart demands. And, assuredly, no thoughtful man ever came to the end of his life, and had time and a little space of calm from which to look back upon it, who did not know and acknowledge that it was what he had done unselfishly and for others, and nothing else, that satisfied him in the retrospect, and made him feel that he had played the man. That alone seems to him the real measure of himself, the real standard of his manhood.

And so men grow by having responsibility laid upon them, the burden of other people's business. Their powers are put out at interest, and they get usury in kind. *They are like men multiplied.* Each counts manifold. Men who live with an eye only upon what is their own are dwarfed beside them — seem fractions while they are integers. The trustworthiness of men trusted seems often to grow with the trust.

It is for this reason that men are in love with power and greatness: it affords them so pleasurable an expansion of faculty, so large a run for their minds, an exercise of spirit so various and refreshing; they have the freedom of so wide a tract of the world of affairs. But if they use power only for their own ends, if there be no unselfish service in it, if its object be only their personal aggrandizement, their love to see other men tools in their hands, they go out of the world small, disquieted, beggared, no enlargement of soul vouchsafed them, no usury of satisfaction. They have added nothing to themselves. Mental and physical powers alike grow by use, as every one knows; but labor for oneself alone is like exercise in a gymnasium. No healthy man can remain satisfied with it, or regard it as anything but a preparation for tasks in the open, amid the affairs of the world — not sport, but business — where there is no orderly apparatus, and every man must devise the means by which he is to make the most of himself. To make the most of himself means the multiplication of his activities, and he must turn away from himself for that. He looks about him, studies the face of business or of affairs, catches some intimation of their larger objects, is guided by the intimation, and presently finds himself part of the motive force of communities or of nations. It makes no difference how small a part, how insignificant, how unnoticed. When his powers begin to play outward, and he loves the task at hand, not because it gains him a livelihood, but because it makes him a life, he has come to himself.

There is a negative side also. Men come to themselves by discovering their limitations no less than by discovering their deeper endowments and the mastery that will make them happy. It is the discovery of what they can *not* do, and ought not to attempt, that transforms reformers into statesmen; and great should be the joy of the world over every reformer who comes to himself. The spectacle is not rare; the method is not hidden.

The practicability of every reform is determined absolutely and always by "the circumstances of the case," and only those who put themselves into the midst of affairs, either by action or by observation, can know what those circumstances are or perceive what they signify.

No statesman dreams of doing whatever he pleases; he knows that it does not follow that because a point of morals or of policy is obvious to him it will be obvious to the nation, or even to his own friends; and it is the strength of a democratic polity that there are so many minds to be consulted and brought to agreement, and that nothing can be wisely done for which the thought, and a good deal more than the thought, of the country, its sentiment and its purpose, have not been prepared. Social reform is a matter of cooperation, and, if it be of a novel kind, requires an infinite deal of converting to bring the efficient majority to believe in it and support it. Without their agreement and support it is impossible.

Every man has both an absolute and a relative capacity: an absolute in that he has been endued with such a nature and with such parts and faculties; and a relative in that he is part of the universal community of men, and so stands in such a relation to the whole. When we say that a man has come to himself, it is not of his absolute capacity that we are thinking, but of his relative. He has begun to realize that he is part of a whole, and to know *what* part, suitable for what service and achievement.

It was once fashionable — and that not a very long time ago — to speak of political society with a certain distaste, as a necessary evil, an irritating but inevitable restriction upon the "natural" sovereignty and entire self-government of the individual.

That was the dream of the egotist. It was a theory in which men were seen to strut in the proud consciousness of their several and "absolute" capacities. It would be as instructive as it would be difficult to count the errors it has bred in political thinking. As a matter of fact, men have never dreamed of wishing to do without the "trammels" of organized society, for the very good reason that those trammels are in reality no trammels at all, but indispensable aids and spurs to the attainment of the highest and most enjoyable things man is capable of.

Political society, the life of men in states, is an abiding natural relationship. It is neither a mere convenience nor a mere necessity. It is not a mere voluntary association, not a mere corporation. It is nothing deliberate or artificial, devised for a special purpose.

It is in real truth the eternal and natural expression and embodiment of a form of life higher than that of the individual — that common life of mutual helpfulness, stimulation, and contest which gives leave and opportunity to the individual life, makes it possible, makes it full and complete.

It is in such a scene that man looks about to discover his own place and force. In the midst of men organized, infinitely cross-related, bound by ties of interest, hope, affection, subject to authorities, to opinion, to passion, to visions and desires which no man can reckon, he casts eagerly about to find where he may enter in with the rest and be a man among his fellows. In making his place, he finds, if he seeks intelligently and with eyes that see, more than ease of spirit and scope for his mind. He finds himself — as if mists had cleared away about him and he knew at last his neighborhood among men and tasks.

What every man seeks is satisfaction. He deceives himself so long as he imagines it to lie in self-indulgence, so long as he deems himself the center and object of effort. His mind is spent in vain upon itself. Not in action itself, not in "pleasure," shall it find its desires satisfied, but in consciousness of right, of powers greatly and nobly spent. It comes to know itself in the motives which satisfy it, in the zest and power of rectitude.

Christianity has liberated the world, not as a system of ethics, not as a philosophy of altruism, but by its revelation of the power of pure and unselfish love. Its vital principle is not its code, but its motive. Love, clear-sighted, loyal, personal, is its breath and immortality. Christ came, not to save Himself, assuredly, but to save the world. His motive, His example, are every man's key to his own gifts and happiness. The ethical code he taught may no doubt be matched, here a piece and there a piece, out of other religions, other teachings and philosophies. Every thoughtful man born with a conscience must know a code of right and of pity to which he ought to conform; but without the motive of Christianity, without love, he may be the purest altruist and yet be as sad and as unsatisfied as Marcus Aurelius.

Christianity gave us, in the fullness of time, the perfect image of right living, the secret of social and of individual well-being; for the two are not separable, and the man who receives and verifies that secret in his own living has discovered not only the best and only way to serve the world, but also the one happy way to satisfy himself. Henceforth he knows what his powers mean, what spiritual air they breathe, what ardors of service clear them of lethargy, relieve them of all sense of effort, put them at their best. After this fretfulness passes away, experience mellows and strengthens and makes more fit, and old age brings, not senility, not satiety, not regret, but higher hope and serene maturity.

Wilson had now "come to himself." From now on, the principles, the fundamentals, which he had found out for himself, by looking for them in the lives of men, in institutions, in books, in life itself, were to be applied in trying to make those phases of life "come to themselves" in accordance with these principles — and with the least possible use of expediency, but use of expediency where necessary.

JANUARY 21, 1902 [TO FREDERICK J. TURNER]

I was forty-five three weeks ago, and between forty-five and fifty-five, I take it, is when a man ought to do the work into which he expects to put most of himself.

I was born a politician, and must be at the task for which, by means of my historical writings, I have all these years been in training.

In June, 1902, the Board of Trustees of Princeton University unanimously elected Wilson as president of the institution — the first time in its history that a layman had been so honored.

JULY 12, 1902 [TO MRS. EDITH G. REID]

I have received hundreds of letters about my election to the presidency of the University, and many of them have been from very dear friends, but yours struck a note unlike any of the rest, and roused in me a special sort of gratitude, a deep sense of the genuine affection of a nature deeper, of surer instinct for the heart of friendship, than the others. *You* were thinking of *me* — of the office hardly at all; the rest of the office chiefly and of their pleasure that I should have been honoured with it. It is not egotism that I should like your way best. You give me a friendship which is for *myself* — and that I crave more than all the honours and all the praises it were possible to win.

No doubt I shall have to give up writing for the next three or four years, and that is a heartbreaking thing for a fellow who has not yet written the particular thing for which he has been training all his life; but when I can tell you the circumstances I am sure that you will say that it was my duty to accept. It was a singularly plain, a *blessedly* plain, case.

Sometimes I am a bit ashamed of myself when I think how few friends I have amidst a host of acquaintances. Plenty of people offer me their friendship; but, partly because I am reserved and shy, and partly because I am fastidious and have a narrow, uncatholic taste in friends, I reject the offer in almost every case; and then am dismayed to look about and see how few persons in the world stand near and know me as I am — in such wise that they can give me sympathy and close support of heart. Perhaps it is because when I give at all I want to give my whole heart, and I feel that so few want it all, or would return measure for measure. Am I wrong, do you think, in that feeling? And can one as deeply covetous of friendship and close affection as I am afford to act upon such a feeling? In any case, you know why such a friendship as yours is a priceless treasure to me.

JULY 19, 1902 [TO ELLEN AXSON WILSON]

Fortunately, I never worked out the argument on liberal studies, which is the theme of my inaugural, before, never before having treated myself as a professional "educator," and so the matter is not stale but fresh and interesting.

I am quite straightening out my ideas! — and that amuses me. I feel like a new prime minister getting ready to address his constituents.

PART II

When a University Comes to
Itself

CHAPTER EIGHT

"Princeton for the Nation's Service"

≫≪≫≪≫≪≫≪≫≪≫≪≫≪≫≪≫≪≫≪≫≪≫≪

OCTOBER 25, 1902

In his inaugural address as president of Princeton, Wilson set forth his ideas of what a university in a democracy should be. Here is his declaration of "democratic education" which he tried to put into effect later.

In planning for Princeton, we are planning for the country. The service of institutions of learning is not private, but public. It is plain what the nation needs as its affairs grow more and more complex and its interests begin to touch the ends of the earth. It needs efficient and enlightened men. The universities of the country must take part in supplying them.

American universities serve a free nation whose progress, whose power, whose prosperity, whose happiness, whose integrity depend upon individual initiative and the sound sense and equipment of the rank and file. Their history, moreover, has set them apart to a character and service of their own. Their task is two-fold: the production of a great body of informed and thoughtful men and the production of a small body of trained scholars and investigators.

These two functions are not to be performed separately, but side by side, and are to be informed with one spirit, the spirit of enlightenment, a spirit of learning which is neither superficial nor pedantic, which values life more than it values the mere acquisitions of the mind.

When we insist that a certain general education shall precede all special training which is not merely mechanic in its scope and purpose, we mean simply that every mind needs for its highest serviceability a certain preliminary orientation, that it may get its bearings and release its perceptions for a wide and catholic view. We must deal in college with the spirits of men, not with their fortunes. Here, in history and philosophy and literature and science, are the experiences of the world summed up.

There are two ways of preparing a young man for his life work. One is to give him the skill and special knowledge which shall make a good tool, an excellent bread-winning tool, of him; and for thousands of young men that way must be followed. It is a good way. It is honorable, it is indispensable. But it is not for the college, and it never can be.

The college should seek to make the men whom it receives something more than excellent servants of a trade or skilled practitioners of a profession. It should give them elasticity of faculty and breadth of vision, so that they shall have a surplus of mind to expend, not upon their profession only, for its liberalization and enlargement, but also upon the broader interests which lie about them, in the spheres in which they are to be, not breadwinners merely, but citizens as well, and in their own hearts, where they are to grow to the stature of real nobility.

It is this free capital of mind the world most stands in need of — this free capital that awaits investment in undertakings, spiritual as well as material, which advance the race and help all men to a better life.

The true American university seems to me to get its best characteristic, its surest guarantee of sane and catholic learning, from the presence at its very heart of a college of liberal arts. Its vital union with the college gives it, it seems to me, the true university atmosphere, a pervading sense of the unity and unbroken circle of learning.

It is not the education that concentrates that is to be dreaded, but the education that narrows — that is narrow from the first.

I should wish to see every student made, not a man of his task, but a man of the world, whatever his world may be. If it be the world of learning, then he should be a conscious and a broad-minded citizen of it. If it be the world of letters, his thought should run free upon the whole field of it. If it be the world of affairs, he should move amidst affairs like a man of thought.

What we seek in education is a full liberation of the faculties, and the man who has not some surplus of thought and energy to expend outside the narrow circle of his own task and interest is a dwarfed, uneducated man. We judge the range and excellence of every man's abilities by their play outside the task by which he earns his livelihood.

We mean to build a notable graduate college, not apart, but as nearly as may be at the very heart, the geographical heart, of the university; and its comradeship shall be for young men and old, for the novice as well as for the graduate. It will constitute but a single term in the scheme of coordination which is our ideal.

Our generation must be supplied with men who care more for principles than for money, for the right adjustments of life than for the gross accumulations of profit. The problems that call for sober thoughtfulness and mere devotion are as pressing as those which call for practical efficiency. We are here not merely to release the faculties of men for their own use, but also to quicken their social understanding, instruct their consciences, and give them the catholic vision of those who know their just relations to their fellow men. Here in America, for every man touched with nobility, for every man touched with the spirit of our institutions, social service is the high law of duty, and every American university must square its standards by that law or lack its national title.

We are not put into this world to sit still and know; we are put into it to act.

I have studied the history of America; I have seen her grow great in the paths of liberty and of progress by following after great ideals. Every concrete thing that she has done has seemed to rise out of some abstract principle, some vision of the mind. Her greatest victories have been the victories of peace and of humanity. A new age is before us, in which, it would seem, we must lead the world.

The spirit of the age will lift us to that great enterprise. The ancient spirit of sound learning will also rule us. We shall demonstrate in our lecture rooms again and again the old principles that have made us free and great.

There are some drill subjects which are just as necessary as the measles in order to make a man a grown-up person. But there are other subjects, what I call reading subjects, like philosophy, like literature, like law, like history. In those subjects it is futile to try to instruct men by mere classroom methods. The only way to instruct them is to provide a certain number of men sufficiently qualified as instructors, as scholars, who will be the companions and coaches and guides of the men's reading, just as if we supplied the university with a score or more, with fifty or more, reference librarians, to say "If you want to get up such and such a subject here is the central and most authoritative literature on that subject, these are the books to read. If there are hard places in them we will explain them, if you lose your compass in the journey we will find your whereabouts again. You may report to us from time to time, you may consort with us every evening, we are your companions and coaches in the business, we are at your service."

That, you will say, is the English tutorial system. Yes, but the English make an old-fashioned mistake about it; they appoint their tutors for life and their tutors go to seed. No man can do that sort of thing for youngsters without getting tired of it. It makes it necessary that he should always be understanding the difficulties of beginners, and after awhile, ceasing to be a beginner himself, the thing becomes intolerable to him. He wants to go on about the independent research for which his beginnings have made him fit, and, therefore, I do not believe you could afford to keep an ordinary tutor for more than five years at that particular job.

If we could get a body of such tutors at Princeton we could transform the place from a place where there are youngsters doing tasks to a place where there are men doing thinking, men who are conversing about the things of thought, men who are eager and interested in the things of thought.

Wherever you have a small class and they can be intimately associated with their chief in the study of an interesting subject they catch the infection of the subject; but where they are in big classes and simply hear a man lecture two or three times a week, they cannot catch the infection of anything, except it may be the voice and enthusiasm of the lecturer himself.

In brief, the system will be a method of study, a means of familiarizing the undergraduate with the chief authorities, conceptions and orders of work in his fields of study. The preceptors will not set the examinations. That would turn them into mere coaches, coaching for final tests which they themselves were to set. They are, rather, to be fellow-students, expositors, advisers, to see that the right work is done by themselves taking part in it.

They will not be a body of men segregated and set apart from the general body of the faculty. The present staff of the university will also do preceptorial work; the new preceptors will take some part in the lecture and regular class work, which will still go forward; they will be members of the faculty, indistinguishable in privilege and rank from their colleagues.

The fundamental object of the system would be defeated if any sharp line of division were drawn in the faculty between the several kinds of teachers, for the fundamental object is to draw faculty and undergraduates together into a common body of students, old and young, among whom a real community of interest, pursuit and feeling will prevail. The preceptors will only have more conference work to do than their colleagues. It will be their chief, if not their distinctive, function to devote their energies to the intimate work of counsel and guidance I have tried to characterize and describe.

It is our confident hope that such changes will bring about very gratifying results: that the undergraduate will take more pleasure in his studies, derive more profit and stimulation from them, and that the instructor will find vital intercourse with his pupils takes the place of dull routine. There will be more work done, but it will be less burdensome both to teacher and pupil, more normal, less like a body of tasks and more like a natural enjoyment of science and letters.

CHAPTER NINE

Education and Democracy

⊱⊰⊱⊰⊱⊰⊱⊰⊱⊰⊱⊰⊱⊰⊱⊰⊱⊰⊱⊰⊱⊰⊱⊰⊱⊰

As a college president, Wilson began getting closer contacts with life, began to realize that things in theory did not always work out in practice. From now on he was to get a thorough indoctrination in what "makes the mare go" — namely, money, even in a university.

OCTOBER 13, 1904 ["THE YOUNG PEOPLE AND THE CHURCH" FROM THE *Sunday School Times*]

When you think of it, we are engaged in the somewhat questionable practice of making all the world uniform.

There are two means by which we carry on this interesting work of making the next generation like the last. There is life itself, and that is the most drastic school there is. There is no school so hard in its lessons as the school of life. You are not excused from any one of its exercises. You are not excused for mistakes in any one of its lessons. We say a great many things that are harsh, and deservedly harsh, I will admit, about college hazing; but there is a more subtle hazing than that.

The world hazes the persons that will not conform. It hazes after a manner that is worse than hazing their bodies — it hazes their spirits, and teases them with the pointed finger and the curl of the lip, and says, "That man thinks he knows the whole thing."

That, I say, is a very much more refined torture than making a man do a great many ridiculous things for the purpose of realizing that he is ridiculous, and so getting out of conceit with himself. I do not believe in hazing, but I do believe that there are some things worse than hazing. And I have suffered worse things from my fellow-men since I got out of college than I suffered while I was in college.

The other means we have of indoctrinating the next generation and making the world uniform is organization.

In the first place, there is the home; then there is the school; then there is the church; then there are all the political means, the means which we call social in their character, by which to mold and control the rising generation. All of these have their part in controlling the youth of the country and making them what we deem it necessary that they should be.

What do we wish that they should be? If forced to reason about it, we say they ought to be what we have found by experience it is prudent and wise to be; and they ought to be something more — they ought to go one stage beyond the stage we have gone.

But we cannot conduct them beyond the stage we have reached. We can only point and say, "Here are the boundaries which we have reached; beyond is an undiscovered country; go out and discover it. We can furnish you with a few probabilities; we can supply you with a few tendencies; we can say to you that we think that wisdom points in this direction; but we cannot go with you; we cannot guide you; we must part with you at the opening of the door, and bid you Godspeed. But we want you to go on; we do not want you to stop where we stopped."

All the wise saws and prudent maxims and pieces of information that we supply to the generation coming on are of no consequence whatever in themselves *unless they get into the blood and are transmuted.*

And how are you going to get these things into the blood? You know that nothing communicates fire except fire. In order to start a fire you must originate a fire. You must have a little spark in order to have a great blaze. I have often heard it said that a speaker is dry, or that a subject is dry.

Well, there isn't any subject in the world that is dry. It is the person that handles it and the person who receives it that are dry.

The subject is fertile enough. But the trouble with most persons when they handle a subject is that they handle it as if it were a mere aggregate mass meant to stay where it was placed; whereas it is something to be absorbed into the pores, to have the life circulation communicated to it, and the moment you communicate that to it, it itself becomes a vehicle of life. Every one who touches a live thing knows he has touched living tissue, and not a dead hand.

The moral of which is simply this, that the truths which are not translated into lives are dead truths, and not living truths.

In his first three years as president of Princeton, Wilson made extraordinary progress. His preceptoral system was an instant success.

MAY 19, 1906 ["THE PRECEPTORAL SYSTEM," IN THE *Alumni Weekly*]

One of the undergraduates the other day said, in a tone of great condemnation, that Princeton was not the place it used to be — that men were actually talking about their studies at the clubs. He evidently regretted that as an invasion of the privileges of undergraduate life.

But the beauty of the situation is that the studies of the University are becoming a part of the life of the University, and for my part I don't care a peppercorn for studies which do not constitute a part of the life of the men who are pursuing them.

I believe that there has been in all our universities in years past too much of the spirit of schoolboys; not because the men there were not often really interested in their studies, but because the processes of the University kept them schoolboys in their attitude toward their studies; now at Princeton they are beginning to feel that they are coming into the privileges of manhood.

The new thing we are introducing is the independent pursuit of certain studies by men old enough to study for themselves and accorded the privilege in their studies of having the counsel of scholars older than themselves. It is not merely that they are being led, but that they are becoming what every university student ought to be, reading men.

MARCH 15, 1907 [TO MRS. EDITH G. REID]

Why any sane man who wishes *some* of the reasonable delights of life — friendship, for example — should ever allow himself to be made a college president I can understand only because I know at least one case in which the victim had no notion what he was getting into! I literally have not had *time* to write.

Although his single-track mind was concerned mostly with the university, Wilson knew what was going on in the field of politics. Teddy Roosevelt had become President in 1901 and had been re-elected in 1904. This was the beginning of the period of the "muck-rakers." Problems of great wealth, of labor and capital, of graft and misgovernment, were widely discussed. Ida Tarbell, Jacob Riis, Lincoln Steffens, Charles E. Hughes, and others, were making significant criticisms of the American way of life. Over it all Teddy Roosevelt, "booted and spurred, rode the wild horses of reform."

Wilson not only heard the noise but knew what it meant. Much of the screaming and yelling were to him wasted "evangelism." What was needed was constructive action; governments should have high-minded leadership; the university should prepare men for just this. What we needed was "not more heat but more light."

By 1906 he was turning his attention to constructive ways to eliminate from the campus at Princeton the same harmful influences that were working such devastation on the world outside. He saw primarily in the eating clubs — the upper-class clubs that filled the role of fraternities in other colleges — a "decrease of democratic, increase of social feeling." The answer was to reintegrate by creating a college comradeship based not on a social distinction but on letters. "We now have tutor and pupil, now we must have pupil and pupil in a comradeship of studies," he wrote in a memorandum in 1906.

All the while he was becoming, by his writing and speaking, more of a national figure.

On February 3, 1906, Colonel George Harvey, editor of Harper's, at a dinner of the Lotos Club in New York, proposed Wilson for the Presidency of the United States.

By now Wilson had definitely shifted his political viewpoint from that of a mild "Federalist" (although he never shared Hamilton's economic views nor his contempt of the people) to the Jeffersonian.

He phrased it this way:

I follow Jefferson because of his objects and his principles. It is indeed his spirit that rules us from his urn.

His principles were the right of the individual to opportunity and the right of the people to a development not monopolized by the few.

JUNE 10, 1907 ["REPORT ON THE SOCIAL CO-ORDINATION OF THE UNIVERSITY," IN THE *Alumni Weekly*]

In this report Wilson dropped the bomb that was ultimately to catapult him out of the university into politics. In many ways it might be called the "Declaration of Educational Independence." In it he set forth the reasons why, if democracy is to live, democracy first must be made an integral part of the education of and for democracy.

Leisure and study ought not to be separated in airtight compartments. Leisure ought to be enriched and diversified by the interests which study creates. In the midst of play there ought to be a constant consciousness of what the place means and must be made to stand for — a place of thoughtful, manly, disinterested men, disciples of university ideals.

When we introduced the preceptorial system we made the greatest strategic move in that direction that has been made in the whole history of American universities. By it we meant to say that the intellectual life of a college did not consist of attendance upon class exercises or of preparation for recitations, but consisted, rather, of constant contact with study and the intimate association of teacher and pupil outside the class room, where the tradition of lectures and recitations was forgotten, rejected, and a thoroughly natural and human relationship, the relationship of fellow-students, substituted. And that meaning has at once been made evident to the whole country.

The contrast with the old order of things is most marked in the case of the intercourse of undergraduates with those preceptors who invite them often to their houses or who live in the same dormitories with them. A natural and easy social relationship, an informal, frequent exchange of calls, the easy, unconstrained talks of ordinary comradeship make study itself seem a thing natural and human, a thing not so much of formal exaction under rules as of the vital contact of minds. It is, by intention and in actual fact, a widening of the atmosphere of study to seem a natural medium of life and serious enjoyment.

But the new process, vital as it is in itself, suited as it is to the object we have had in view, may be checked and even nullified by hostile or unfavorable influences.

Our new methods of study require as their soil an indispensable environment, a new social coordination — a coordination which will not only make sure of a constant and natural intercourse between teacher and pupil, but also knit the student body itself together in some truly organic way which will ensure vital intellectual and academic contacts, the comradeships of a common life with common ends.

This can best be done by combining the undergraduates in residential groups — groups so made up that the forms and conditions under which each man in residence lives may so far as possible be the forms and conditions which are common to all.

Our social life for generations together has formed itself around the boarding house and club tables. Men have associated themselves with congenial groups of companions to eat together, and, when no sufficiently comfortable boarding house could be found, have rented or built quarters of their own in which they could command their own comforts and their own bill of fare in pleasing independence.

The outcome in our own day has been the development of the upper-class clubs with their attractive club houses, in each of which there are not only dining rooms and kitchens and servants' quarters, but also well-appointed common rooms, libraries, billiard rooms, smoking rooms, private dining rooms for parties, and sleeping rooms for visitors.

The evident peculiarity of this life is that it severs the social from the intellectual interests of the place, and does not, with its scattered clubs and divided classes, make us up into a community even on the social side. The vital units are the club units.

They divide all four classes into segments and sharply separate the classes as wholes from one another during the two earlier years of the undergraduate course, when characters are being formed and points of view established.

Their organization is entirely outside university action; has no organic connection whatever with anything academic; produces interests which absorb the attention and the energy of the best undergraduates as of all others, and yet nowhere interpenetrates the associations which arise out of study, carries no flavour with it which it might not as well have in any other town or in any other similar environment.

It absorbs the attention and all the planning faculties of the undergraduates because all social ambitions turn upon it. It would be difficult to exaggerate the importance in the life of the undergraduate of the question whether at the end of his Sophomore year he is going to be taken into one of the upper-class clubs. His thought is constantly fixed upon that object throughout the first two years of his university course with a great intensity and uneasiness whenever he thinks either of his social standing, his comradeships, or his general social consideration among his fellows. The clubs do not take in all the members of the Junior and Senior classes.

About one-third are left out in the elections; and their lot is little less than deplorable. They feel that they cannot continue to associate on terms of intimacy with friends who have been elected into the clubs, for fear that they will be thought to be seeking to make favour with them and obtain a belated invitation to join; and, even when many of them as individuals are not disappointed at having been passed by, they must seek their comradeships with other classmates who are very much disappointed and who feel their isolation with a good deal of bitterness. It is difficult for them to arrange for comfortable eating places; and the places at which they do board are only too much like caves of Adullam.

They go forward to their graduation almost like men who are in the University and yet not of it. Often they are cheerful and steadfast enough; individuals here and there are sometimes quite indifferent to their comparative isolation, being absorbed in their books or in the task of earning the money necessary to pay their college expenses, but as a class their position is most trying, and most discreditable to our university democracy. It often happens that men who fail of election into one of the clubs at the end of the Sophomore year leave the University and go to some other college or abandon altogether the idea of completing their university course.

Two very significant and very undesirable, and even dangerous, things have thus come about: the two lower classes, who need above all things the forming and guiding influence of the upper classes, have been almost completely segregated, and the very influences which seemed to render their segregation necessary from the point of view of the clubmen have brought about the very result their segregation was meant to prevent — that is, they have cut them up into groups and cliques whose social ambitions give them separate and rival interests quite distinct from, plainly hostile to, the interests of the University as a whole.

Along with the steadily increasing concentration of the attention of the undergraduates upon the social question and the centering of all social ambitions upon the upper-class clubs has gone a very noticeable, a very rapid, increase in the luxury of the upper-class club houses. The two oldest clubs now have houses of extraordinary elegance and luxury of appointment and five other clubs are maturing plans for replacing their present comfortable structures with buildings which will rival the others in beauty, spaciousness, and comfort. The University, which gives life to these clubs, seems in danger of becoming, if the present tendencies of undergraduate organization are allowed to work out their logical results, only an artistic setting and background for life on Prospect Avenue.

That life, as it becomes more and more elaborate, will become more and more absorbing, and university interests will fall more and more into the background. The interest of the lower classes will more and more centre upon it and the energies of the upper classes will be more and more engrossed by it. The vital life of the place will be outside the University and in large part independent of it.

Before the establishment of the preceptorial system, with its necessary corollary of the intimate association of teacher and pupil — the coordination of the undergraduate life with the teaching of the University — these things were not so near the heart of our plans and hopes for Princeton's intellectual development and academic revitalization. But now they are of the essence of everything we are striving for, whether on the undergraduate or on the graduate side of the University's work, and we are bound to consider the means by which to effect an immediate reintegration of our academic life.

The only adequate means of accomplishing this is the grouping of the undergraduates in residential quadrangles, each with its common dining hall, its common room for intercourse and diversion, and its resident master and preceptors; where members of all four of the classes shall be associated in a sort of family life, not merely as neighbors in the dormitories but also as comrades at meals and in many daily activities — the upper classes ruling and forming the lower, and all in constant association with members of the Faculty fitted to act in sympathetic cooperation with them in the management of their common life. The only way in which the social life of the undergraduates can be prevented from fatally disordering, and perhaps even strangling, the academic life of the University is by the actual absorption of the social life into the academic.

JULY 1, 1907 [TO CLEVELAND H. DODGE]

Richardson, the physicist, the other day expressed in a very striking manner his astonishment at the social conditions here, and said that they were such as would strangle the university.

When I was at Harvard the other day, the men I talked with up there were most deeply interested and most warmly congratulatory. Their general sentiment was, "If you do it, we must; and we ought all long ago to have done it."

The fight is on, and I regard it, not as a fight for the development, but as a fight for the restoration of Princeton. My heart is in it more than it has been in anything else, because it is a scheme of salvation.

At first it seemed that Wilson was going to succeed in his program for the social co-ordination of Princeton. But not for long. Opposition developed against the plan as one that took away property rights, that killed class spirit; the largest group simply resented the move as an attempt to dictate to the students how they should arrange their social life. "No man can make a gentleman associate with a mucker," became the motto of this group — a mucker being a nonmember of the eating clubs.

Pretty soon the opposition reached alarming proportions. This merely made Wilson fight all the harder — it convinced him that the evil was much worse than he had suspected.

The board accepted Wilson's proposal — which had been given to it as a committee's report — in June. Then in October, by pressure from the alumni, the board reversed its stand. It seemed to him that vested property rights, social privileges, empty ceremonies, were more powerful than the intellectual vitality of Princeton.

"You'll win yet," said his brother-in-law, Stockton Axson.

"No, I won't," said Wilson. "What I am opposing is privilege. They would let me do anything in educational reform, but here I am attacking social privilege."

In an article in the Atlantic Monthly, *November, 1907, Wilson pointed out that "business organization is so different from our old, to which we had adjusted our morals and our economic analyses, that we find ourselves confused when we try to think out its problems." Above all, he warned, "the individual is lost in the organization."*

He further warned that if individual responsibility was not again recovered, by law, further and further governmental regulation was to be expected, which ultimately would result in government own-ership.

He reiterated over and over that to solve the problem would re-quire the right sort of thinking and the right sort of trained men.

Thus it was, to him, that the trouble besetting Princeton — the trend there away from democracy — was just a little pimple in the larger "national disease."

The political scene did not offer much hope. In 1908 the Republi-cans nominated William H. Taft and the Democrats put up Wil-liam J. Bryan. The former, to Wilson, represented the vested inter-ests, and the latter represented "evangelistic" methods of reform that were not soberly or properly thought out.

In a speech on April 13, 1908, Wilson set forth the crux of his ideas on government:

The familiar Jeffersonian maxim that that government is the best which governs least, translated into the terms of modern experience, means that that government is best whose processes least expose the individual to arbitrary interference and the choices of governors, which makes him most secure of the regular and impartial admin-istration of fixed and uniform rules, which makes no distinction between class and class, aims always at eliminating undesirable transactions rather than at setting up official interference with the management of business, and looks to individuals, not to the general public to bear the penalties of infraction.

Law, and the government as umpire; not discretionary power, and the government as master, should be the program of every man who loves liberty and the established character of the Republic.

SEPTEMBER 30, 1908

In a speech, "The Banker and the Nation," he pointed out what the real struggle in the United States was:

For the first time in the history of America there is a general feel-ing that the issue is now joined, or about to be joined, between the power of accumulated capital and the privileges and opportunities of the masses of the people. The power of accumulated capital is now, as at all other times and in all other circumstances, in the hands of a comparatively small number of persons, but there is a very widespread impression that those persons have been able in recent years as never before to control the national development in their own interest.

The contest is sometimes said to be between capital and labor, but that is a too narrow and too special conception of it. It is, rather, between capital in all its larger accumulations and all other less concentrated, more dispersed, smaller, and more individual economic forces; and every new policy proposed has as its immediate or ultimate object the restraint of the power of accumulated capital for the protection and benefit of those who cannot command its use.

This process of segregation and contrast is always a symptom of deep discontent. It is not set afoot accidentally. It generally comes about, as it has come about now, because the several parts of society have forgotten their organic connections, their vital interdependence, and have become individually selfish or hostile — because the attention of a physician is in fact necessary.

The most striking fact about the actual organization of modern society is that the most conspicuous, the most readily wielded, and the most formidable power is not the power of government, but the power of capital.

Men of our day in England and America have almost forgotten what it is to fear the Government, but have found out what it is to fear the power of capital, to watch it with jealousy and suspicion, and trace to it the source of every open or hidden wrong. Our memories are not of history, but of what our own lives and experiences and the lives and experiences of the men about us have disclosed. We have had no experience in our day, or in the days of which our fathers have told us, of the tyranny of governments, of their minute control and arrogant interference and arbitrary regulation of our business and of our daily life, though it may be that we shall know something of it in the near future.

We have forgotten what the power of government means and have found out what the power of capital means; and so we do not fear government and are not jealous of political power. We fear capital and are jealous of its domination.

There will be need of many cool heads and much excellent judgment amongst us to curb this new power without throwing ourselves back into the gulf of the old from which we were the first of the nations of the world to find a practicable way of escape.

The only forces that can save us from the one extreme or the other are those forces of social reunion and social reintegration which every man of station and character and influence in the country can in some degree and within the scope of his own life set afoot.

We must open our minds wide to the new circumstances of our time, must bring about a new common understanding and effect a new coordination in the affairs which most concern us.

Capital must give over its too great preoccupation with the business of making those who control it individually rich and must study to serve the interests of the people as a whole. It must draw near to the people and serve them in some intimate way of which they will be conscious.

Voluntary cooperation must forestall the involuntary cooperation which legislators will otherwise seek to bring about by the coercion of law. Capital now looks to the people like a force and interest apart, with which they must deal as with a master and not as with a friend.

Wilson then went on to tell the bankers that "bankers, like men of every other interest, have their lot and part in the nation," and that how "capital is to draw near to the people and serve them at once obviously and safely is the question, the great and now pressing question, which it is the particular duty of the banker to answer." In conclusion he said, "There is a sense in which in a democratic country statesmanship is forced upon every man capable of leading anybody."

Since the bankers did not choose to do this voluntarily, it was left up to Wilson, as President, to do it through the Federal Reserve System.

The question of yielding private interest to public welfare, to the betterment of others, brought forth from Wilson an important distinction:

JANUARY 19, 1909 [AN ADDRESS ON "ROBERT E. LEE"]

I have sometimes noted with a great deal of interest how careless we are about most words in our language, and yet how careful we are about some others; for example, there is one word which we do not use carelessly and that is the word "noble." We use the word "great" indiscriminately. A man is great because he has had great material success and has piled up a fortune; a man is great because he is a great writer, or a great orator; a man is great because he is a great hero. We notice in him some distinct quality that overtops like qualities in other men. But we reserve the word "noble" carefully for those whose greatness is not spent in their own interest.

In this speech he also warned:

There is one lesson that the peoples of the world have learned so often that they ought to esteem themselves contemptible if they have to learn it again, and that is that if you concentrate the management of a people's affairs in a single central government and carry that concentration beyond a certain point of oversight and regulation, you will certainly provoke again those revolutionary processes by which individual liberty was asserted. We have had so little excess of government in this country that we have forgotten that excess of government is the very antithesis of liberty. We want to see to it that, though there is control, it is control of law and not the discretionary control of executive officials. We want to see to it that while there is the restraint of abuses, it is persons who are restrained, and not unnamed bodies of persons. There is only, historically speaking, one possible successful punishment of abuses of law, and that is, that when a wrong thing is done you find the man who did it and punish him.

FEBRUARY 12, 1909 [ON CAUTIOUS MEN]

God save a free country from cautious men — men, I mean, cautious for themselves — for cautious men are men who will not speak the truth if the speaking of it threatens to damage them. Caution is the confidential agent of selfishness.

Life is a very complex thing. No theory I ever heard will match its varied pattern; and the men who are dangerous are the men who are not content with understanding, but go on to propound theories, things which will make a new pattern for society and a new model for the universe. Those are the men who are not to be trusted. Because, although you steer by the North Star, when you have lost the bearings of your compass, you nevertheless must steer a pathway on the sea — you are not bound for the North Star.

A new element entered Wilson's struggle at Princeton — the location of a new building for the graduate school. As Wilson had stated in his inaugural address, it was essential to him that the graduate school should be near the "geographical" heart of the university so that his entire program of integration — of making the university a democratic place — should be of a whole. Now, with money ready for building, the dean of the graduate school, Andrew F. West, insisted that it should be built at a great distance from the rest of the campus. The man giving the money sided with West. The details of the struggle are not important; the principle is. But before the entire struggle came to an end, Wilson had gone to Abraham Lincoln for his answers on many things and from them had formulated some important conclusions.

FEBRUARY 12, 1909 [IN AN ADDRESS, "A MAN OF THE PEOPLE: ABRAHAM LINCOLN"]

This country is going to have crisis after crisis. God send they may not be bloody crises; but they will be intense and acute. No body politic so abounding in life and so puzzled by problems as ours is can avoid moving from crisis to crisis. We must have the leadership of sane, genial men of universal use like Lincoln, to save us from mistakes and give us the necessary leadership in such days of struggle and of difficulty. And yet, such men will hereafter have to be produced among us by processes which are not characteristically American, *but which belong to the whole world.*

It seems to me serviceable, therefore, to ask ourselves what it is that we must reproduce in order not to lose the splendid breed of men of this calibre. Mr. Lincoln we describe as "a man of the people," and he was a man of the people, essentially. But what do we mean by a "man of the people"?

We mean a man who has his rootage deep in the experiences and the consciousness of the ordinary mass of his fellow-men; but we do not mean a man whose rootage is holding him at their level. We mean a man who, drawing his sap from such sources, has, nevertheless, risen above the level of the rest of mankind and has got an outlook over their heads, seeing horizons which they are too submerged to see; a man who finds and draws his inspiration from the common plane, but nevertheless has lifted himself to a new place of outlook and of insight; who has come out from the people and is their leader, not because he speaks from their ranks, but because he speaks for them and for their interests.

A great nation is not led by a man who simply repeats the talk of the street-corners or the opinions of the newspapers. A nation is led by a man who hears more than those things; or who, rather, hearing those things, understands them better, unites them, puts them into a common meaning; speaks, not the rumors of the street, but a new principle for a new age; a man in whose ears the voices of the nation do not sound like the accidental and discordant notes that come from the voice of a mob, but concurrent and concordant like the united voices of a chorus, whose many meanings unite in his understanding in a single meaning and reveal to him a single vision, so that he can speak what no man else knows, the common meaning of the common voice. Such is the man who leads a great, free, democratic nation.

How shall we know him when he emerges to our view?

Well, in the first place, it seems to me that a man of the people is a man who sees affairs as the people see them, and not as a man of particular classes or the professions sees them. You cannot afford to take the advice of a man who has been too long submerged in a particular profession — not because you cannot trust him to be honest and candid, but because he has been too long immersed and submerged, and through the inevitable pressure and circumstances of his life has come to look upon the nation from a particular point of view.

The man of the people is a man who looks far and wide upon the nation, and is not limited by a professional point of view. A man of the people is not subdued by any stuff of life that he has happened to work in; he is free to move in any direction his spirit prompts.

Why was it that Mr. Lincoln was wiser than the professional politicians? Because the professional politicians had burrowed into particular burrows and Mr. Lincoln walked on the surface and saw his fellow-men. He was detached from every point of view and therefore superior to every point of view. You must have a man of this detachable sort.

Moreover, you must not have a man, if he is to be a man of the people, who is standardized and conventionalized. Look to it that your communities, your great cities, do not impose too arbitrary standards upon the men whom you wish to use.

And then, last and greatest characteristic of all, a man of the people is a man who has felt that unspoken, that intense, that almost terrifying struggle of humanity, that struggle whose object is, not to get forms of government, not to realize particular formulas or make for any definite goal, but simply to live and be free. He has participated in that struggle; he has felt the blood stream against the tissue; he has known anxiety; he has felt that life contained for him nothing but effort, effort from the rising of the sun to the going down of it. He has, therefore, felt beat in him, if he had any heart, a universal sympathy for those who struggle, a universal understanding of the unutterable things that were in their hearts and the unbearable burdens that were upon their backs.

The tasks of the future call for men like Lincoln more audibly, more imperatively, than did the tasks of the time when civil war was brewing and the very existence of the Nation was in the scale of destiny. For the things that perplex us at this moment are the things which mark, I will not say a warfare, but a division among classes; and when a nation begins to be divided into rival and contestant interests by the score, the time is much more dangerous than when it is divided into only two perfectly distinguishable interests, which you can discriminate and deal with. It is then I need a man of the people, detached from this struggle yet cognizant of it all, sympathetic with it all, saturated with it all, to whom I can say, "How do you sum it up, what are the signs of the day, what does the morning say, what are the tasks that we must set our hands to?"

The most dangerous thing you can have in an age like this is a man who is intense and hot. We have heat enough; what we want is light. Anybody can stir up emotions, but who is master of men enough to take the saddle and guide those awakened emotions? Anybody can cry a nation awake to the necessities of reform, but who shall frame the reform but a man who is cool, who takes his time, who will draw you aside for a jest?

The most valuable thing about Mr. Lincoln was that in the midst of the strain of war, in the midst of the crash of arms, he could sit quietly in his room and enjoy a book that led his thoughts off from everything American, could wander in fields of dreams, while every other man was hot with the immediate contest. Always set your faith in a man who can withdraw himself, because only the man who can withdraw himself can see affairs as they are.

We should not be Americans deserving to call ourselves the fellow-countrymen of Lincoln if we did not feel the compulsion that his example lays upon us — the compulsion, not to heed him merely but to look to our own duty, to live every day as if that were the day upon which America was to be reborn and remade; to attack every task as if we had something here that was new and virginal and original, out of which we could make the very stuff of life, by integrity, faith in our fellow-men, wherever it is deserved, absolute ignorance of any obstacle that is insuperable, patience, indomitable courage, insight, universal sympathy — with that programme opening our hearts to every candid suggestion, listening to all the voices of the nation, trying to bring in a new day of vision and of achievement.

On June 3, 1909, Wilson said:

A danger surrounding our modern education is the danger of wealth. So far as the colleges go, the sideshows have swallowed up the circus, and we don't know what is going on in the main tent: and I don't know that I want to continue as ringmaster under those circumstances.

At the same time, before he went out of the business, he was determined to make "as many of my countrymen as uncomfortable as possible." In a speech on January 17, 1910, with J. P. Morgan present, he told the bankers:

The trouble today is that you bankers are too narrow minded. You don't know the country or what is going on in it and the country doesn't trust you. There is a higher law than the law of profit. You bankers sitting in this provincial community of New York see nothing beyond your own interests and are content to sit at the receipt of customs and take tolls of all passers-by. You should be broader-minded and see what is the best for the country in the long run.

Heresy, heresy. Then, when he went on to say, in another speech, that "We do not die by corporations. We do not die by societies. We do not withdraw into our closets by companies," and that "Every man has to live with himself, remember what he did during the day, the things that he yielded to, the things that he shrugged his shoulders at and let go by," he was condemning men who had eased their consciences by thinking that they were doing things for the group, for the company.

In holding individuals responsible for what masses of individuals did, Wilson set forth a doctrine which must be understood if he is to be understood.

NOVEMBER 2, 1909 ["THE MINISTRY AND THE INDIVIDUAL"]

I have often preached in my political utterances the doctrine of expediency, and I am an unabashed disciple of that doctrine. What I mean to say is, you cannot carry the world forward as fast as a few select individuals think. The individuals who have the vigour to lead must content themselves with a slackened pace and go only so fast as they can be followed. They must not be impracticable. They must not be impossible. They must not insist upon getting at once what they know they cannot get.

But that is not inconsistent with their telling the world in very plain terms whither it is bound and what the ultimate and complete truth of the matter, as it seems to them, is. You cannot make any progress unless you know whither you are bound. The question is not a pace. That is a matter of expediency, not of direction; that is not a matter of principle.

Where the individual should be indomitable is in the choice of direction, saying: "I will not bow down to the golden calf of fashion. I will not bow down to the weak habit of pursuing everything that is popular, everything that belongs to the society to which I belong. I will insist on telling that society, if I think it so, that in certain fundamental principles it is wrong; but I won't be fool enough to insist that it adopt my programme at once for putting it right."

What I do insist upon is, speaking the full truth to it and never letting it forget the truth; speaking the truth again and again and again with every variation of the theme, until men will wake some morning and the theme will sound familiar, and they will say, "Well, after all, is it not so?" That is what I mean by the indomitable individual. Not the defiant individual, not the impracticable individual, but the individual who does try, and cannot be ashamed, and cannot be silenced; who tries to observe the fair manner of just speech but who will not hold his tongue.

It is, I suppose, a high intellectual plane upon which we think that we live, but we do not live upon intellectual planes at all; we live upon emotional planes; we live upon planes of resolution and not upon planes of doctrine, if I may put it so. And the reason that we differ so is that we hold ourselves too far above the practical levels of life and are constantly forgetting that the whole vitality of Christianity consists not in its texts, but in their translation; not in the things that we set up as the abstract standard, but in the actions which we originate as the concrete examples.

For my part, I do not see any promise of vitality either in the church or in society except upon the true basis of individualism. A nation is strong in proportion to the variety of its originative strength, and that is in proportion to the vitality of its individuals. It is rich in direct proportion to the independence of the souls of which it is made up. And so every promising scheme that unites us must still be illuminated and checked and offset by those eternal principles of individual responsibility which are repeated not only in the gospel but in human nature, in physical nature.

The struggle at Princeton had come to a head by the spring of 1910. Wilson was able to write his wife: "We have no compromise to look back on, the record of our conscience is clear in this whole trying business." The attack was now personal — as it was to become to a great extent in 1916 and 1919 — to destroy the prophet, to maintain that even if his way was right, his methods were wrong.

In a last-ditch fight, Wilson took the cause to the alumni.

APRIL 16, 1910 [ADDRESS TO ALUMNI AT PITTSBURGH]

I trust I may be thought among the last to blame the churches, yet I feel it my duty to say that they — at least the Protestant churches — are serving the classes and not the masses of the people. They have more regard for the pew rents than for men's souls. They are depressing the level of Christian endeavour.

It is the same with the universities. We look for the support of the wealthy and neglect our opportunities to serve the people.

While attending a recent Lincoln celebration I asked myself if Lincoln would have been as serviceable to the people of this country had he been a college man, and I was obliged to say to myself that he would not. The process to which the college man is subjected does not render him serviceable to the country as a whole. It is for this reason that I have dedicated every power in me to a democratic regeneration.

The American college must become saturated in the same sympathies as the common people. The colleges of this country must be reconstructed from the top to the bottom. The American people will tolerate nothing that savours of exclusiveness. Their political parties are going to pieces. They are busy with their moral regeneration and they want leaders who can help them accomplish it. Only those leaders who seem able to promise something of a moral advance are able to secure a following. The people are tired of pretense, and I ask you, as Princeton men, to heed what is going on.

In a speech on August 31, 1910, Wilson told the lawyers of the Bar Association that they had ceased to be "the mediators of progress," and that they had turned their backs on stupendous, far-reaching questions which needed lawyers with wide horizons and the public welfare at heart to settle. The country vitally needs lawyers, he summed up, "who can think in the terms of society itself, mediate between interests, accommodate right to right, establish equity, and bring the peace that will come with genuine cooperation, and will come in no other way." He went on:

The whole history of society has been the history of a struggle for law. Law is simply that part of the established thought and habit which has been accorded general acceptance and which is backed and sanctioned by the force and authority of the regularly constituted government of the body politic.

The whole history of liberty has been a struggle for the recognition of rights not only, but for the embodiment of rights in law, in courts and magistrates and assemblies.

We do not fight to establish theses. We do not pour our blood out to vindicate a philosophy of politics.

There are two great empires of human feeling, the realm of religion and the realm of political aspiration. In the one realm we work spiritually, our liberty is of the thought; in the other we work structurally, our liberty abides in institutions, is real only when it is tangible, a thing that can be put into operation — not in our own souls merely, but in the world of action outside of us as well.

A right in the field of politics is a power to command the action of others in our own behoof; and that is also a right in law.

Religions are mighty forces of belief, and the church, when it has its genuine and entire liberty, lies outside the state; but political liberty lives and moves and has its being in the structure and practice of society.

The two fields are not, indeed, sharply separated: religious freedom must be safeguarded by institutional arrangements; but religious freedom is the right to be ungoverned, political freedom the right to be governed justly and with equity as between man and man.

In the late spring of 1910 a man died in Massachusetts (whom neither Wilson nor Dean West had met) who left his entire fortune to Princeton for building a graduate college provided it was built as West wanted it built.

Stockton Axson tells how Mrs. Wilson heard him laughing. He showed her a telegram announcing the gift.

"The game is up," he said.

PART III

When a "State" Comes to Itself

CHAPTER TEN
"The Profession I Chose"

❧❧❧❧❧❧❧❧❧❧❧❧❧

The emergence of Woodrow Wilson upon the American political scene came at a time of extraordinary political unrest. Many political observers felt that even if it wasn't the time for a political revolution, it was a time for great and far-reaching change — that prevailing unrest might mean revolution if the right leaders did not arise to guide it back into safer channels.

Someday the year 1910 will be pointed to as perhaps the most eventful in the history of the United States — if for no other reason than that Woodrow Wilson and Franklin D. Roosevelt entered politics that year.

The Democratic party in New Jersey needed a candidate to sacrifice on the altar of "respectability." Its boss, James Smith, former senator, needed whitewashing. Feelers were put out on the question of running Wilson.

JUNE 23, 1910 [LETTER CONCERNING DEMOCRATIC BOSS, JAMES SMITH]
I would be perfectly willing to assure Mr. Smith that I would not, if elected Governor, set about "fighting and breaking down the existing Democratic organization and replacing it with one of my own." The last thing I should think of would be building up a machine of my own. So long as the existing Democratic organization was willing to work with thorough heartiness for such policies as would re-establish the reputation of the State and the credit of the Democratic Party in serving the State, I should deem myself inexcusable for antagonizing it, so long as I was left absolutely free in the matter of measures and men.

JULY, 1910

Wilson later wrote:

I was asked to allow myself to be nominated, and for a long time it was impossible for me to understand why I had been asked. The gentlemen who wanted to nominate me were going outside the ranks of recognized politicians and picking out a man who they knew would be regarded as an absolutely independent person and who I thought they knew was an absolutely independent person. I tried to form a working theory as to why they should do it. I asked very direct and impertinent questions of some of the gentlemen as to why they wanted me to make the run. They didn't give me any very satisfactory explanation, so I had to work one out for myself.

I concluded on the whole that these gentlemen had been driven to recognize that a new day had come in American politics, and that they would have to conduct themselves henceforth after a new fashion. Moreover, there were certain obvious practical advantages to be gained by the old-time managers. Whether they could control the governor or not, a Democratic victory would restore their local prestige.

JULY 14, 1910 [TO DAVID B. JONES]

After much doubt and perplexity, I have told the New Jersey men that, if the nomination for governor comes to me without any effort on my part, unanimously, and with no requirement that I pledge myself to anybody about anything, I will accept it. I did not see, in the circumstances, how I could say anything else, particularly in view of my lifelong teaching, in my college classes, that it was the duty of educated men to accept just such opportunities of political service as this.

On September 15, 1910, Wilson was nominated by the Democratic party as its candidate for governor of New Jersey.

SEPTEMBER 15, 1910 [FROM HIS ACCEPTANCE SPEECH]

As you know, I did not seek this nomination. It has come to me absolutely unsolicited, with the consequence that I shall enter upon the duties of the office of Governor, if elected, with absolutely no pledges of any kind to prevent me from serving the people of the State with singleness of purpose. Not only have no pledges of any kind been given, but none have been proposed or desired.

The future is not for parties "playing politics," but for measures conceived in the largest spirit, pushed by parties whose leaders are statesmen, not demagogues, who love, not their offices but their duty and their opportunity for service. We are witnessing a renaissance of public spirit, a reawakening of sober public opinion, a revival of the power of the people, the beginning of an age of thoughtful reconstruction that makes our thought hark back to the great age in which democracy was set up in America. With the new age we shall show a new spirit. We shall serve justice and candour and all things that make for right. Is not our own ancient party the party disciplined and made ready for this great task? Shall we not forget ourselves in making it the instrument of righteousness for the State and for the Nation?

SEPTEMBER 25, 1910 [TO DAVID B. JONES]

I know that you will forgive me for returning the cheque, because I know the spirit in which it was sent, and hope that I know the trust and affection it stands for. I do not remember anything that ever touched me more or made me happier. You have treated me as you would have treated your own brother. I feel as I never did before the value and the beauty of the friendship you have honoured me with.

But I want to say, if possible, that I paid every cent of my own personal expenses in this campaign out of my own pocket. I do not think that they will run above a few hundred dollars; and I have arranged to deliver three addresses after the election which will net me five hundred dollars in fees. I made the engagements with the express purpose of earning the money for that object. Friends at every turn are putting their automobiles at my service; I shall have only hotel bills, the fares for short railway journeys, and the fees for extra stenographic services to pay. It will not come to much, all put together. If I get stuck, I will not hesitate to call on you for what I cannot do. You have made that possible by the way you have done this and by what I see between the lines of your generous letters.

SEPTEMBER 29, 1910 [IN A CAMPAIGN SPEECH]

I hope sincerely that you will never hear me, in the course of this campaign, say anything against that great body of our fellow citizens who have believed in the principles of the Republican party. What I want you to understand me as doing is this: I believe that that great body of citizens is now led by persons who are not capable of realizing in a proper spirit the great principles of the Republican party any more than they can win the acquiescence of those persons who believe in the great principles of the Democratic party.

I want to speak very plainly to this audience to-night. I have now been into every county of the state, and I have seen audiences that would move the heart of any man, thronging in numbers and rallying around, not a party, not a person, not to accomplish some selfish purpose of interest, but to enjoy the experience of hearing the genuine interest of the entire commonwealth candidly discussed. I have tried throughout this campaign to be as candid and as fair as I knew how to be; I have tried always to dwell upon the merits of every question.

I want to say that I understand the present campaign to mean this — that if I am elected governor I shall have been elected leader of my party and shall have been elected governor of all the people of New Jersey, to conduct the government in their interest and in their interest only, using party and party adherents for that service. If the Democratic party does not understand it in that way, then I want to say to you very frankly that the Democratic party ought not to elect me governor.

We have begun a fight that, it may be, will take many a generation to complete, the fight against special privilege, but you know that men are not put into this world to go the path of ease; they are put into this world to go the path of pain and struggle. No man would wish to sit idly by and lose the opportunity to take part in such a struggle. All through the centuries there has been this slow, painful struggle forward, forward, up, up, a little at a time, along the entire incline, the interminable way.

What difference does it make if we ourselves do not reach the uplands? We have given our lives to the enterprise, and that is richer and the moral is greater.

NOVEMBER 5, 1910 [ABOUT PRESIDENT TAFT]

If I were to sum up all the criticisms that have been made against the President of the United States, I could express them all in this: The American people are disappointed because he has not led them. They clearly long for someone to put the pressure of the opinion of all the people of the United States upon Congress.

NOVEMBER 8, 1910 [STATEMENT AT THE TIME OF HIS ELECTION AS GOVERNOR]

I shall, of course, put every power I possess into the service of the people as governor of the state. It will be my pleasure and privilege to serve them, not as the head of a party but as the servant of all classes and of all interests, in an effort to promote the common welfare.

NOVEMBER 15, 1910

Boss Smith had promised that, if the Democrats were returned to power, he would not again be a candidate for the United States Senate. But with victory, it looked as though he would change his mind. Wilson made no bones of what he would do.

If Senator Smith should become a candidate, I would have to fight him; and there is nothing I would more sincerely deplore. It would offend every instinct in me, except the instinct as to what was right and honest from the point of view of public service. I have had to do similar things in the University.

DECEMBER 5, 1910

It looks as if we had Smith safely beaten for the Senatorship. I hope tomorrow to see Senator Smith, and tell him very plainly what my position is in order to induce him, if possible, to decline the candidacy. If he will not do that I will come out openly against him.

DECEMBER 8, 1910 [OFFICIAL STATEMENT]

The question, Who should be chosen by the incoming legislature of the state to occupy the seat in the Senate of the United States, which will presently be made vacant by the expiration of the term of Mr. Kean, is of such vital importance to the people of the state, both as a question of political good faith and as a question of genuine representation in the Senate, that I feel constrained to express my own opinion with regard to it in terms which cannot be misunderstood. I had hoped that it would not be necessary for me to speak, but it is.

I realize the delicacy of taking any part in the discussion of the matter. As governor of New Jersey I shall have no part in the choice of a senator. Legally speaking, it is not my duty even to give advice with regard to the choice.

But there are other duties besides legal duties.

The recent campaign has put me in an unusual position. I offered, if elected, to be the political spokesman and adviser of the people. I even asked those who did not care to make their choice of governor upon that understanding not to vote for me. I believe that the choice was made upon that understanding; and I cannot escape the responsibility involved. I have no desire to escape it. It is my duty to say, with a full sense of the peculiar responsibility of my position, what I deem it to be the obligation of the legislature to do in this gravely important matter.

I know that the people of New Jersey do not desire Mr. James Smith, Jr., to be sent again to the Senate. If he should be, he will not go as their representative. The only means I have of knowing whom they do desire to represent them is the vote at the recent primaries, where 48,000 Democratic voters, a majority of the whole number who voted at the primaries, declared for their preference for Mr. Martine of Union City. For me that vote is conclusive. I think it should be for every member of the legislature.

Absolute good faith in dealing with the people, an unhesitating fidelity to every principle avowed, is the highest law of political morality under a constitutional government.

The Democratic party has been given a majority in the legislature; the Democratic voters of the state have expressed their preference under a law advocated and supported by the opinion of their party, declared alike in platforms and in enacted law. It is clearly the duty of every Democratic legislator who would keep faith with the law of the state, and with the avowed principles of his party, to vote for Mr. Martine. It is my duty to advocate his election — to urge it by every honourable means at my command.

DECEMBER 16, 1910 [TO MARY A. HULBERT, A FRIEND OF THE FAMILY]
Smith has at last come openly out and defied me to defeat him: and defeated he must be if it takes every ounce of strength out of me. I feel pretty confident it can be done; but a nasty enough fight is ahead, and I shall have to do some rather heartless things which I had hoped might be avoided. They are against all the instincts of kindliness in me.

But you cannot fight the unscrupulous without using very brutal weapons. I only hope I shall use them like a gentleman and a man of honour. Probably I shall have to go out on the stump again and conduct something like a systematic campaign against the whole gang: for Smith is only one of a gang that has had its grip upon the throat of the State for a generation. He is no Democrat. He has been in close alliance with men calling themselves Republicans and their purposes have been wholly non-partisan, as non-partisan as those of the plain (and much more picturesque) highwayman.

I cannot say whether I relish the new job or not. It is grim and forbidding in many ways, and there is a certain indomitable something in me that gets satisfaction out of it all; and, for the rest, I have not time to think whether I like it or not. It does not matter. It has to be faced and carried through.

JANUARY 2, 1911 [TO OSWALD GARRISON VILLARD]
The plot thickens about me here; the Smith forces are trying to coil me about with plans of their own which it will take more knowledge of past transactions here than I now have to checkmate and defeat. I am therefore going to ask one of the ablest of the young

Democratic politicians of the State [*Joseph P. Tumulty*] if he will not act as my secretary in order that I may have a guide at my elbow in matters of which I know almost nothing.

JANUARY 6, 1911 [AT A MASS MEETING IN TRENTON]

Do not allow yourselves to be dismayed. You see where the machine is entrenched, and it looks like a real fortress. It looks as if real men were inside, as if they had real guns. Go and touch it. It is a house of cards. Those are imitation generals. Those are playthings that look like guns. Go and put your shoulder against the thing and it collapses.

JANUARY 13, 1911 [TO MARY A. HULBERT]

We have just left "Prospect" [*the president's home at Princeton*] and I am writing from a little den, quite strange to me, in the Princeton Inn.

Alas! It is not pleasant; my heart aches at the break-up of the old life, interesting and vital as the new life is. I did not realize it until it touched our home and sent us into lodgings at an inn. I feel like a nomad! The idea of a man of fifty-four (no less!) leaving a definite career and a settled way of life of a sudden and launching out into a vast sea of Ifs and Buts! It sounds like an account of a fool. At any rate, there is nothing in it of private advantage! Every private comfort and satisfaction (for example and chief of all, the freedom to go to Bermuda) is destroyed and broken up and one's life is made to turn upon public affairs altogether. What can be snatched from the public (from office seekers and reporters and an occasional serious discussion of something really interesting and important) one *can* devote to his family or his friends or some hastily enjoyed pleasure. Even his *thinking*, which used to be done deliberately and upon the independent impulse of his own mind, he must do as bidden, at any moment, upon expected or unexpected summons — at the call of the casual acquaintance or the exaction of the newest correspondence! I shall get used to it, but at present I am in revolt.

CHAPTER ELEVEN

"We Are Put into This World to Act"

Wilson made it plain — painfully plain — that he meant to carry out absolutely, item by item, the reforms pledged in the platform on which he had been elected.

These included: direct primaries, a corrupt-practice act, laws regulating public utilities, and an employers' liability act. It was certainly a progressive — almost radical — program, especially for New Jersey, which had, in many respects, the most corrupt government of all the states.

JANUARY 23, 1911 [WILSON'S DEFINITION OF DIFFERENT GROUPS]
RADICAL — one who goes too far.
CONSERVATIVE — one who does not go far enough.
REACTIONARY — one who does not go at all.
Hence we have invented the term, label
PROGRESSIVE, to mean one who (a) recognizes new facts and adjusts law to them, and who (b) attempts to think ahead, constructively. Progress must build, build tissue, must be cohesive, must have a plan at its heart.

JANUARY 29, 1911 [TO MARY A. HULBERT]
I pitied Smith at the last. It was so plain that he had few real friends — that he held men by fear and power and the benefits he could bestow, not by love or loyalty or any genuine devotion. The minute it was seen that he was defeated his adherents began to desert him like rats leaving a sinking ship. He left Trenton (where his headquarters had at first been crowded) attended, I am told,

only by his sons, and looking old and broken. He wept, they say, as he admitted himself utterly beaten. Such is the end of political power — particularly when selfishly obtained and heartlessly used. It is a pitiless game, in which, it would seem, one takes one's life in one's hands — and for me it has only begun!

FEBRUARY 10, 1911

The people of the United States are just like the people of New Jersey. If they believe in an issue, once it is stated to them in terms they understand, they will force their leaders to adopt it.

FEBRUARY 19, 1911 [TO MARY A. HULBERT]

All these men are strangely interested in the enterprise of making me President of the United States. I cannot help them in the least. There is something in me that makes it inevitable that I should go on as I have begun, doing things as it seems to me they ought to be done, square with my own individual sense of conviction of right, whether it is expedient or not; and I may, by that token, at any moment spoil all they are generously trying to do! I think every man instinctively likes to play the role of king-maker. I am at present, apparently, suitable material for their favourite sport, and so the game is on the boards.

MARCH 5, 1911 [TO MARY A. HULBERT]

Things are getting intense and interesting again. The bills for which we are pledged and on whose passage the success and prestige of my administration as governor largely depend are ready for report to the legislature, and the question is,

Can we pass them?

I think we can, and my spirits rise as the crisis approaches: it is like the senatorial contest all over again — the same forces arrayed against me; and no doubt the same sort of fight will enable me to win. I have begun my speech-making (this time at various dinners of boards of trade, which afford me a convenient platform) and am pouring shot into the enemy in a way which I hope reaches the heart of his defenses. To-morrow I meet all the Democratic members of the Assembly in conference and shall have my first shot at them direct. Besides that, I shall draw various individuals into my office and have talks with them.

After the difficulties of the House are overcome, there is the Senate to deal with, which is Republican, by a majority of three. I do not know just how they will act. The senators gave me a dinner on Friday night (the customary thing, it seems) at the new Ritz-Carlton hotel, 46th St. and Madison Avenue, and in the little speech I made them I established as natural and cordial relations as I knew how to suggest.

They are good and honest men, for the most part, and I could warmly feel all the things I said. I am hoping for the best even with them — though from just which of them I am to get the necessary votes I do not yet know. There are so many "personal equations" to bring into these puzzling calculations that I do not know till the last moment how the "sum" is going to work out. It's a fascinating, as well as nerve-racking, business.

And somehow, through all of it, I keep my stubborn optimism. I cannot manage to think ill of my fellow men as a whole, though some of them are extraordinary scoundrels. Fortunately in this strange game most of the scoundrels are cowards also. The right, boldly done, intimidates them. Above all, they shrink away from the light. I spoke at three dinners last week: on Tuesday night before the West Hudson Board of Trade; on Thursday night before the Hoboken Board of Trade; on Friday night to the senators.

The Democratic members of the legislature called a caucus to discuss the new election law proposed by Wilson — which they considered too radical.

"All right," Wilson said, "why don't you invite me?"

"What constitutional right has the governor to interfere with legislation?" demanded one of the legislators.

"Since you appeal to the constitution, I can satisfy you," said Wilson, drawing a copy from his pocket. He then read: "The governor shall communicate by message to the legislature at the opening

of each session, and at such other times as he may deem necessary, the condition of the state and recommend such measures as he may deem expedient."

He was then told that such a law would wreck the organization that nominated him.

"It was the people who elected me," Wilson answered. "Does the gentleman charge that this bill attacks the interests of the people?"

Wilson spoke to the group for three hours on his proposed bill. He not only knew what he was talking about but he let the caucus know in no uncertain terms that if they did not pass the bill the people would know who was responsible.

"You can," he said, "turn away from this measure if you choose; you can decline to follow me; you can deprive me of office and turn away from me, but you cannot deprive me of power so long as I steadfastly stand for what I believe to be the interests and legitimate demands of the people themselves. I beg you to remember you are settling the question of the power or impotence, the distinction or the ignominy, of the party to which the people with singular generosity have offered the conduct of their affairs."

MARCH 13, 1911 [TO MARY A. HULBERT]

I hurried back to greet Mr. Bryan! He was in Princeton to-day, to address the Theological Seminary, at their Sunday afternoon conference. They held it in Alexander Hall, which was packed; and the address, which was on Faith, was most impressive. He held the audience easily for an hour and a half. It was the first time I had ever heard him speak, and I was exceedingly pleased. After the meeting he came over to the Inn and dined with Ellen, Jessie, Nellie, a Mr. Birch (in whose car he had come up from Burlington), and me, and I feel that I can now say that I know him, and have a very different impression of him from that I had before seeing him thus close at hand. He has extraordinary force of personality, and it seems the force of sincerity and conviction. He has himself well in hand at every turn of the thought and talk, too; and his voice is

wholly delightful. A truly captivating man, I must admit. He had
to be off by half past seven, so I had only a little while with him —
only through the short dinner.

*Nugent, Smith's lieutenant, came to see Wilson, trying to per-
suade him not to support the election law. When he told Wilson
that it couldn't be passed without using the state patronage, Wilson
arose and pointed his hand at the door.*
"Good afternoon, Mr. Nugent."
"You're no gentleman," cried Nugent.
"You're no judge," responded Wilson.

MARCH 26, 1911 [TO MARY A. HULBERT]
It was a most unpleasant incident, which I did not at all enjoy;
but apparently it did a lot of good. It has been spoken of with glee
all over the country, and editorials written about it, of which the
enclosed is a specimen. One paper had a cartoon entitled "Good
afternoon," in wh. Nugent was to be seen flying head foremost
from a door out of which protruded a foot marked "Wilson." In the
distance, nursing his bruises, sat Smith. It is all very well to get
applause and credit for such things, but I need not tell you that
they are not at all to my taste. I cannot help feeling a bit vulgar
after them. They commend me to the rank and file, and particularly
to the politicians themselves, I believe, but they do not leave me
pleased with myself. I feel debased to the level of the men whom
I feel obliged to snub. But it all comes in the day's work.

APRIL 2, 1911 [TO MARY A. HULBERT]
The Senate of the State has, you must know, a Republican majority of two: I must obtain at least two votes to get my bills through.
The senator from — — is one, a sly old fraud who likes to increase
his consequence by posing as something of an independent. At an
early stage of the game he came to me and intimated that he was
going to stand by me and vote for the administration measures.
He dropped into my office frequently, and I began to realize that
something was in the wind.

As if to assist my diagnosis, the sheriff of — — up and died. The senator promptly showed his hand. He came to me and said very plainly that, since he was going to vote for my bills, he expected to be allowed to say what the appointments in his county should be. Needless to say, I did not indulge him. I appointed the man who seemed to be most acceptable to the Democrats of good standing in the county. He thereupon renounced me. I was not the broad man he had taken me to be, he said. He was loud and not at all parliamentary in speaking of the breach. He certainly would not vote for the bills.

A day or two after his disappointment, I was invited, by the Adjutant General, Sadler, to go out with the senators to the country club and eat a fried chicken and waffle supper (which was delicious, by the way), and at the supper things happened! The senators are as jolly as boys when they let themselves "go" on such an occasion, and that night they were in fine fettle. In the middle of the meal Freling-huysen, of Somerset, got up and said, "By special request, Senator — — has consented to sing 'I Love Him No More.'" Then the fun began! — — got up to speak, but for almost five minutes they would not let him, throwing all sorts of jibes at him, very good natured and very witty, but very teasing. When they let him, he said that the trouble was, not that he did not love me more, but that I loved him less. I reminded him that I had high example, for "Whom the Lord loveth he chasteneth," and then we were off. The rest of the evening was one unbroken romp. After we got up from the table we danced in every comical combination anyone could think of, and I led Senator — — several times around the big dining room in a cakewalk, in which we pranced together to the perfect content of the whole company. He seemed quite mollified before we got through with him. Such are the processes of high politics! This is what it costs to be a leader! But it remains to be seen whether the sly old fox votes for the bills or not. I would not trust him out of my sight. But this at least seems gained: I am on easy and delight-ful terms with all the senators. They know me for something else than "an ambitious dictator."

APRIL 23, 1911 [TO MARY A. HULBERT]

The Legislature adjourned yesterday morning at three o'clock, with its work done. I got absolutely everything I strove for — and more besides: all four of the great acts that I had set my heart on (the primaries and election law, the corrupt practices act, as stringent as the English, the workingmen's compensation act, and the act giving a public commission control over the railways, the trolley lines, the water companies, and the gas and electric light and power companies), and besides them I got certain fundamental school reforms and an act enabling any city in the State to adopt the commission form of government, which simplifies the electoral process and concentrates responsibility. Everyone, the papers included, are saying that none of it could have been done, if it had not been for my influence and tact and hold upon the people. Be that as it may, the thing was done, and the result was as complete a victory as has ever been won, I venture to say, in the history of the country. I wrote the platform, I had the measures formulated to my mind, I kept the pressure of opinion constantly on the legislature, and the programme was carried out to its last detail. This with the senatorial business seems, in the minds of the people looking on, little less than a miracle, in the light of what has been the history of reform hitherto in this State. As a matter of fact, it is just a bit of natural history. I came to the office in the fulness of time, when opinion was ripe on all these matters, when both parties were committed to these reforms, and by merely standing fast, and by never losing sight of the business for an hour, but keeping up all sorts of (legitimate) pressure *all the time*, kept the mighty forces from being diverted or blocked at any point. The strain has been immense, but the reward is great. I feel a great reaction to-day, for I am, of course, exceedingly tired, but I am quietly and deeply happy that I should have been of just the kind of service I wished to be to those who elected and trusted me. I can look them in the face, like a servant who has kept faith and done all that was in him, given every power he possessed, to them and their affairs. There could be no deeper source of satisfaction and contentment!

I have no doubt that a good deal of the result was due to the personal relations I established with the men in the Senate, the Republican Senate which, it was feared at the outset, might be the stumbling block. You remember the dinner in New York and the supper at the Trenton country club which I described to you. Those evenings undoubtedly played their part in the outcome. They brought us all close together on terms not unlike friendly intimacy; made them realize just what sort of *person* I was. Since then Republicans have resorted to my office for counsel and advice almost as freely as Democrats (an almost unprecedented circumstance at Trenton) and with several of them I have established relations almost of affection. Otherwise I do not believe that the extraordinary thing that happened could possibly have come about: for all four of the great "administration" measures passed the Senate *without a dissenting voice!* The newspaper men seem dazed. They do not understand how such things *could* happen. They were impressed, too, with the orderly and dignified way in which the session ended, despite the long strain of the closing night, when the houses sat from eight until three. Generally there is wild horseplay, like that on the stock exchange, but this time everything was done decently and with an air of self-respect.

I took several naps in my office during the long hours of the session, coming out into the outer office in the intervals to talk and swap stories with the men who were sitting there, my secretary, the reporters who were coming and going, and interested friends who had come down to see how things ended. Then a committee from each House called on me to ask if there was anything more I had to lay before them before adjournment — and the session was over. Most of the members dropped in to say good bye, and by four o'clock your tired and happy friend was in bed in the noisy little Hotel Sterling, with the strong odours of late suppers in the nostrils, floating in at the open window. It's a great game, thoroughly worth playing!

What a vigil it has been! I am certainly in training for almost anything that may come to me by way of public tasks. There are serious times ahead. It daunts me to think of the possibility of my playing an influential part in them. There is no telling what deep waters may be ahead of me. The forces of greed and the forces of justice and humanity are about to grapple for a bout in which men will spend all the life that is in them. God grant I may have strength enough to count, to tip the balance in the unequal and tremendous struggle! This week I turn to speech-making again (much the easier task of the two) and to preparation for my western trip.

In one session of the legislature, New Jersey moved from one of the most ill-governed states to one of the most progressive. And Wilson used none of the old political devices, made no threats, promised no rewards — just did what he had been teaching and preaching for the past generation that leaders in politics should do. He said:

The main object of what we are attempting is to establish a close connection, a very sensitive connection, between the people and their government, both in the states and in the nation, in order that we may restore liberty and opportunity to all of the people.

CHAPTER TWELVE

"The New Freedom"

⫸⫷⫸⫷⫸⫷⫸⫷⫸⫷⫸⫷⫸⫷⫸⫷⫸⫷⫸⫷⫸⫷⫸⫷

The attention of the nation was turning more and more to Woodrow Wilson, and with that turning he was invited to different sections to make addresses. In them he set forth the credo of his political beliefs as they were crystallizing into what might be political action.

MAY, 1911 [TO MARY A. HULBERT]

It's an awful thing to be President of the United States. It means giving up nearly everything that one holds dear. When a man enters the White House, he might as well say, "all hope abandon, ye who enter here." The presidency becomes a barrier between a man and his wife, between a man and his children. He is no longer his own master — he is a slave to the job. He may indulge no longer in the luxury of free action or even free speech.

In spite of what I said to you, I do want to be President and I will tell you why: I want this country to have a President who will do certain things. There are men who could do these things better than I can. Of that I am sure; but the question is, *would they do them?* I cannot have any positive assurance that the man who becomes President will do, or even attempt to do, the things which I want to see done. But I am sure that I will at least try to the utmost to do them.

MAY 1, 1911 [TO THE REVEREND THOMAS B. SHANNON, ON PROHIBITION]

I am in favour of local option. I am a thorough believer in local self-government and believe that every self-governing community which constitutes a social unit should have the right to control the matter of regulation or of the withholding of licenses.

But the questions involved are social and moral and are not susceptible of being made parts of a party programme. Whenever they have been made the subject matter of party contests, they have cut the lines of party organization and party action athwart to the utter confusion of political action in every other field.

They have thrown every other question, however important, into the background and have made constructive party action impossible for long years together. So far as I am concerned, therefore, I can never consent to have the question of local option made an issue between political parties in this State.

My judgment is very clear in this matter. I do not believe that party programmes of the highest consequence to the political life of the State and of the Nation ought to be thrust on one side and hopelessly embarrassed for long periods together by making a political issue of a great question which is essentially non-political, non-partisan, moral and social in its nature.

May 2, 1911

When ex-Governor Pennypacker of Pennsylvania stated in an interview that Wilson was a charlatan and was courting oblivion because Wilson was too much for government regulation of business — and that "something should be left to the Lord," Wilson dryly remarked:

He says I am courting oblivion. Not at all. I may find it, but I am not courting it, surely. The reference to divine interference in legislation reminds me of a talk I had with Mark Twain a year or so before the humorist's death.

He was talking about some man, but could not recall the gentleman's name. "Anyhow," said Twain, "he was one of those fellows who had been appointed to a committee at Washington to straighten out some matter that the Almighty had overlooked."

Of his "New Freedom," Wilson wrote:

It is an attempt to express the new spirit of our politics and to set forth, in large terms which may stick in the imagination, what it is that must be done if we are to restore our politics to their full spiritual vigor again, and our national life, whether in trade, in industry, or in what concerns us only as families and individuals, to its purity, its self-respect, and its pristine strength and freedom. The New Freedom is only the old revived and clothed in the unconquerable strength of modern America.

Stated another way, it is merely democracy a-making.

June 15, 1911 ["Democracy's Opportunity"]

In this speech Woodrow Wilson set forth the political credo as he saw it, of the Democratic Party.

Other parties have risen and fallen, have come into existence and passed utterly away, but the Democratic party has renewed itself from generation to generation with an indomitable youth. It is never the party of the past, but always the party of the present and the future, always taking new life with the changing circumstances of the nation.

Whenever things are to be done in a new way, in response to a new popular impulse, in obedience to the great democratic traditions of the nation itself, it is to the Democratic party that the country naturally turns.

Other parties have tied themselves up to particular lines of action to which they presently became wholly subject, upon which they at length became dependent, but the Democratic party has remained free to act, free to take on the new elements of popular impulse, free to read new times in new terms.

Its freedom is now about to serve it in an extraordinary degree. Those who look about them see parties apparently breaking up; but if they will look closer what they will see is simply this, that men are turning away by the thousands from those courses of policy and of action to which the alliances and practices of the Republican party have at last bound the country as if with a grip of iron.

The free elements of thought in the country are asserting themselves with an extraordinary energy and majesty that must presently work profound changes and mark this as one of the most noteworthy eras of our politics.

The Democratic party has always had the impulse of reform because it has always been based upon deep and fundamental sympathy with the interests of the people at large. It has now only to prove that its impulse can find expression in a wise and feasible programme in order to capture both the imagination and the allegiance of the country.

It is this power of self-removal, this power of looking forward, this power of realizing the present and projecting itself into the future that has kept it young and which must now make it the party of young men, the party to which those must resort who are coming for the first time into the activities of politics; with which those must ally themselves whose hopes are forming into purposes, whose impulses are framing themselves by sober thought into concrete judgments, who know what they want and are fast finding out by what means they can get what they want.

The first item of that programme is that the machinery of political control must be put in the hands of the people.

Another great item of the programme is that the service rendered the people by the national government must be of a more extended sort and of a kind not only to protect it against monopoly, but also to facilitate its life.

The revision of the tariff, of course, looms big and central in the programme, because it is in the tariff schedules that half the monopolies of the country have found covert and protection and opportunity.

The regulation of corporations is hardly less significant and central. We are beginning to see, for one thing, how public service corporations, at any rate, can be governed with great advantage to the public and without serious detriment to themselves, as undertakings of private capital.

Again there is the great question of conservation. We are not yet clear as to all the methods, but we are absolutely clear as to the principle and the intention and shall not be satisfied until we have found the way, not only to preserve our great national resources, but also to conserve the strength and health and energy of our people themselves by protection against wrongful forms of labour and by securing them against the myriad forms of harm which have come from the selfish uses of economic power.

Beyond all these, waiting to be solved, lying as yet in the hinterland of party policy, *lurks the great question of banking reform.* The plain fact is that control of credit — at any rate of credit upon any large scale — is dangerously concentrated in this country.

The large money resources of the country are not at the command of those who do not submit to the direction and domination of small groups of capitalists, who wish to keep the economic development of the country under their own eye and guidance.

The great monopoly in this country *is the money monopoly.* So long as that exists our old variety and freedom and individual energy of development are out of the question. A great industrial nation is controlled by its system of credit. Our system of credit is concentrated. This is the greatest question of all, and to this statesmen must address themselves with an earnest determination to serve the long future and the true liberties of men.

The American people are an eminently just and an intensely practical people. They do not wish to lay violent hands upon their own affairs, but they do claim the right to look them over with close and frank and fearless scrutiny from top to bottom; to look at them from within as well as from without, in their most intimate and private details, as well as in their obvious exterior proportions; and they do hold themselves at liberty, attacking one point at a time, to readjust, correct, purify, rearrange; not destroying or even injuring the elements, but filling their altered combination with a new spirit. This is the task of the Democratic party. It is the task of all statesmanship.

It is a task which just at this particular juncture in our affairs looms particularly big. It is not ominous, but inviting; not alarming, but inspiriting.

JULY 30, 1911 [TO MARY A. HULBERT]

Truly, I know what "public life" is now! I have no private life at all. It is entertaining to see the whole world surge about you — particularly the whole summer world — but when a fellow is like me — when, i.e., he *loves* his own privacy, loves the liberty to think of his friends (live with them in his *thought,* if he can have them no other way) and to dream his own dreams — to conceive a life which he cannot share with the crowd, can share, indeed with only one or two, who seem part of him, rebellion comes into his heart and he flings about like a wild bird in a cage — denied his sweet haunts and his freedom. Sometimes (as I must have told you more than once) my whole life seems to me rooted in dreams — and I do not want the roots of it to dry up. I lived a dream life (almost too exclusively, perhaps) when I was a lad and even now my thought goes back for refreshment to those days when all the world seemed to me a place of heroic adventure, in which one's heart must keep its own counsel while one's hands worked at big things. And *now* this is that dreaming boy's *Sunday:* he must sit at the edge of his front piazza flanked by a row of militia officers and be gazed at, while a chaplain conducts service on his lawn, with a full brass band to play the tunes for the hymns; then he must have the chaplains of the two regiments in camp, plus the Catholic priest, and anybody else that happens along, in for lunch. In the afternoon he must receive and pay military calls and attend a review. The evening brings callers galore from all along the coast. Where and when does one's own heart get a chance to breathe and to call up the sweet memories and dreams upon wh. it lives?

JANUARY 7, 1912 [TO MARY A. HULBERT]

I am on my way down to Washington, where I am to speak to-morrow evening. The Democratic National Committee is to meet there to-morrow (which is Jackson's birthday) and the banquet in the evening is to be a grand dress parade of candidates for the presidential nomination on the Democratic ticket. I hate the whole thing, but it is something "expected" of me by my friends and backers, and, after all, an honest and sincere man need not be embarrassed by being put on exhibition.

There is a merry war on against me. I am evidently regarded as the strongest candidate at present, for all the attacks are directed against me, and the other fellows are not bothered. Kind one-time friends are giving to the newspapers letters I wrote them before I became of public consequence in which I expressed uncomplimentary opinions of Mr. Bryan. Rumours are sedulously set afoot that there is a letter which various persons have seen or been told the contents of in which Mr. Cleveland said that he thought I "lacked intellectual integrity," or words to that effect, — &c. &c. No doubt these things will have their effect and will turn various people against me, and this rain of small missiles makes me feel like a common target for the malicious (by the way, practically all the darts are supplied by the Princetonians who hate me), and somewhat affect my spirits for a day at a time (the strongest nerves wince under persistent spite); but for the most part I go serenely on my way. I believe very profoundly in an overruling Providence, and do not fear that any real plans can be thrown off the track. It may not be intended that I shall be President — but that would not break my heart — and I am content to await the event — doing what I honourably can, in the meantime, to discomfit mine enemies!

JANUARY 27, 1912 [TO MARY A. HULBERT]

I was saying to-day that I wished I had been born 20 years later, so that I could have had 20 years more of this exhilarating century upon which we have entered, a century which greets the challenge to originative effort. This is no century for any man who looks over his shoulder; it is no century for any man who has no stomach for the facts that change even while he tries to digest them; a century in which America is to prove once more whether she has any right to claim leadership in the world of originative politics and originative economic effort. This is a century just as worth living in as was

the eighteenth century, better worth living in than was the nineteenth century.

FEBRUARY 1, 1912 [IN AN ADDRESS AT RICHMOND, VIRGINIA]

I have heard men complain of the changes of the times. I have
heard men counsel that we stand still and do nothing. How futile
the counsel is! Do you remember the quaint story of the Scottish
highlander who went into the market of Edinburgh, followed by his
dog? He went to a fishmonger's stall and the dog incautiously
dropped his tail into a basket of lobsters, and one of the lobsters
nipped his tail. Whereupon the dog went yelping down the street,
with the lobster bouncing after. The fishmonger said, "Hoot, mon:
whussle to your dog!" "Hoot!" said the Scotchman, "whussle to your
lobster."

Now if you think some of your leaders are going too fast a pace,
don't whistle to them. Whistle to the spirit of the age. Whistle to the
questions that have whipped their consciences and dominated their
understandings. They cannot stop if they are going to keep up with
the great transmutations of affairs.

I have heard men say that it was un-American to criticise the institutions we are living under. I wonder if they remember the significance of the American flag — the first insurgent flag that was flung
to the breeze — the flag that represented the most colossal "kick" that
was ever taken in political transactions; a flag that I cannot look at
without imagining that it consists of alternate strips of parchment
upon which are written the fundamental rights of man, alternating
with the streams of blood by which those rights had been vindicated
and validated. In the blue sky of the corner there are swung star
after star of commonwealths of free men who were setting up their
own homes upon the principles of those vindicated rights.

Do you suppose that I will believe, or that any one knowing the
history of America will believe, that it is inconsistent with being an
American to propose that you construct liberty for each successive
age, and that if necessary you reconstruct liberty for each successive
age?

It made the sleep of some men, in some quarters, uneasy that they should be haunted by those visions, but they never went out of the thought or the sleepless eyes of those great multitudes of men for whom happiness depends upon freedom, for whom self-respect depends upon freedom and principle by which we constantly renew our youth, and devote ourselves generation after generation to the preservation of the institutions of America.

If I knew my business and were a manufacturer, what would I do? I would create such conditions of sanitation, such conditions of life and comfort and health as would keep my employees in the best physical condition, and I would establish such a relationship with them as would make them believe that I was a fellow human being, with a heart under my jacket, and that they were not my tools, but my partners.

Then you would see the gleam in the eye, then you would see that human energy spring into expression which is the only energy which differentiates America from the rest of the world. Men are used everywhere, men are driven under all climes and flags, but we have boasted in America that every man was a free unit of whom we had to be as careful as we would of ourselves.

America's economic supremacy depends upon the moral character and the resilient hopefulness of our workmen.

We have got to get a *modus vivendi* in America for happiness, and that is our new problem. And I call you to witness it *is* a new problem. America never had to finish anything before; she has been at liberty to do the thing with a broad hand, quickly, improvise something and go on to the next thing; leave all sorts of waste behind her, push on, blaze trails through the forest, beat paths across the prairie.

There is another new question in America, and that is the question of business. Business is in a situation in America that it was never in before; it is in a situation to which we have not adjusted our laws. Our laws are still meant for business done by *individuals;* they have not been satisfactorily adjusted to business done by great *combinations,* and we have got to adjust them.

I do not say we may or may not, I say we have got to, there is no choice. If your laws do not fit your facts, the facts are not injured, the law is damaged; so much the worse for the law, because the law, unless I have studied it amiss, is the expression of the facts in legal regulation.

I am not here to enter an indictment against business. No man indicts natural history. No man undertakes to say that the things that have happened by operation of irresistible forces are immoral things, though some men may have made deeply immoral use of them.

I am not here to suggest that the automobile be destroyed because some fools take joy rides in it.

I want to catch the fools.

I was trying to analyze the other day what a Republican is. I do not want to say anything about that great body of my fellow-countrymen in various parts of America who have formed the bad habit of voting the Republican ticket. They are not the men I am talking about, but the Republican leaders, the men who establish the ideals and policies of that party, how would you describe them?

Why, I would say that they are men who actually believe that the only men whose advice it is safe to take with regard to the happiness and prosperity of America are the men who have the biggest material stake in the enterprises of America.

They believe, therefore, that America ought to be governed by trustees and that those trustees are the managers of the oldest and greatest "vested interests" of the country.

That is a workable theory, that is a theory that has obtained time out of mind.

It happens, though these gentlemen have forgotten it, that America was established to get rid of it, but, having forgotten that, reading only the older books, I dare say, reading back of the birth of America, they say that there are only a few men with grasp enough of affairs and knowledge enough of what are the bases of prosperity to run a big, complicated government like this.

Now, as a Democrat I define myself by absolutely protesting against that view of public affairs.

I will not live under trustees if I can help it. No group of men less than the majority has a right to tell me how I have got to live in America.

I know that there are some gum-shoe politicians in both camps who do not agree with that theory at all. They say, "You need not say much about it out loud, but we have got to run these people; this enterprise of free government has to be personally conducted — that the people want this or that we do not deny, but they do not know what is good for them."

So there are two theories of trusteeship, a trusteeship of the big interests and a trusteeship of the machine.

I do not see my way to subscribe to either kind of trusteeship. Not that I am an insurgent, because I believe in organization; I believe that party success is impossible without organization; but I make this distinction between organization and the machine — *organization is a systematic cooperation of men for a common purpose, while the machine is a systematic cooperation of men for a private purpose.*

I know what I am talking about, because we have a perfect specimen in New Jersey.

Now I know what supports the machine, because I have seen them eat out of a spoon. It is a golden spoon, and I have seen the nurse that fed them, and I have seen that nurse absolutely impartial as between the Republican machine and the Democratic machine and the price of the food, the price of the nutrition, is that the machine will be good, that it will see that nothing is done that will hurt the nurse, that nothing is done which will interfere with the private understanding that is established in the nursery.

FEBRUARY 12, 1912 [ADDRESS ON LINCOLN'S BIRTHDAY]

When I hear you say to me let business alone, I say I will do it upon one condition; that you will let politics alone. Politics did not enter business. *Let me tell you that business entered politics.* Now if you want this thing remedied take business out of politics.

Take your own condition, if you want the politician to give business a chance, then all I have to say is, give politics a chance to act independently of the influence of money and of privilege.

These are some of the things to which my eyes have been opened since I got on the inside.

I sometimes think it is a singular circumstance that the present Republican party should have sprung from Lincoln, but that is one of the mysteries of Providence and for my part I feel the closest kinship in principle and in political lineament to that great mind. I wonder if we appreciate just how apposite his example is to the present moment.

Here was a case where the nation had come to a critical turning point in its history, where it had to make a choice whether it would divide or remain united upon a fundamental question of social structure — a question which was all the more difficult to approach and more difficult to solve because it involved so much passion, because it involved some of the deepest feelings that men can acquire.

At that critical juncture what happened? Was a man picked out who had become experienced and sophisticated among the ruling class of the community?

Is it not an interesting circumstance that a man should have come almost untutored from the mass of the people, who had the wisdom, who had the vision as well as the courage and sagacity to handle a great crisis with a steadiness which made it possible to save the nation?

I do not know any life which more illustrates the fundamental faith of democracy. The fundamental faith of democracy is that out of a mass of uncatalogued men you can always count upon genius asserting itself, genius suited to mankind, genius suited to the task. The richness of a democracy is in this — that it never has to predict who is going to save it. It never relies upon those of established influence. The gates of opportunity are wide open and he may enter who is fit.

MARCH 10, 1912 [TO MARY A. HULBERT]

Nothing new is happening in politics, except Mr. Roosevelt, who is always new, being bound by nothing in the heavens above or in the earth below. He is now rampant and very diligently employed in splitting the party wide open — so that we may get in!

MARCH 15, 1912 [TO WILLIAM JENNINGS BRYAN]

I altogether subscribe to your view, that the publication of pre-nomination subscriptions should be made obligatory by law. Signs multiply that the nomination will again be determined by money — the indications of a combination are palpable; and there is danger that things are being done which may render the use of the party, *as a unit,* in the free service of the people impossible. Alliances are being made that I would have thought impossible and which may rise up to discredit us.

We are engaged in a war for emancipation — emancipation of our institutions and our life — from the control of the concentrated and organized power of money. There are men — many men — who have come by their money perfectly cleanly and honestly — who are as keen to be emancipated as we are and who would gladly subscribe the money absolutely needed to organize opinion and the scattered forces of the people. They dare not subscribe, if their names are to be published. They would be squeezed and put out of business. I know such men. They are victims of the system — are caught in its toils — and cannot get free without our assistance and guidance, for which they are eager. Shall we make any temporary abatement of our programme for their sake?

My own managers have not been able to obtain the sums needed for an adequate campaign — and I have refused to promise rewards.

APRIL 13, 1912 ["WHAT JEFFERSON WOULD DO"]

The circumstances of our day are so utterly different from those of Jefferson's day that it may seem nothing less than an act of temerity to attempt to say what Jefferson would do if he were now alive and guiding us with his vision and command. The world we live in is no longer divided into neighbourhoods and communities. The ends of the earth touch one another and exchange impulse and purpose.

America has swung out of her one-time isolation and has joined the family of nations. She is linked to mankind by every tie of blood and circumstance. She is more cosmopolitan in her make-up than any other nation of the world; is enriched by a greater variety of energy drawn from strong peoples the world over. She is not the simple, homogeneous, rural nation that she was in Jefferson's time, making only a beginning at development and the conquest of fortune; she is great and strong; above all she is infinitely varied; her affairs are shot through with emotion and the passion that comes with strength and growth and self-confidence. We live in a new and strange age and reckon with new affairs alike in economics and politics of which Jefferson knew nothing.

And yet we may remind ourselves that Jefferson's mind did not move in a world of narrow circumstances; it did not confine itself to the conditions of a single race or a single continent. It had commerce with the thought of men old and new; it had moved in an age of ample air, in which men thought not only of nations but of mankind, in which they saw not only individual policies, but a great field of human need and of human fortune.

We may be sure, therefore, that had Jefferson lived in our time he would have acted upon *the facts as they are*. In the first place, because he would have seen them as they actually are, and in the second place because he would have been interested in theory only as he could adjust it to the reality of the life about him.

He would not have been content with a philosophy which he could fit together only within the walls of his study.

To determine what Jefferson would have done, therefore, requires only that we should ourselves clearly see the facts of our time as they are, whether in the field of government or in the field of our economic life, and that we should see how Jefferson's principle of the rule and authority of the people stands related to these facts.

We are constantly quoting Jefferson's fundamental thought: it was that no policy could last whose foundation is narrow, based upon the privileges and authority of a few, but that its foundations must be as broad as the interests of all the men and families and neighbourhoods that live under it.

Monopoly, private control, the authority of privilege, the con-

cealed mastery of a few men cunning enough to rule without showing their power — he would have at once announced them rank
weeds which were sure to choke out all wholesome life in the fair
garden of affairs. If we can detect these things in our time; if we can
see them and describe them and touch them as they are, then we
know what Jefferson would have done.

He would have moved against them, sometimes directly, sometimes indirectly, sometimes openly, sometimes subtly; but whether
he merely mined about them or struck directly at them, he would
have set systematic war against them at the front of all his purpose.

MAY 23, 1912 [IN A SPEECH]

Mr. Milburn said that everybody here knew what I am, but that
depends upon which newspaper he has read. Most persons are so
thoroughly uninformed as to my opinions that I have concluded that
the only things they have not read are my speeches.

MAY 26, 1912 [TO MRS. EDITH G. REID]

You must have *known* that I needed a letter from you and that an
expression of your generous confidence in me was just the tonic that
would put me in form again! Everybody over here seems to agree
that there has never been a Campaign in which there was such a
systematic and malevolent attempt to destroy a man's reputation for
character and intellectual integrity as has been made by my opponents all over the country, including the representatives of the other
Candidates for the Democratic nomination, and in such circumstances one *needs* to hear the voice of true and loyal friends to keep
him in heart.

Not that I actually lose heart. I find I am of too firm a fibre, and
of too firm a faith, for that; but the world grows sometimes to seem
so brutal, so naked of beauty, so devoid of chivalrous sentiment and
all sense of fair play, that one's own spirit hardens and is in danger
of losing its fineness.

JUNE 30, 1912 [STATEMENT ABOUT THE DEMOCRATIC CONVENTION]

It has become evident that the present deadlock is being maintained for the purpose of enabling New York, a delegation controlled

by a single group of men, to control the nomination and tie the candidate to itself. In these circumstances it is the imperative duty of each candidate for the nomination to see to it that his own independence is beyond question. I can see no other way to do this than to declare that he will not accept a nomination if it cannot be secured without the aid of that delegation. For myself, I have no hesitation in making that declaration. The freedom of the party and its candidate and the security of the government against private control constitute the supreme consideration.

After a long and weary deadlock, Woodrow Wilson was finally nominated by the Democratic party as its candidate for the Presidency.

In his acceptance speech he reiterated the principles which he had been expressing in his talks leading up to the convention. His was to be the "people's cause" brought into effective action. What he would try to create was

a government that cannot be used for private purposes, either in the field of business or politics; a government that will not tolerate the use of the organization of a great party to serve personal aims and ambitions of any individual, and that will not permit legislation to be employed to further any private interest.

AUGUST 25, 1912 [TO MARY A. HULBERT]

I feel that Roosevelt's strength is altogether incalculable. He appeals to their imagination; I do not. He is a real, vivid person, whom they have seen and shouted themselves hoarse over and voted for, millions strong; I am a vague, conjectural personality, more made up of opinions and academic prepossessions than of human traits and red corpuscles. We shall see what will happen!

AUGUST 30, 1912

I drew a picture of a group of men sitting around the stove in a country store chewing tobacco and spitting in a sawdust box, conferring about the affairs of the neighbourhood, and I got into trouble by indulging in this harmless pleasantry. I said, "Whatever may be said against the chewing of tobacco, this at least can be said for it, that it gives a man time to think between sentences." An enterprising newspaper published only that part of my speech and headed it, "Advocates the Chewing of Tobacco." And a facsimile of that article was, I understand, circulated with the advertisements of certain tobacco firms. The whole point of the thing was missed. I wasn't advocating the chewing of tobacco, but I was advocating thinking between sentences!

OCTOBER 7, 1912

I remember distinctly when the first feeling came over me that I had "arrived" in politics. It was when an old fellow back East a few weeks ago slapped me on the back and shouted:

"Doc, you're all right; give it to 'em!"

Wilson put on a campaign that had the old-time politicians goggle-eyed. He talked the people's language and they liked it. He ended the campaign at a great meeting in Madison Square Garden.

When he had won the election, and was greeted by a wildly cheering group of Princeton students, he said:

I have no feeling of triumph to-night, but a feeling of solemn responsibility. I know the very great task ahead of me. I look almost with pleading to you, the young men of America, to stand behind me, to support me in the new administration.

PART IV

When a Nation Comes to Itself

CHAPTER THIRTEEN

Full Realization of His Powers

➤➤≪≪➤➤≪≪➤➤≪≪➤➤≪≪➤➤≪≪➤➤≪≪➤➤≪≪➤➤≪≪➤➤≪≪➤➤≪≪➤➤≪≪➤➤≪≪

DECEMBER 17, 1912 [ADDRESS AT THE WALDORF-ASTORIA, NEW YORK]
People make all sorts of sinister predictions as to the trouble we
are going to get into down at Washington. They say that business is
going to be disturbed by the changes which are going to be undertaken by the Democratic party.

Business cannot be disturbed unless the minds of those who conduct it are disturbed.

A panic is a state of mind because, obviously, when a panic occurs
there is just as much wealth in the country the day after the panic
as the day before. Nothing in material circumstances has changed,
but the whole state of mind of the financial community has changed.
They dare not part with their money. They call in their loans. They
are excited, and they do not always know exactly why. That is a
natural panic, but you know there are unnatural panics, and sometimes panics are said to occur because certain gentlemen want to
create the impression that the wrong thing is going to be done.

Frankly I do not believe there is any man living at the present
moment who dares use that machinery for that purpose. If he does,
I promise him, not for myself but for my countrymen, a gibbet as
high as Haman.

*Immediately after the first of the year he made another speech in
which he outlined Four Points:*

JANUARY 11, 1913
1. We must husband and administer the common resources of this
country for the common benefit.

2. The raw materials obtainable in this country for every kind of manufacture and industry must be at the disposal of everybody in the United States upon the same terms.

3. There is a third thing which you must do which has not yet been done. You must put the credit of this country at the disposal of everybody upon equal terms. Now, I am not entering into an indictment against the banking methods of this country. The banking system of this country does not need to be indicted. It is convicted.

4. And then in addition and on top of all this, we must see to it that the business of the United States is set absolutely free of every feature of monopoly. I notice you do not applaud that. I am somewhat disappointed because unless you feel that way the thing is not going to happen except by duress, the worst way to bring anything about.

I have no intimate knowledge of the processes of business. I never was engaged in business in my life. I must take counsel with the men who do understand business, and I dare not take counsel with them unless they intend the same things that I intend. The man who does not hold the people's interests dearer than his own, I cannot admit into my counsel. I am a trustee for the prosperity of the United States in counsel, and the counsel that is not common counsel, the counsel that does not include you, is imperfect counsel, is counsel which will mislead. Won't you come in? There is no bright prospect otherwise.

FEBRUARY 5, 1913

When Wilson was asked to favor a single six-year single term for the President of the United States, he wrote A. Mitchell Palmer:

Four years is too long a term for a President who is not the true spokesman of the people, who is imposed upon and does not lead. It is too short a term for a President who is doing, or attempting a great work of reform, and who has not had time to finish it.

To change the term to six years would increase the likelihood of its being too long, without any assurance that it would, in happy cases, be long enough. A fixed constitutional limitation to a single term of office is highly arbitrary and unsatisfactory from every point of view.

The argument for it rests upon temporary conditions which can easily be removed by law. Presidents, it is said, are effective for one-half of their term only because they devote their attention during the last two years of the term to building up the influences, and above all, the organization, by which they hope and purpose to secure a second nomination and election.

It is their illicit power, not their legitimate influence with the country, that the advocates of a constitutional change profess to be afraid of, and I heartily sympathize with them.

It is intolerable that any President should be permitted to determine who should succeed him — himself or another — by patronage or coercion, or by any sort of control of the machinery by which delegates to the nominating convention are chosen.

There ought never to be another presidential nominating convention; and there need never be another. The nominations should be made directly by the people at the polls.

Conventions should determine nothing but party platforms and should be made up of the men who would be expected, if elected, to carry those platforms into effect. It is not necessary to attend to the people's business by constitutional amendment if you will only actually put the business into the people's own hands.

Put the present customary limitation of two terms into the Constitution, if you do not trust the people to take care of themselves, but make it two terms (not one, because four years is often too long), and give the President a chance to win the full service by proving himself fit for it.

As things stand now the people might more likely be cheated than served by further limitations of the President's eligibility. His fighting power in their behalf would be immensely weakened. No one will fear a President except those whom he can make fear the elections.

We singularly belie our own principles by seeking to determine by fixed constitutional provision what the people shall determine for themselves and are perfectly competent to determine for themselves. We cast a doubt upon the whole theory of popular government.

If we want our Presidents to fight our battles for us, we should give them the means, the legitimate means, the means their opponents will always have.

Strip them of everything else but the right to appeal to the people, but leave them that; suffer them to be leaders; absolutely prevent them from being bosses.

We would otherwise appear to be going in two opposite directions. We are seeking in every way to extend the power of the people, but in the matter of the Presidency we fear and distrust the people and seek to bind them hand and foot by rigid constitutional provision. My own mind is not agile enough to go both ways.

I am very well aware that my position on this question will be misconstrued, but that is a matter of perfect indifference to me. The truth is much more important than my reputation for modesty and lack of personal ambition. My reputation will take care of itself, but constitutional questions and questions of policy will not take care of themselves without frank and fearless discussion.

I am not speaking for my own re-election; I am speaking to redeem my promise that I would say what I really think on every public question and take my chances in the court of public opinion.

FEBRUARY 23, 1913 [TO JOSEPHUS DANIELS]

I have been sweating blood over the cabinet choices, and have decided to beg of you that you will do me the very great service of accepting the Secretaryship of the Navy. I know of no one I trust more entirely or affectionately, and I am sure that you will trust and believe me when I assure you that you will, in my judgment, best serve the party and its new leader by accepting this post. I cannot spare you from my council table.

MARCH 4, 1913 [INAUGURAL ADDRESS]

This is not a day of triumph; it is a day of dedication.

Here muster, not the forces of party, but the forces of humanity. Men's hearts wait upon us; men's lives hang in the balance; men's hopes call upon us to say what we will do. Who shall live up to the great trust? Who dares fail to try? I summon all honest men, all patriotic, all forward-looking men, to my side. God helping me, I will not fail them, if they will but counsel and sustain me!

MARCH 5, 1913 [TO MARY A. HULBERT]

The old kink in me is still there. Everything is persistently *impersonal* — I am administering a great office — no doubt the greatest in the world — but I do not seem to be identified with it: it is not me, and I am not it. I am only a commissioner, in charge of its apparatus, living in its offices, and taking upon myself its functions. This impersonality of my life is a very odd thing, and perhaps robs it of intensity, as it certainly does of pride and self-consciousness (and, maybe, of enjoyment) but at least prevents me from becoming a fool, and thinking myself *It!*

APRIL 8, 1913 [TO MARY A. HULBERT]

Today I break another precedent by reading my message to Congress in person. The town is agog about it. The President has not addressed Congress in person since John Adams's day — and yet what is more natural and dignified?

And a president is likely to read his own message rather better than a clerk would. Here is what I am going to say, by way of preface:

I am very glad indeed to have this opportunity to address the two Houses directly and to verify for myself the impression that the President of the United States is a person, not a mere department of the Government hailing Congress from some isolated island of jealous power, sending messages, not speaking naturally and with his own voice — that he is a human being trying to cooperate with other human beings in a common service.

APRIL 8, 1913 [TO CONGRESS]

I have called the Congress together in extraordinary session because a duty was laid upon the party now in power at the recent elections which it ought to perform promptly, in order that the burden carried by the people under existing law may be lightened as soon as possible, and in order, also, that the business interests of the country may not be kept too long in suspense as to what the fiscal changes are to be to which they will be required to adjust themselves. It is clear to the whole country that the tariff duties must be altered.

We must abolish everything that bears even the semblance of privilege or of any kind of artificial advantage, and put our business men and producers under the stimulation of a constant necessity to be efficient, economical, and enterprising, masters of competitive supremacy, better workers and merchants than any in the world.

APRIL 9, 1913

Wilson went to the Capitol to confer with senators, breaking another precedent.

It is something that I hope the Senators will permit me to do very often.

APRIL 12, 1913 [TO MARY A. HULBERT]

Last night I dined with the Gridiron Club (where public men are periodically grilled) and received my first public discipline as President, responsible to all who look on. It was very amusing and very instructive, in a way, and I was treated with singular sympathy and consideration, as if they really liked and admired me, and were a wee bit in awe of me! Fancy! Can you imagine it? I was a good deal moved, and very much stimulated. And so, step by step, am I being more and more thoroughly inducted into office.

APRIL 16, 1913 [TO SENATOR OSCAR W. UNDERWOOD ON INCOME-TAX LAW]

If the lower limit of incomes is to be $4,000, would it not be wise and fair to exempt all persons receiving less than $3,000 a year income from the necessity of making income returns at all, in order to burden as small a number of persons with the obligations involved in the administration of what will at best be an unpopular law?

APRIL 22, 1913 [TO HIS BROTHER, J. R. WILSON]

I never in my life had anything quite so hard to do as this that I must do about the Nashville Post Office. Knowing as I do that a better man could not possibly be found for the place, and sure though I am that it would meet with the general approval of the citizens of Nashville, I yet feel that it would be a very serious mistake both for you and for me if I were to appoint you to the Postmastership there. I cannot tell you how I have worried about this or how much I have had to struggle against affection and temptation, but I am clear in the conviction and I am sure that in the long run, if not now, you will agree with me that I am deciding rightly.

I can't write any more just now, because I feel too deeply.

MAY 26, 1913 [STATEMENT ON LOBBYISTS]

I think that the public ought to know the extraordinary exertions being made by the lobby in Washington to gain recognition for certain alterations of the Tariff bill. Washington has seldom seen so numerous, so industrious or so insidious a lobby.

The newspapers are being filled with paid advertisements calculated to mislead the judgment of public men not only, but also the public opinion of the country itself.

There is every evidence that money without limit is being spent to sustain this lobby and to create an appearance of a pressure of opinion antagonistic to some of the chief items of the Tariff bill.

It is of serious interest to the country that the people at large should have no lobby and be voiceless in these matters, while great bodies of astute men seek to create an artificial opinion and to overcome the interests of the public for their private profit. It is thoroughly worth the while of the people of this country to take knowledge of this matter. Only public opinion can check and destroy it.

The Government in all its branches ought to be relieved from this intolerable burden and this constant interruption to the calm progress of debate. I know that in this I am speaking for the members of the two houses, who would rejoice as much as I would to be released from this unbearable situation.

JUNE 12, 1913 [TO SECRETARY OF THE INTERIOR FRANKLIN K. LANE]

I realize very keenly how unfortunate it is that so many circumstances should be combined to render it an anxious and ticklish business to change the tariff and also the basis of the currency, but I feel that if we allow ourselves to be forced to a modification of plan by the alarms and embarrassments of the moment, we shall never find the time more suited to what we wish to do, because whenever action is contemplated, the same obstructions will arise. A steady purpose and a just execution of it seem to me the only course open to us.

JUNE 28, 1913 [TO MARY A. HULBERT]

Stern visaged Duty lifted its hand and said "Not on your life, my dear sanguine boy! You seem to forget that you are, my lad, that you are President of the United States and not your own master, — no not for a minute." "What is it now?" I said, savage like, and with scant manners. "You forget, lad, that this fourth of July is the fiftieth anniversary of the battle of Gettysburg, the battle that turned the tide of the civil war. A big celebration is on. Old men in blue and in gray are to be there. It would be nothing less than scandal were the President to prefer a personal holiday instead of being present. Besides they would say, 'This is what comes of making a southerner President: he is not in sympathy, deep down in his heart, with this celebration at all.'" Again I clapped my heels together, saluted, and prepared to obey orders, not give them. I may take a turn down the river on one of the Government's boats to get a whiff of the sea before Friday; but to Cornish I cannot go. I shall have to content myself with a week end later on.

JULY 15, 1913 [TO SENATOR J. R. THORNTON]

Undoubtedly, you should have felt yourself perfectly free in the caucus to make every effort to carry out the promises you had made to your own people, but when it comes to the final action, my own judgment is perfectly clear. No party can ever for any length of time control the Government or serve the people which can not command the allegiance of its own minority. I feel that there are times, after every argument has been given full consideration and men of equal public conscience have conferred together, when those who are overruled should accept the principle of party government and act with the colleagues through whom they expect to see the country best and most permanently well served.

AUGUST 3, 1913 [TO MARY A. HULBERT]

Do not believe what you read in the newspapers. According to them everything is in a pretty coil and tangle here; but, as a matter of fact, there is no tangle that cannot easily be unravelled, if I am not mistaken. One has constantly to be on the job, it would appear. It is not safe to withdraw one's attention even for an hour. No one but the President seems to be expected, or to expect himself, to look out for the general interests of the country. Everybody else is special counsel for some locality or some group of persons or industries. Everybody, but he, is to look out for something in particular. He alone has the acknowledged duty of studying the pattern of affairs as a whole and of living all the while in his thoughts with the people of the whole country. It is a lonely business. He needs company. Where is he to find it in Washington? His friends are his constituents in that difficult and responsible matter. I am very well. I play ten or eleven holes of golf almost every day, heat or no heat, and on as hilly and sporty a course as one could wish, for beauty or fun, and twice every week I go to the theatre, clad in white and looking, I would fain believe, as cool and care free as I often am on those occasions. Fortunately, I have a special gift for relaxation and for being amused. But even then it is lonely, very lonely. And it is then that I have *time* to miss my friends and consciously wish for them.

AUGUST 21, 1913 [TO OSWALD GARRISON VILLARD]

It would be hard to make any one understand the delicacy and difficulty of the situation I find existing here with regard to the colored people. You know my own disposition in the matter, I am sure, but I find myself absolutely blocked by the sentiment of Senators; not alone Senators from the South, by any means, but Senators from various parts of the country. I want to handle the matter with the greatest possible patience and tact, and am not without hope that I may succeed in certain directions. But just because the situation is extremely delicate and because I know the feeling of irritation that comes with every effort at systematic inquiry into conditions because of the feeling that there is some sort of indictment involved in the very inquiry itself — I think that it would be a blunder on my part to consent to name the commission you speak of and which we discussed at our conference in Trenton. I never realized before the complexity and difficulty of this matter in respect of every step taken here. I not only hope but I pray that a better aspect may come upon it before many months.

Woodrow Wilson had remarked at the beginning of his administration that the worst thing that could happen would be for him to have to give most of his attention to foreign affairs before the domestic problems were cured.

This happened. Almost immediately after his inauguration there developed a serious crisis in Mexico. Just a month before it, Huerta had overthrown President Madero, and shortly thereafter had had him assassinated.

The ambassador to Mexico was a strong advocate of "dollar diplomacy" and was more the representative of the big-business interests in the United States than the government itself. He had strongly advocated the recognition of Huerta. President Taft, however, had refused and had stanchly maintained the status quo *until Wilson took over.*

AUGUST 24, 1913 [TO MARY A. HULBERT]

Our friend Huerta is a diverting brute! He is always so perfectly in character: so false, so sly, so full of bravado (the bravado of ignorance, chiefly), and yet so courageous, too, and determined — such a mixture of weak and strong, of ridiculous and respectable! One moment you long for his blood, out of mere justice for what he has done, and the next you find yourself entertaining a sneaking admiration for his nerve. He will not let go till he pulls the whole house down with him. He loves only those who advise him to do what he wants to do. He has cold lead for those who tell him the truth. He is seldom sober and always impossible, and yet what an admirable

fighter for his own hand! Every day the news from Mexico City un-
settles the news of the day before. The whole thing is quicksilver.
I dare not finish my message to Congress intended for Tuesday till
Tuesday's news comes, for fear the things I say in it might turn out
to be untrue in fact! Any hour of the day or night I may have to
revise my judgment as to what it is best to do. Do you wonder that
I have lost flesh a bit?

AUGUST 27, 1913

*Wilson sent a message to Congress on the Mexican situation,
which was growing worse daily.*

The peace, prosperity, and contentment of Mexico mean more,
much more to us than merely an enlarged field for our commerce
and enterprise. They mean an enlargement of the field of self-government and the realization of the hopes and rights of a nation with
whose best aspirations, so long suppressed and disappointed, we
deeply sympathize. We shall yet prove to the Mexican people that
we know how to serve them without first thinking how we shall
serve ourselves.

SEPTEMBER 10 [TO MISS FLORENCE GRISWOLD]

The matter of patronage is a thorny path which daily makes me
wish I had never been born.

SEPTEMBER 17, 1913 [TO CHARLES W. ELIOT]

In the matter of the diplomatic service, there are difficulties which
I cannot within the space of a letter more than indicate to you.
We find that those who have been occupying the legations and
embassies have been habituated to a point of view which is very
different, indeed, from the point of view of the present administration. They have had the material interests of individuals in the
United States very much more in mind than the moral and public
considerations which it seems to us ought to control. They have
been so bred in a different school that we have found, in several
instances, that it was difficult for them to comprehend our point of
view and purpose. I have been genuinely distressed at the necessity

of seeming to act contrary to the spirit of the merit system in any case or particular, but there are circumstances which seem to me to make a certain amount of this necessary at the opening of a new order of things.

SEPTEMBER 21, 1913 [TO MARY A. HULBERT]

If you read the papers I see, they are utterly untrustworthy. They represent the obstacles as existing which they wish to have exist, whether they are actual or not. Read the editorial page and you will know what you will find in the news columns. For unless they are grossly careless the two always support one another. Their lying is shameless and colossal! Editorially the papers which are friendly (and some which are not) represent me, in the most foolish way, as master of the situation here, bending Congress to my indomitable individual will.

That is, of course, silly. Congress is made up of thinking men who want the party to succeed as much as I do, and who wish to serve the country effectively and intelligently. They have found out that I am honest and that I have no personal purpose of my own to serve (except that "If it be a sin to covet honour, then am I the most offending soul alive!") and accept my guidance because they see that I am attempting only to mediate their own thoughts and purposes. I do not know how to wield a big stick, but I do know how to put my mind at the service of others for the accomplishment of a common purpose. They are using me; I am not driving them . . . and what a pleasure it is, what a deep human pleasure, to work with strong men, who do their own thinking and know how to put things in shape! Why a man should wish to be the whole show, and surround himself with weak men, I cannot imagine! How dull it would be! How tiresome to watch a plot which was only the result of your own action and every part of which you could predict before it was put on the boards!

That is not power. Power consists in one's capacity to link his will with the purpose of others, to lead by reason and a gift of cooperation. It is a multiple of combined brains.

SEPTEMBER 28, 1913 [TO MARY A. HULBERT]

The struggle goes on down here without intermission. Why it should *be* a struggle it is hard (cynicism put on one side) to say. Why *should* public men, senators of the United States, have to be led and stimulated to what all the country knows to be their duty! Why should they see less clearly, apparently, than anyone else what the straight path of service is! To whom are they listening? Certainly not to the voice of the people, when they quibble and twist and hesitate. They have strangely blunted perceptions, and exaggerate themselves in the most extraordinary degree. Therefore it *is* a struggle and must be accepted as such. A man of my temperament and my limitations will certainly wear himself out in it; but that is small matter: the danger is that he may lose his patience and suffer the weakness of exasperation. It is against these that I have constantly guarded myself.

How does the game look to you, and the actors in it, as you sit at a distance and look on at it? It is more important to me to know how it looks outside of Washington than how it looks inside. The men who think *in Washington* only cannot think for the country. It is a place of illusions. The disease is that men think of themselves and not of their tasks of service, and are more concerned with what will happen to them than what will happen to the country. I am not complaining or scolding or holding myself superior; I am only analyzing, as a man will on Sunday, when the work pauses and he looks before and after. My eye is no better than theirs; it is only fresher, and was a thoughtful spectator of these very things before it got on the inside and tried to see straight there.

OCTOBER 3, 1913

Wilson signed the tariff bill, which was a move away from high protection.

He said:

I have had the accomplishment of something like this at heart ever since I was a boy, and I know men standing around me who can say the same thing, who have been waiting to see the things done which it was necessary to do in order that there might be justice in the United States.

We have set the business of this country free from those conditions which have made monopoly not only possible, but in a sense easy and natural. But there is no use taking away the conditions of monopoly if we do not take away also the power to create monopoly; and that is a financial rather than a merely circumstantial and economic power.

The power to control and guide and direct the credit of the country is the power to say who shall and who shall not build up the industries of the country, in which direction they shall be built, and in which direction they shall not be built. We are now about to take the second step, which will be the final step in setting the business of this country free.

OCTOBER 6, 1913 [TO SAMUEL UNTERMYER]

Just now my whole thought and purpose is so preoccupied with the matter of passage of the currency bill that I am giving absolutely no thought to the formulation, or even to the subject matter, of my annual message.

OCTOBER 8, 1913

The Washington Post *had reported the President as calling certain of the recalcitrant Democratic senators "rebels and no Democrats."*

I am quoted in your issue of this morning as saying that any one who does not support me is no Democrat but a rebel. Of course, I never said any such thing. It is contrary both to my thought and to my character, and I must ask that you give a very prominent place in your issue of tomorrow to this denial.

OCTOBER 9, 1913 [TO REPRESENTATIVE H. ROBERT FOWLER]

I need not tell you that I heartily agree with you that real dissolution in the case of the trusts is the only thing we can rest satisfied with, and I am ready to cooperate with you in every way possible to accomplish that object.

OCTOBER 9, 1913 [TO RALPH PULITZER]

Now for the currency. The influences which are working against it cannot be traced like the others, but they are very subtle and powerful, and this is our opportunity to prove that we have the knowledge and the ability to set the business of the country free from the forces which have too long controlled it.

OCTOBER 11, 1913 [TO SENATOR JOHN SHARP WILLIAMS]

Things are going on in the banking world which are evidently based upon a desire to make the members of the two houses uneasy in the presence of the bankers' power, and it is possible that with expanding business and contracting credits a panic may be brought on while we wait. There is absolutely no excuse for the fall in the market value of the two-per-cents. It is being brought about by those who misunderstand or misrepresent or have not read the bill.

OCTOBER 12, 1913 [TO MARY A. HULBERT]

I have been under a terrible strain, if the truth must be told, and am still under it, and my little spell of indigestion (for that is what it was) was due, undoubtedly, to my being worn out and unable to run both my stomach and the government. I realize when I stop to think about it at all that I never before knew such a strain as I have undergone ever since Congress convened in April. The more I succeed in directing things the more I am depended on for leadership and expected to do everything, make all paths straight and carry every plan to its completion. I take the best care I can of myself. The doctor, who is one of my regularly appointed staff, is with me practically at all times of the day, and this summer, while the family has been away, has lived in the house here with me, being very watchful and very competent, and I shall fare very well; but I was a bit bored this past week to find myself so "poorly" that I almost lost interest in golf itself and lay down to rest instead of going out to play. When I did play I hardly had spunk enough to drive the ball a hundred yards. But that is all gone by now. For one thing the weather has changed. The lassitude that was in the air has been replaced, within the last twenty-four hours, by bracing airs, and I am feeling very different.

This is indeed a complicated job I have undertaken down here. It uses up all the grey matter there is in my brain, and I have to borrow much of fellows as I go. What you read in the papers (if I may judge from what I read myself) is for the most part idle gossip, made up for the purposes of each particular paper. We shall get the currency bill through in due time, and the difficulties offered by the attitude of several of the Senators will in due process of argument and persuasion be overcome.

OCTOBER 24, 1913 [TO CHALMERS MARTIN]

It is interesting to learn that I own property in Ohio, though the fact that the property consists of a burial-ground robs me of any satisfaction and pride of ownership I might otherwise feel.

OCTOBER 27, 1913

A new Latin-American policy was given in an address at Mobile, Alabama, that was the forerunner of the "good neighbor" policy.

The States lying to the south of us, which have always been our neighbors, will now be drawn closer to us by innumerable ties, and, I hope, chief of all, by the tie of a common understanding of each other. Interest does not tie nations together; it sometimes separates them. But sympathy and understanding does unite them. It is a spiritual union which we seek.

There is one peculiarity about the history of the Latin American States which I am sure they are keenly aware of. You hear of "concessions" to foreign capitalists in Latin America. You do not hear of concessions to foreign capitalists in the United States. They are not granted concessions. They are invited to make investments. The work is ours, though they are welcome to invest in it. We do not ask them to supply the capital and do the work. It is an invitation, not a privilege; and States that are obliged, because their territory does not lie within the main field of modern enterprise and action, to grant concessions are in this condition, that foreign interests are apt to dominate their domestic affairs, a condition of affairs always dangerous and apt to become intolerable.

What these States are going to see, therefore, is an emancipation from the subordination, which has been inevitable, to foreign enterprise and an assertion of the splendid character which, in spite of these difficulties, they have again and again been able to demonstrate.

The dignity, the courage, the self-possession, the self-respect of the Latin American States, their achievements in the face of all these adverse circumstances, deserve nothing but the admiration and applause of the world.

They have had harder bargains driven with them in the matter of loans than any other peoples in the world. Interest has been exacted of them that was not exacted of anybody else, because the risk was said to be greater; and then securities were taken that destroyed the risk — an admirable arrangement for those who were forcing the terms!

I rejoice in nothing so much as in the prospect that they will now be emancipated from these conditions, and we ought to be the first to take part in assisting in that emancipation.

We must prove ourselves their friends, and champions upon terms of equality and honor. You cannot be friends upon any other terms than upon the terms of equality. You cannot be friends at all except upon the terms of honor. We must show ourselves friends by comprehending their interest whether it squares with our own interest or not.

It is a very perilous thing to determine the foreign policy of a nation in the terms of material interest. It not only is unfair to those with whom you are dealing, but it is degrading as regards your own actions.

Comprehension must be the soil in which shall grow all the fruits of friendship, and there is a reason and a compulsion lying behind all this which is dearer than anything else to the thoughtful men of America.

I mean the development of constitutional liberty in the world. Human rights, national integrity, and opportunity as against material interests — that is the issue which we now have to face.

I want to take this occasion to say that the United States will never again seek one additional foot of territory by conquest. She will devote herself to showing that she knows how to make honorable and fruitful use of the territory she has, and she must regard it as one of the duties of friendship to see that from no quarter are material interests made superior to human liberty and national opportunity. I say this, not with a single thought that anyone gainsay it, but merely to fix in our consciousness what our real relationship with the rest of America is. It is the relationship of a family of mankind devoted to the development of true constitutional liberty. We know that that is the soil out of which the best enterprise springs. We know that this is a cause which we are making in common with our neighbors, because we have had to make it for ourselves.

I know what the response of the thought and heart of America will be to the program I have outlined, because America was created to realize a program like that.

This is not America because it is rich. This is not America because it has set up for a great population great opportunities of material prosperity.

America is a name which sounds in the ears of men everywhere as a synonym with individual opportunity because it is a synonym of individual liberty.

I would rather belong to a poor nation that was free than to a rich nation that had ceased to be in love with liberty. But we shall not be poor if we love liberty, because the nation that loves liberty truly sets every man free to do his best and be his best, and that means the release of all the splendid energies of a great people who think for themselves. A nation of employees cannot be free any more than a nation of employers can be.

In emphasizing the points which must unite us in sympathy and in spiritual interest with the Latin American peoples we are only emphasizing the points of our own life, and we should prove ourselves untrue to our own traditions if we proved ourselves untrue friends to them.

Do not think, therefore, that the questions of the day are mere questions of policy and diplomacy.

They are shot through with the principles of life.

We dare not turn from the principle that morality and not expediency is the thing that must guide us and that we will never condone iniquity because it is most convenient to do so.

DECEMBER 2, 1913 [TO CONGRESS]

We have allowed the industry of our farms to lag behind the other activities of the country in its development. I need not stop to tell you how fundamental to the life of the Nation is the production of its food. And yet the farmer does not stand upon the same footing with the forester and the miner in the market of credit. He is the servant of the seasons. Nature determines how long he must wait for his crops, and will not be hurried in her processes. He may give his note, but the season of its maturity depends upon the season when his crop matures, lies at the gates of the market where his products are sold. And the security he gives is of a character not known in the broker's office or as familiarly as it might be on the counter of the banker.

We must add the means by which the farmer may make his credit constantly and easily available and command when he will the capital by which to support and expand his business. We lag behind many other great countries of the modern world in attempting to do this. Systems of rural credit have been studied and developed on the other side of the water while we left our farmers to shift for themselves in the ordinary money market. You have but to look about you in any rural district to see the result, the handicap and embarrassment which have been put upon those who produce our food.

On December 23, 1913, the Federal Reserve Act was signed. It accomplished four very important things. It made twelve money centers in the country where there had only been one before, and broke the absolute control over the finances of the nation that had previously been exercised by Wall Street. It created a flexible cur-

rency to meet the needs of expanding or contracting business. It furnished protection to otherwise solvent banks against runs made upon them for ulterior purposes or by hysterical depositors, and it laid the foundation for furnishing credit abroad for the benefit of our exporters.

DECEMBER 23, 1913 [TO CARTER GLASS]

May I not express my admiration for the way in which you have carried the fight for the currency bill to an extraordinarily successful issue. I hope and believe that the whole country appreciates the work you have done at something like its real value and I rejoice that you have so established yourself in its confidence.

JANUARY 4, 1914 [TO JOSEPH P. TUMULTY]

I have been deeply disturbed by what I have seen in the newspapers about the promotions and demotions that Ford has been making in the Public Printing Office. I am afraid, if any considerable part of what the newspapers charge is true, I shall have to ask the Civil Service Commission to make a careful investigation and report to me.

The single and most threatening danger to our party just at this moment is that it will yield to the "spoils" impulse and make a partisan use of the power of appointment to office and promotion and demotion in the departments. I hope that you will get into communication with Ford and let him know how warmly I feel on this subject, though I am sure you already know it, and how anxious I am to have this matter satisfactorily cleared up. Such editorials as the one in the World entitled "Stop It" are more ominous than perhaps we realize.

JANUARY 23, 1914 [TO ROBERT BRIDGES]

My frank wish in this matter is that during my visit to Princeton at Commencement time the fact is to be absolutely ignored that I am President of the United States. My personal enjoyment of the occasion depends upon that being done. If I am to be treated as President, I simply cannot come. It would be too heavy a burden to me personally and rob the occasion of all the fun that I might otherwise get out of it.

I am sure all concerned will understand this point of view and I sincerely hope that they will be willing to give me this freedom.

FEBRUARY 5, 1914

Wilson wrote to W. L. Marbury on the exemption of American ships from tolls contrary to a treaty with Great Britain. This became an extremely bitter controversy between the vested interests and President Wilson.

With regard to the question of the Canal tolls, my opinion is very clear. The exemption constitutes a very mistaken policy from every point of view. It is economically unjust; as a matter of fact, it benefits, for the present at any rate, only a monopoly; and it seems to me in clear violation of the terms of the Hay–Pauncefote Treaty. There is, of course, much honest difference of opinion as to the last point, as there is, no doubt, as to the others; but it is at least debatable, and if the promises we make in such matters are debatable, I for one do not care to debate them. I think the country would prefer to let no question arise as to its wholehearted purpose to redeem its promises in the light of any reasonable construction of them rather than debate a point of honor.

FEBRUARY 28, 1914 [TO SECRETARY OF THE TREASURY WILLIAM GIBBS McADOO]

I find that I have overlooked until the last moment my returns under the income tax. Will you be kind enough to tell me just what I have to do and how I have to do it?

MARCH 17, 1914 [TO DR. ALBERT SHAW]

The tolls matter is a very deep one. The truth is, just between you and me, until we straighten this matter out we shall not enjoy for a moment the confidence of foreign governments in our promises, for they all interpret the treaty one way. It is not merely England that I am thinking of. The distrust runs all through Europe and all through Central and South America and is expressed by the press of South America, for example, in the most marked degree in this very connection.

MARCH 20, 1914 [TO THE GRIDIRON CLUB]

I have never read an article about myself in which I have recognized myself, and I have come to have the impression that I must be some kind of a fraud, because I think a great many of these articles are written in absolute good faith.

I tremble to think of the variety and falseness in the impressions I make — and it is being borne in on me so that it may change my very disposition — that I am a cold and removed person who has a thinking machine inside which he adjusts to the circumstances, which he does not allow to be moved by any winds of affection or emotion of any kind, that turns like a cold searchlight on anything that is presented to his attention and makes it work.

I am not aware of having any detachable apparatus inside of me. On the contrary, if I were to interpret myself, I would say that my constant embarrassment is to restrain the emotions that are inside of me.

You may not believe it, but I sometimes feel like a fire from a far from extinct volcano, and if the lava does not seem to spill over it is because you are not high enough to see the caldron boil.

Because, truly, in the position which I now occupy there is a sort of passionate sense of being connected with my fellow men in a peculiar relationship of responsibility, not merely the responsibility of office, but God knows there are enough things in this world that need to be corrected.

I was amused the other day at a remark that Senator Newlands made. I had read him the trust message that I was to deliver to Congress some ten days before I delivered it, and I never stop "doctoring" things of that kind until the day I have to deliver them. When he heard it read to Congress he said: "I think it was better than it was when you read it to me." I said: "Senator, there is one thing which I do not think you understand. I not only use all the brains I have, but all I can borrow, and I have borrowed a lot since I read it to you first."

I am listening; I am diligently trying to collect all the brains that are borrowable in order that I will not make more blunders than it is inevitable that a man should make who has great limitations of knowledge and capacity. And the emotion of the thing is so great that I suppose I must be some kind of a mask to conceal it. I really feel sometimes as if I were masquerading when I catch a picture of myself in some printed description. In between things that I have to do as a public officer I never think of myself as the President of the United States, because I never have had any sense of being identified with that office.

I feel like a person appointed for a certain length of time to administer that office, and I feel just as much outside of it at this moment as I did before I was elected to it. I feel just as much outside of it as I still feel outside of the Government of the United States.

No man could imagine himself the Government of the United States; but he could understand that some part of his fellow-citizens had told him to go and run a certain part of it the best he knew how. That would not make him the Government itself or the thing itself. It would just make him responsible for running it the best he knew how.

The machine is so much greater than himself, the office is so much greater than he can ever be, and the most he can do is to look grave enough and self-possessed enough to seem to fill it.

I can hardly refrain every now and again from tipping the public a wink, as much as to say, "It is only 'me' that is inside this thing. I know perfectly well that I will have to get out presently. I know that then I will look just my own proper size, and that for the time being the proportions are somewhat refracted and misrepresented to the eye by the large thing I am inside of, from which I am tipping you this wink."

I will not say whether it is wise or unwise, simple or grave, but certain precedents have been established that in certain companies the President must leave the room first, and people must give way to him. They must not sit down if he is standing up. It is a very uncomfortable thing to have to think of all the other people every time I get up and sit down, and all that sort of thing.

So that when I get guests in my own house and the public is shut out I adjourn being President and take leave to be a gentleman. If they draw back and insist upon my doing something first, I firmly decline.

There are blessed intervals when I forget by one means or another that I am President of the United States. One means by which I forget is to get a rattling good detective story, get after some imaginary offender, and chase him all over — preferably any continent but this, because the various parts of this continent are becoming painfully suggestive to me.

Some day after I am through with this office I am going to come back to Washington and see it. In the meantime I am in the same category as the National Museum, the Monument, the Smithsonian Institution, or the Congressional Library, and everything that comes down here has to be shown the President. If I only knew the appearance to assume — apparently I can assume other appearances that do not show what is going on inside — I would like to have it pointed out, so that I could practice it before the looking glass and see if I could not look like the Monument. Being regarded as a national exhibit, it will be much simpler than being shaken hands with by the whole United States.

And yet, even that is interesting to me, simply because I like human beings. It is a pretty poor crowd that does not interest you. I think they would have to be all members of that class that devotes itself to "expense regardless of pleasure" in order to be entirely uninteresting. These look so much alike — spend their time trying to look so much alike — and so relieve themselves of all responsibility of thought — that they are very monotonous, indeed, to look at; whereas, a crowd picked up off the street is just a jolly lot — a job lot of real human beings, pulsating with life, with all kinds of passions and desires.

It would be a great pleasure if, unobserved and unattended, I could be knocked around as I have been accustomed to being knocked around all my life; if I could resort to any delightful quarter, to any place in Washington that I chose. I have sometimes thought of going to some costumer's — some theatrical costumer's — and buying an assortment of beards, rouge and coloring and all the known means of disguising myself, if it were not against the law.

You see I have a scruple as President against breaking the law and disguising one's self is against the law, but if I could disguise myself and not get caught I would go out, be a free American citizen once more and have a jolly time.

APRIL 14, 1914 [TO I. REESE PRICE]

I have always looked back with the greatest pleasure to my connection with the Alpha chapter of the Phi Kappa Psi at the University of Virginia, but my later experience as a college administrator has made me feel that fraternities break up the natural democracy and solidarity of the college boy too much.

APRIL 20, 1914 [STATEMENT TO THE PRESS]

I want to say to you gentlemen, do not get the impression that there is about to be war between the United States and Mexico. That is not the outlook at present, at all. In the first place, in no conceivable circumstance will we fight the people of Mexico.

We are their friends and we want to help them in every way that we can to recover their rights and their Government and their laws, and for the present I am going to Congress to present a special situation and seek approval to meet that special situation.

It is only an issue between the Government and a person calling himself the provisional President of Mexico, whose right to call himself such we have never recognized in any way.

So that I had a feeling of uneasiness as I read the papers this morning as if the country were getting on fire with war enthusiasm. I have no enthusiasm for war. I have an enthusiasm for justice and for the dignity of the United States, but not for war. And this need not eventuate in war if we handle it with firmness and promptness.

The people of Mexico are entitled to settle their own domestic affairs in their own way, and we sincerely desire to respect their right. The present situation need have none of the grave complications of interference if we deal with it promptly, firmly, and wisely.

MAY 13, 1914 [TO FRANK P. GLASS]

As I was saying to one of the Senators last night, I feel as if I ought, amidst my present perplexities and the un-conscionable pressure of such a fluid matter as the Mexican situation, to put up in the office the sign that was put up on the organ loft of a country church for the defense of the organist. On it was written, "Don't shoot; he is doing his damnedest."

MAY 16, 1914

Patriotism is a principle, not a mere sentiment. No man can be a true patriot who does not feel himself shot through and through with a deep ardor for what his country stands for, what its existence means, what its purpose is declared to be in its history and in its policy.

MAY 23, 1914 [AN ARTICLE IN THE *Saturday Evening Post*]

My ideal is an orderly and righteous government in Mexico; but my passion is for the submerged 85 per cent of the people of that Republic who are now struggling toward liberty.

It is a curious thing that every demand for the establishment of order in Mexico takes into consideration, not order for the benefit of the people of Mexico, the great mass of the population, but order for the benefit of the old-time regime, for the aristocrats, for the vested interests, for the men who are responsible for this very condition of disorder. No one asks for order because order will help the masses of the people to get a portion of their rights and their land; but all demand it so that the great owners of property, the overlords, the hidalgos, the men who have exploited that rich country for their own selfish purposes, shall be able to continue their processes undisturbed by the protests of the people from whom their wealth and power have been obtained.

The dangers that beset the Republic are held to be the individual and corporate troubles of these men, not the aggregated injustices that have been heaped on this vastly greater section of the population that is now struggling to recover by force what has always been theirs by right.

They want order — the old order; but I say to you that the old order is dead. It is my part, as I see it, to aid in composing those differences so far as I may be able, that the new order, which will have its foundation on human liberty and human rights, shall prevail.

First. The United States will not seek to gain a foot of Mexican territory in any way or under any pretext. When we have finished with Mexico, Mexico will be territorially intact.

Second. No personal aggrandizement by American investors or adventurers or capitalists, or exploitation of that country, will be permitted. Legitimate business interests that seek to develop rather than exploit will be encouraged.

Third. A settlement of the agrarian land question by constitutional means will be insisted on.

The function of being a policeman in Mexico has not appealed to me, nor does it appeal to our people. Our duty is higher than that. If we are to go in there, restore order, and immediately get out, and invite a repetition of conflict similar to that which is in progress now, we had better have remained out.

What we must do and what we hope to do are twofold: First, we hope to show the world that our friendship for Mexico is a disinterested friendship, so far as our own aggrandizement goes; and, second, we hope to prove to the world that the Monroe Doctrine is not what the rest of the world, including some of the countries in this hemisphere, contends — merely an excuse for the gaining of territory for ourselves.

I hold this to be a wonderful opportunity to prove to the world that the United States of America is not only human but humane; that we are actuated by no other motives than the betterment of the conditions of our unfortunate neighbor, and by the sincere desire to advance the cause of human liberty.

JUNE 1, 1914 [TO CHARLES W. ELIOT]

We have several times considered the possibility of having a publicity bureau which would handle the real facts, so far as the government was aware of them, for all the departments. The real trouble is that the newspapers get the real facts but do not find them to their taste and do not use them as given them, and in some of the newspaper offices news is deliberately invented. Since I came here I have wondered how it ever happened that the public got a right impression regarding public affairs, particularly foreign affairs.

JUNE 4, 1914 [TO WALTER HINES PAGE]

A landless people will always furnish the inflammable material for revolution.

JULY 3, 1914 [TO SECRETARY OF WAR LINDLEY M. GARRISON]

It seems to me that although he proves that the writer of the headlines in the New York Times article did him an injustice and gave a wrong color to what he said, I regard General Evans' letter as a virtual admission that he said in substance the things attributed to him, and he seems to me to have committed a grave indiscretion.

No officer of the Army ought ever to refer to our foreign policy in a way to illustrate specific dangers or ought ever to say in public that our country is held in disfavor and is likely to be attacked out of ill feelings which its established policy has aroused.

Ellen Axson Wilson, who had been Wilson's balance wheel and constant companion for twenty-seven years, died on August 6, 1914, and was buried at Rome, Georgia, on August 12. A few days earlier the First World War had broken out.

CHAPTER FOURTEEN

The World Comes Apart

➤➤➤➤➤➤➤➤➤➤➤➤➤➤➤➤➤➤➤➤➤➤➤➤

The First World War burst upon an America — if not a world — totally unprepared for it. The Hague Court, the arbitration treaties of President Taft and those under way by Wilson's Secretary of State, William Jennings Bryan, indicated a need for a new approach to settling the affairs of the world.

In many ways Wilson's "New Freedom," aimed at settling problems on the domestic level, struck out at the same forces that were upsetting the world: greed, selfishness, growing autocracy on both the economic and political level — in a phrase, men and nations that loved themselves more than they loved humanity.

Few people in the United States had any grasp of the international scene and even fewer of these were in the government. In his foreign policy as it worked out with Mexico, Wilson had shown a clear concept of a new morality. The big question was, could he implement it as far as the world was concerned?

AUGUST 19, 1914 [STATEMENT TO THE PRESS]

The effect of the war upon the United States will depend upon what American citizens say and do. Every man who really loves America will act and speak in the true spirit of neutrality, which is the spirit of impartiality and fairness and friendliness to all concerned. The spirit of the Nation in this critical matter will be determined largely by what individuals and society and those gathered in public meetings do and say, upon what newspapers and magazines contain, upon what ministers utter in their pulpits, and men proclaim as their opinions on the street.

The people of the United States are drawn from many nations, and chiefly from the nations now at war. It is natural and inevitable that there should be the utmost variety of sympathy and desire among them with regard to the issues and circumstances of the conflict. Some will wish one nation, others another, to succeed in the momentous struggle. It will be easy to excite passion and difficult to allay it.

Those responsible for exciting it will assume a heavy responsibility, responsibility for no less a thing than that the people of the United States, whose love of their country and whose loyalty to its Government should unite them as Americans all, bound in honor and affection to think first of her and her interests, may be divided in camps of hostile opinion, hot against each other, involved in the war itself in impulse and opinion if not in action.

The United States must be neutral in fact as well as in name during these days that are to try men's souls. We must be impartial in thought as well as in action, must put a curb upon our sentiments as well as upon every transaction that might be construed as a preference of one party to the struggle before another.

My thought is of America. I am speaking, I feel sure, the earnest wish and purpose of every thoughtful American that this great country of ours, which is, of course, the first in our thoughts and in our hearts, should show herself in this time of peculiar trial a Nation fit beyond others to exhibit the fine poise of undisturbed judgment, the dignity of self-control, the efficiency of dispassionate action; a Nation that neither sits in judgment upon others nor is disturbed in her own counsels and which keeps herself fit and free to do what is honest and disinterested and truly serviceable for the peace of the world.

SEPTEMBER 15, 1914 [TO JOSEPHUS DANIELS]

Every reform we have won will be lost if we go into this war. We have been making a fight on special privilege. We have got new tariff and currency and trust legislation. We don't know yet how they will work. They are not thoroughly set.

SEPTEMBER 17, 1914 [TO J. P. MORGAN]

Mr. Morgan had written Wilson that business was "appalled at the prospects before us," and was fearful under the new laws for "its own capital invested in its own country."

I believe that being blue is just the wrong thing. It is a situation which requires nothing more, in my judgment, than courage and the kind of intelligence which our bankers and men of affairs have shown themselves equal to applying to any circumstances that have yet arisen, and my judgment differs radically from yours with regard to the pending legislation.

SEPTEMBER 20, 1914 [TO MARY A. HULBERT ABOUT THE DEATH OF HIS WIFE]

It is very strange: I feel almost as if I had lost my sense of identity and were living in some new, unfamiliar world! But there are big, imperative things that have not changed: my duty and the big tasks that press, press, press the days through and forbid, prevent, my thinking of myself, thank God. I am trying not to dwell even for a moment at a time on what is going to happen to me personally: and I am happy to say that most of the time I succeed.

You have noticed, I dare say, that the papers and the politicians have been talking lately about a second term for me in the presidency; but you will know that that has not been in *my* thoughts. For the moment I am approved of and trusted by the party and the country and am popular. But I am not deceived. I know by what tenure a man holds popularity. It is only a tenancy at will, and may be terminated without notice. Any day I may find it my duty to do something that will make me intensely unpopular, it may be, the object of fierce and passionate criticism.

The place has brought me no personal blessing, but only irreparable loss and desperate suffering. I am not complaining; I am only stating the facts, and letting you see the very inside of my mind. . . . I want you to know that I manage to live and to be stimulated by work and to love a task that makes me useful. My loss has made me humble. I know that there is nothing *for me* in what

I am doing. And I hope that that will make me more serviceable. I have succeeded so far, I believe, only because I have not sought my own pleasure in the work or in the office, and have, more than my predecessors, devoted my entire time and energy, alike of body and of mind, to the work of administration and of leadership to be done from day to day. And now self is killed more pitilessly than ever — there is *nothing but the work* for me.

OCTOBER 2, 1914 [TO SECRETARY OF STATE BRYAN]

I have the letter, which I return, which General Witherspoon addressed to you. It discloses again the uncomfortable and problematical situation at Veru Cruz. But I am clear in the judgment that we ought not to linger in our departing. I think it would make a very bad impression not only in Mexico, but in Latin–America generally, and I sincerely hope that the department's correspondence with the temporary authorities at Mexico City has resulted in something definite which we can use as a basis for handing over the civil authority on our departure. My wish is to get out at the very earliest possible date.

OCTOBER 2, 1914 [TO J. F. GALLBREATH, SECRETARY OF THE AMERICAN MINING CONGRESS]

I am informed that during the last year more than three thousand men were killed and one hundred thousand injured in the mining and metallurgical industries of the country. At the same time, those in authority tell me that from their observation and experience one-half of such deaths and three-fourths of such injuries may be regarded as easily preventable.

I suggest this situation as an opportunity for further endeavor on your part to cut down this excessive toll of death and injury. I can assure you of the fullest cooperation of all the proper governmental agencies; and also of my earnest desire for your active and continued assistance.

There is one other problem connected with the mining industry in which the Federal Government is vitally interested, and that is proper conservation and proper use of the mineral resources of the nation. I realize that you, too, are interested in this problem and wish merely to call it to your attention because of its fundamental importance to the present and future prosperity of the nation. I am happy to say that the profligacy of the past in the use of these resources is not being continued, at least not on so large a scale. There is, however, great opportunity for further reform along these lines and in this your organization can be of invaluable service.

OCTOBER 17, 1914 [TO REPRESENTATIVE OSCAR W. UNDERWOOD]

The people of the country have been served by the members of this Congress as they have seldom, if ever, been served before. The program has several distinct parts and many items, but, after all, a single purpose, namely, to destroy private control and set business free. That purpose was manifest enough in the case of the tariff and in the legislation affecting trusts; but, though perhaps less evident upon the surface there, it lay at the very heart of the currency bill, too.

May I not add, even though it lies outside the field of legislation, that that, and that chiefly, has been the object of the foreign policy of the Government during the last 18 months?

The European war came before the withdrawal of this much-coveted opportunity for the control of monopoly could show its full effects and active competition bring prices to their normal level again; but it is clear enough already that the reduction of the tariff, the simplification of its schedules so as to cut away the jungle in which secret agencies had so long lurked, the correction of its inequalities, and its thorough recasting with the single honest object of revenue, were an indispensable *first step* to reestablishing competition.

The lobby by which some of the worst features of the old tariff had been maintained was driven away by the mere pitiless turning on of the light. The principle was adopted that each duty levied was to be tested by the inquiry whether it was put at such a figure and levied in such a manner as to provoke competition.

The panic that the friends of privilege had predicted did not follow. Business has already adjusted itself to the new conditions with singular ease and elasticity, because the new conditions are in fact more normal than the old.

The revenue lost by the import duties was replaced by an income tax which in part shifted the burden of taxation from the shoulders of every consumer in the country, great or small, to shoulders more certainly able to bear it.

We had time to learn from the actual administration of the law that the revenues resulting from the double change would have been abundant had it not been for the breaking out of the present war in Europe, which affects almost every route of trade and every market in the world outside of the United States.

Until the war ends and until its effects upon manufacture and commerce have been corrected we shall have to impose additional taxes to make up for the loss of such part of our import duties as the war cuts off by cutting off the imports themselves — a veritable war tax, though we are not at war; for war, and only war, is the cause of it.

With similar purpose and in a like temper the Congress has sought, in the Trade-Commission bill and in the Clayton bill, to make men in a small way of business as free to succeed as men in a big way, and to kill monopoly in the seed.

Before these bills were passed the law was already clear enough that monopolies once formed were illegal and could be dissolved by direct process of law and those who had created them punished as for crime.

But there was no law to check the process by which monopoly was built up until the tree was full grown and its fruit developed, or, at any rate, until the full opportunity for monopoly had been created. With this new legislation there is clear and sufficient law to check and destroy the noxious growth in its infancy.

Monopolies are built up by unfair methods of competition, and the new Trade Commission has power to forbid and prevent unfair competition, whether upon a big scale or upon a little; whether just begun or grown old and formidable. Monopoly is created also by putting the same men in charge of a variety of business enterprises, whether apparently related or unrelated to another, by means of interlocking directorates. That the Clayton bill now in large measure prevents. Each enterprise must depend upon its own initiative and effectiveness for success, and upon the intelligence and business energy of the men who officer it.

Justice has been done the laborer. His labor is no longer to be treated as if it were merely an inanimate object of commerce disconnected from the fortunes and happiness of a living human being, to be dealt with as an object of sale and barter. But that, great as it is, is hardly more than the natural and inevitable corollary of a law whose object is individual freedom and initiative as against any kind of private domination.

In like manner by the currency bill we have created a democracy of credit such as has never existed in this country before. For a generation or more we have known and admitted that we had the worst banking and currency system in the world, because the volume of our currency was wholly inelastic; that is, because there was more than enough at certain seasons to meet the demands of commerce and credit, and at other times far too little; that we could not lessen the volume when we needed less nor increase it when we needed more.

Let bankers explain the technical features of the new system. Suffice it here to say that it provides a currency which expands as it is needed, and contracts when it is not needed; a currency which comes into existence in response to the call of every man who can show a going business and a concrete basis for extending credit to him, however obscure or prominent he may be, however big or little his business transactions.

More than that, the power to direct this system of credits is put into the hands of a public board of disinterested officers of the Government itself who can make no money out of anything they do in connection with it.

No group of bankers anywhere can get control; no one part of the country can concentrate the advantages and conveniences of the system upon itself for its own selfish advantage. The board can oblige the banks of one region to go to the assistance of the banks of another. The whole resources of the country are mobilized, to be employed where they are most needed.

I think we are justified in speaking of this as a democracy of credit.

Credit is at the disposal of every man who can show energy and assets. Each region of the country is set to study its own needs and opportunities and the whole country stands by to assist. It is self-government as well as democracy.

A great work of constructive development remains to be accomplished, in building up our merchant marine and in the completion of a great program for the conservation of our natural resources and the development of the water power of the country — a program which has at this session already been carried several steps toward consummation.

OCTOBER 28, 1914 [TO WALTER HINES PAGE, AMBASSADOR TO ENGLAND]

I was just reading carefully last night your last letter dated the fifteenth of October, written in a way to give me a wonderful impression of the state of mind that prevails among the most thoughtful men connected with the government over there.

The whole thing is very vivid in my mind, painfully vivid, and has been almost ever since the struggle began. I think my thought and imagination contain the picture and perceive its significance from every point of view. I have to force myself not to dwell upon it to avoid the sort of numbness that comes from deep apprehension and dwelling upon elements too vast to be yet comprehended or in any way controlled by counsel.

You need not doubt that we comprehend and look into the murky darkness of the whole thing with the same thoughts that you have, though, of course, on this side of the water our own life is, at any rate, still free, and I fancy we can manage a little more perspective than it is conceivable should be obtainable from any point of view on your side of the water.

I have been distressed to have to maintain our recent debate with Sir Edward Grey, but it was absolutely necessary, because not the least part of the difficulty of this war is going to be the satisfaction of opinion in America and the full performance of our utmost duty as the only powerful neutral. More and more, from day to day, the elements (I mean the several racial elements) of our population seem to grow restless and catch more and more the fever of the contest. We are trying to keep all possible spaces cool, and the only means by which we can do so is to make it demonstrably clear that we are doing everything that it is possible to do to define and defend neutral rights.

This is in the interest of all the belligerents no less than in our own interest. I mean that if we are to remain neutral and to afford Europe the legitimate assistance possible in such circumstances, the course we have been pursuing is the absolutely necessary course. Please do not suppose that we are not able to see the thing from the point of view of others, but always remember that it is as necessary for them as it is for us that we should present and emphasize our neutral point of view.

OCTOBER 29, 1914 [TO COLONEL E. M. HOUSE]

You need not fear that you made a mistake in sending me Page's telegram. His official telegrams and his letters to me disclose his state of mind very fully and, while I do not feel it would be just to criticise him in the least, I fear that there is a slight danger in the intense feeling he has for the English case. I do not mean the danger of his neglecting to carry out our instructions very loyally, but the danger of his putting himself out of touch with American feeling altogether.

NOVEMBER 5, 1914 [TO ROBERT LANSING, UNDERSECRETARY OF STATE]

Thank you for having let me see the enclosed communication from the Chinese Minister. I am sorry to say that I have forgotten what the total sum is that we were intending to return to China. Will you be kind enough to remind me how large a proportion of it one hundred thousand dollars would constitute?

I must say in all frankness that I am not half so much interested in the idea of a museum as I am in an adequate provision for Chinese students in this country, and I should not like to sacrifice too large a proportion of the fund to the object which the Minister suggests.

NOVEMBER 8, 1914 [TO MARY A. HULBERT]

I keep a steady front to the world, but my heart is in a whirl day and night. My own individual life has gone utterly to pieces. I do not care a fig for anything that affects me. I could laugh aloud to see the papers, and those for whom they write, assuming every day that a second term in 1916 is in my thoughts and that I want it! If they only knew my supreme indifference to that and to everything else that affects me personally, they would devote their foolish and futile brains to some other topic that they do not understand!

NOVEMBER 9, 1914 [TO MRS. NANCY TOY]

Is it not strange, does it not bespeak our essential individual littleness, that personal happiness should dwell in the little things (little by comparison with the fate and progress of peoples) and in the things that touch us intimately and privately, and not in the big circumstances of our lives? And yet it is so. The love that embraces mankind does not make us happy, but only the love that gives us the intimacy of a dear one who is in fact part of our very selves. We are sustained by the daily touch, the constant sympathy and union in little things, the little things that make up the life that the world knows nothing about. It is a cold, barren region where these things are not. There is no getting any companionship out of the policies of a state or the fortunes of a nation! We are sunk far, far below the likeness in which we were made: we got the likeness but not the substance and character, God forgive us!

DECEMBER 2, 1914 [TO COLONEL HOUSE]

The Springfield Republican is right; the questions of the immediate future are no doubt to be foreign questions, and I am not at all sure that I have the wisdom to meet and solve them, but with the help of counsellors like yourself I hope that it will be possible to guide the old ship in a way that will bring her credit and make her serviceable to the world.

DECEMBER 6, 1914 [TO MARY A. HULBERT]

It costs to be used by the American people as a means of guiding their affairs! Their affairs are so vast and so complicated! It exhausts a chap utterly to keep up with them.

DECEMBER 8, 1914 [TO CONGRESS, ON "PREPAREDNESS"]

It is said in some quarters that we are not prepared for war.

What is meant by being prepared?

Is it meant that we are not ready upon brief notice to put a nation in the field, a nation of men trained to arms? Of course we are not ready to do that; and we shall never be in time of peace so long as we retain our present political principles and institutions.

And what is it that it is suggested we should be prepared to do? To defend ourselves against attack? We have always found means to do that, and shall find them whenever it is necessary without calling our people away from their necessary tasks to render compulsory military service in times of peace.

We are at peace with all the world. No one who speaks counsel based on fact or drawn from a just and candid interpretation of realities can say that there is reason to fear that from any quarters our independence or the integrity of our territory is threatened. Dread of the power of any other nation we are incapable of. We are not jealous of rivalry in the fields of commerce or of any other peaceful achievement.

We mean to live our own lives as we will; but we mean also to let live.

We are, indeed, a true friend to all the nations of the world, because we threaten none, covet the possessions of none, desire the overthrow of none. Our friendship can be accepted and is accepted without reservation, because it is offered in a spirit and for a purpose which no one need ever question or suspect. Therein lies our greatness.

We are the champions of peace and of concord. And we should be very jealous of this distinction which we have sought to earn. Just now we should be particularly jealous of it, because it is our dearest present hope that this character and reputation may presently, in God's providence, bring us an opportunity such as has seldom been vouchsafed any nation, the opportunity to counsel and obtain peace in the world and reconciliation and a healing settlement of many a matter that has cooled and interrupted the friendship of nations.

This is the time above all others when we should wish and resolve to keep our strength by self-possession, our influence by preserving our ancient principles of action.

From the first we have had a clear and settled policy with regard to military establishments. We never have had, and while we retain our present principles and ideals we never shall have, a large standing army.

If asked, Are you ready to defend yourself? we reply, Most assuredly, to the utmost; and yet we shall not turn America into a military camp. We will not ask our young men to spend *the best years of their lives* making soldiers of themselves.

There is another sort of energy in us. It will know how to declare itself and make itself effective should occasion arise. And especially when half the world is on fire we shall be careful to make our moral insurance against the spread of the conflagration very definite and certain and adequate indeed.

Let us remind ourselves, therefore, of the only thing we can do or will do. We must depend in every time of national peril, in the future as in the past, not upon a standing army, nor yet upon a reserve army, but upon a citizenry trained and accustomed to arms.

A powerful navy we have always regarded as our proper and natural means of defense; and it has always been of defense that we have thought, never of aggression or of conquest. We shall take leave to be strong upon the seas, in the future as in the past; and there will be no thought of offense or of provocation in that. Our ships are our natural bulwarks.

Our policy will not be for an occasion. It will be conceived as a permanent and settled thing, which we will pursue at all seasons, without haste and after a fashion perfectly consistent with the peace of the world, the abiding friendship of states, and the unhampered freedom of all with whom we deal. Let there be no misconception. The country has been misinformed. We are not unmindful of the great responsibility resting upon us. We shall learn and profit by the lesson of every experience and every new circumstance; and what is needed will be adequately done.

DECEMBER 12, 1914 [TO MRS. NANCY TOY]

I have not yet learned how to throw off the incubus of my grief and live as I used to live, in thought and spirit, in spite of it. Even books have grown meaningless to me. I read detective stories to forget, as a man would get drunk!

What I do love to talk about, however, is things and persons very near to me, not as President (for I am merely administering the presidency) but as a human being, a traveler between life and death. Human friendship means an infinite deal to me; and I find my thoughts going out to my friends now as never before, trying to make a circle of them close about me no matter how far away in space they may be, and no matter whether they all know one another or not.

JANUARY 3, 1915 [TO MRS. NANCY TOY]

My life would not be worth living if it were not for the driving power of religion, for *faith,* pure and simple. I have seen all my life the arguments against it without ever having been moved by them. There are people who *believe* only so far as they *understand* — that seems to me presumptuous and sets their understanding as the standard of the universe. Why shouldn't Helen's dog, Hamisch here, set up *his* understanding as a standard! I am sorry for such people.

JANUARY 3, 1915 [AFTER READING ALOUD THE CHAPTER ON THE PRESI-
DENT IN HIS *Constitutional Government*]

I am discouraged by the eternal talk with senators one by one. The ideal form of leadership in this country (and I am going to write a book about it one of these days) would be the leadership in the Senate. Now I have to talk with senators one by one — what they say on the floor all the country knows — what I say to them nobody hears. The President should be a mere figurehead like the King of England. The leader of the party should be the leader in Congress and should be heard in debate fully.

CHAPTER FIFTEEN

"Too Proud to Fight"

JANUARY 17, 1915 [TO MARY A. HULBERT, ON THE BIRTH OF HIS FIRST GRANDSON]

None of us can think straight. I forget where the keys of the typewriter are as I absent mindedly try to write this. My own heart is full of the pity that the sweet, sweet mother could not have been here to share her daughter's joy!

JANUARY 28, 1915 [TO CONGRESS ON HIS VETO OF AN IMMIGRATION BILL]

In two particulars of vital consequence this bill embodies a radical departure from the traditional and long-established policy of this country, a policy in which our people have conceived the very character of their Government to be expressed, the very mission and spirit of the Nation in respect of its relations to the peoples of the world outside their borders.

It seeks to all but close entirely the gates of asylum which have always been open to those who could find nowhere else the right and opportunity of constitutional agitation for what they conceived to be the natural and inalienable rights of men; and it excludes those to whom the opportunities of elementary education have been denied, without regard to their character, their purposes, or their natural capacity.

Restrictions like these, adopted earlier in our history as a Nation, would very materially have altered the course and cooled the humane ardors of our politics.

The right of political asylum has brought to this country many a man of noble character and elevated purpose who was marked as an outlaw in his own less fortunate land, and who has yet become an ornament to our citizenship and to our public councils.

The literacy test and the tests and restrictions which accompany it constitute an even more radical change in the policy of the Nation. Hitherto we have generously kept our doors open to all who were not unfitted by reason of disease or incapacity for self-support or such personal records and antecedents as were likely to make them a menace to our peace and order or to the wholesome and essential relationships of life.

In this bill it is proposed to turn away from tests of character and of quality and impose tests which exclude and restrict; for the new tests here embodied are not tests of quality or of character or of personal fitness, but tests of opportunity. Those who come seeking opportunity are not to be admitted unless they have already had one of the chief of the opportunities they seek, the opportunity of education. The object of such provisions is restriction, not selection.

If the people of this country have made up their minds to limit the number of immigrants by arbitrary tests and so reverse the policy of all the generations of Americans that have gone before them, it is their right to do so. I am their servant and have no license to stand in their way. But I do not believe that they have.

JANUARY 29, 1915 [TO COLONEL HOUSE, ON HIS MISSION TO EUROPE]

It gives me peculiar pleasure to give you my commission to go, as my personal representative, on the mission you are now so generously undertaking, a mission fraught with so many great possibilities, and which may, in the kind providence of God, prove the means of opening a way to peace.

It is altogether right and fortunate that you are to act only as my private friend and spokesman, without official standing or authority; for that will relieve both you and those with whom you confer of any embarrassment. Your conferences will not represent the effort of any government to urge action upon another government, but only the effort of a disinterested friend whose suggestions and offers of service will not be misunderstood and may be made use of to the advantage of the world.

The object of this letter is not merely to furnish you with an informal commission but also to supply you with what I know you desire, a definite statement of our attitude with regard to the delicate and important matters you are to discuss and the sort of service we wish to render.

Please say, therefore, very clearly to all with whom you may confer that we have no thought of suggesting, either now or at any other time, the terms and conditions of peace, except as we may be asked to do so as the spokesman of those whose fortunes are involved in the war. Our single object is to be serviceable, if we may, in bringing about the preliminary willingness to parley which must be the first step towards discussing and determining the conditions of peace. If we can be instrumental in ascertaining for each side in the contest what is the real disposition, the real wish, the real purpose of the other with regard to a settlement, our mission and my whole desire in this matter will have been accomplished.

I do not know how better to express my conception of your mission than by saying that it is my desire to supply through you a channel of confidential communication through which the nations which are now at war may make certain that it is right and wise and consistent with their safety and dignity to have a preliminary interchange of views with regard to the terms upon which the present conflict may be brought to an end and future conflicts rendered less likely.

There is nothing to which we wish to bind them. It has occurred to us that to ascertain each other's views in this informal way might be less embarrassing to them than to ascertain them in any other way; that they might possibly be glad to avail themselves of our services, offered in this way, rather than run the risk of missing any honorable opportunity to open a way to peace; and that they might be willing to make use of us the more readily because they might be sure that we sought no advantage for ourselves and had no thought or wish to play a part of guidance in their affairs.

The allies on both sides have seemed to turn to the United States as to a sort of court of opinion in this great struggle, but we have no wish to be judges; we desire only to play the part of disinterested friends who have nothing at stake except their interest in the peace of the world.

FEBRUARY 3, 1915 [ON THE CHAMBERS OF COMMERCE]

I have attended banquets of chambers of commerce in various parts of the country and have got the impression at each of those banquets that there was only one city in the country. It has seemed to me that those associations were meant in order to destroy men's perspective, in order to destroy their sense of relative proportions. Worst of all, if I may be permitted to say so, they were intended to boost something in particular.

Boosting is a very unhandsome thing.

Advancing enterprise is a very handsome thing, but to exaggerate local merits in order to create disproportion in the general development is not a particularly handsome thing or a particularly intelligent thing.

A city cannot grow on the face of a great state like a mushroom on that one spot. Its roots are throughout the state, and unless the state it is in, or the region it draws from, can itself thrive and pulse with life as a whole, the city can have no healthy growth. You forget the wide rootages of everything when you boost some particular region.

FEBRUARY 4, 1915 [TO MRS. NANCY TOY]

I am painfully aware that I am liable to make mistakes, big mistakes; and it is the privilege not only, but the duty of a friend to tell me that I have made them, when the evidence seems against me. That is a proof of loyalty, not a disproof of it! If, in answer to criticism, I reply in what may seem rather grim earnest, it is because I am realizing now, as I have not realized before, even during the fight on the currency bill, that the influences that have so long dominated legislation and administration here are making their last and most desperate stand to regain their control. They are mustering every force they have in this very fight on the shipping bill. It is a very grim business, in which they will give no quarter and in which, so far as I am concerned, they will receive none. If they cannot be mastered, we shall have to have a new struggle for liberty in this country, and God knows what will come of it. Only reform can prevent revolution.

It is not to be wondered at that you do not see the inside of these things, as I am forced to. The wonder would be if you did. And it is a real service to me to be told what is being said by the thoughtful people about you. They are exceedingly critical; but so much the better, if they are fair. There is no harm in their speaking out their minds or my hearing what they say. It is necessary tonic and test of men in public life.

I want to be told exactly what is in your mind; and I shall always understand exactly the spirit in which you utter it. Even if it hurts, it will not wound my heart. Things are desperately hard here, but there is no sense in trying to make them soft; for they cannot be. A man must eat meat.

FEBRUARY 6, 1915 [AN APPEAL TO BUSINESS FOR CO-OPERATION]
I have always maintained that the only way in which men could understand one another was by meeting one another. If I believed all that I read in the newspapers I would not understand anybody. I have met many men whose horns dropped away the moment I was permitted to examine their character.

The important thing is for the different enterprises of the country to understand one another; and the most important thing of all is for us to comprehend our life as a nation and understand each other as fellow-citizens.

The great forces of a country like this can not pull separately; they have got to pull together. And except upon a basis of common understanding as to the law and as to the proprieties of conduct, it is impossible to pull together.

The era of private business in the sense of personal ownership is practically passed, not only in this country, but almost everywhere.

Therefore, almost all business has this direct responsibility to the public in general. We owe a constant report to the public, whose money we are constantly asking for in order to conduct the business itself. Therefore, we have got to trade not only on our efficiency, not only on the service that we render, but *on the confidence that we cultivate.*

We want for business hereafter the same kind of liberty that we want for the individual. The liberty of the individual is limited with the greatest sharpness where his actions come into collision with the interests of the community he lives in.

My liberty consists in a sort of parole. Society says to me, "You may do what you please until you do something that is in violation of the common understanding, of the public interest; then your parole is forfeited. We will take you into custody. We will limit your activities. We will penalize you if you use this thing that you call your liberty against our interest."

Business does not want, and ought not to ask for, more liberty than the individual has; and I have always in my own thought summed up individual liberty, and business liberty, and every other kind of liberty, in the phrase that is common in the sporting world, "A free field and no favor."

You are not going to be barred from the contest because you are big and strong, and you are not going to be penalized because you are big and strong, but you are going to be made to observe the rules of the track and not get in anybody's way except as you can keep ahead of him by having more vigor and skill than he has.

Some men are going to be beaten because they have not the brains, they have not the initiative, they have not the skill, they have not the knowledge, they have not the same capacity that other men have. They will have to be employees, they will have to be used where they can be used.

We do not need to conceal from ourselves that there are varieties of capacities in the world. Some men have heads, but they are not particularly furnished.

Now, liberty does not consist in framing laws to put such men at the front and say they have got to be allowed to keep pace with the rest, because that would hold the whole process of civilization back.

But it does consist in saying no matter how feather-weight the other man is you must not arbitrarily interfere with him; that there must be an absolutely free field and no favor to anybody. There are certain rules of the game. I will mention what seem to me some of them.

First of all, is the rule of publicity, not doing anything under cover, letting the public know what you are doing and judge of it according as it is.

In the second place, there is a full equivalent for the money you receive, the full equivalent in service; not trying to skimp in the service in order to increase profits above a reasonable return, but trying to make the profits proportioned to the satisfaction of the people that you serve.

In the third place, this game requires a certain kind of conscience in business, a certain feeling that we are, after all, in this world because we are expected to make good according to the standards of the people we live with. That, after all, is the chief compulsion that is laid on all of us. We are sustained by the moral judgment of honorable men, and there isn't anything else in this world that I know of that is worth while.

The fourth rule is the rule of having the spirit of service.

When I talk about the spirit of service I am not meaning a sentiment; I am not meaning a state of mind; I am meaning something very concrete, that you want to see to it that the thing that you do for the public and get money for is the best thing of that kind that can be done.

So I say that if your earning capacity is the capacity to earn the public confidence you can go about your business like free men.

It is in this spirit that we all ought to regard the laws, that we all ought to criticize the laws, and that we all ought to cooperate in the enforcement of the laws.

Government is merely an attempt to express the conscience of everybody, the average conscience of the nation, in the rules that everybody is commanded to obey.

FEBRUARY 14, 1915 [TO MARY A. HULBERT]

The last two weeks have been like a fever. Together, England and Germany are likely to drive us crazy, because it looks oftentimes as if they were crazy themselves, the unnecessary provocations they invent.

To keep cool heads and handle each matter composedly and without excitement as it arises, seeking to see each thing in the large, in the light of what is likely to happen as well as in the light of what is happening now, involves a nervous expenditure such as I never dreamed of, and drives every private matter into the background to wait for a time of exemption from these things which never comes.

I go to bed every night absolutely exhausted, trying not to think about anything, and with all my nerves deadened, my own individuality as it were blotted out.

MARCH 4, 1915

Wilson had urged passage of the Shipping Bill to provide sorely needed ships.

Seven Democratic senators united with the Republican senators to defeat the plan, by filibuster when they realized the weakness of debate, and they have achieved their object.

The members of that ill-omened coalition must bear the whole responsibility for it, the very grave responsibility for infinite damage to the business of the United States, to farmers, to laborers, to manufacturers, to producers of every class and sort.

They have fastened the control of the selfish shipping interests on the country and the prospect is not a little sinister. Their responsibility will be very heavy, heavier and heavier as the months come and go; and it will be very bitter to bear.

I shall not call an extra session of Congress. Unless circumstances arise which I cannot at present foresee, I cannot in good faith deny the business of the country this time of adjustment in many large matters, even to remedy the perhaps irremediable damage this unnatural and unprecedented alliance has brought upon our business. Their opportunity to rectify their grievous disloyalty has passed.

The Wilson honeymoon was over. This bill cut down deep into hidden selfish interests. The fight developed personal animosities and rancors that were never healed.

MARCH 7, 1915 [TO MARY A. HULBERT]

Both sides are seeing red on the other side of the sea, and neutral rights are left, for the time being, out of their reckoning altogether. They listen to necessity (and to necessity as they interpret it), not to reason, and there is therefore no way of calculating or preparing for anything. That is what makes the situation such a strain on the nerves, such an exaction on the judgment. One waits for he does not know what, and must act amidst a scene that shifts without notice, without precedent. In such circumstances it is clearly impossible for me to get away from Washington. I must stay where I can, as nearly as may be, keep in touch with all the elements all the time — a large order!

But I can at least regulate my days now so as to be at my own disposal rather than at the disposal of anybody and everybody who wishes to use it all the day long; and that will be an immense relief, if for no other reason, because I can take time enough to look into things thoroughly and comprehend them and think them through. And maybe I shall be able to get a little rest, too, at intervals, instead of spending my strength on trifles all the while, as now. I am well, singularly well: my only trouble is with my spirits, which are distinctly bad, when I give them time to be anything that I am conscious of!

MARCH 15, 1915 [TO SENATOR THOMAS W. HARDWICK ON PARTY GOVERNMENT]

You are right in thinking that differences of opinion upon public questions cannot alter my personal feeling towards men whom I respect and with whom it is a pleasure for me to work and I thank you for judging me so truly.

I must in frankness say, however, that the recent situation in the

Senate distressed and disturbed me not a little. I do not see how party government is possible, indeed I can form no working idea of the successful operation of popular institutions, if individuals are to exercise the privilege of defeating a decisive majority of their own party associated in framing and carrying out the policy of the party.

In party conference personal convictions should have full play and should be most candidly and earnestly presented, but there does not seem to me to be any surrender either of personal dignity or of individual conviction in yielding to the determinations of a decisive majority of one's fellow workers in a great organization which must hold together if it is to be serviceable to the country as a governing agency.

This conviction on my part lies back of and supports every conclusion that I have come to in years of study not only, but in recent years of experience, with regard to the feasibility and efficiency of party government, and I beg, my dear Senator, that you will allow me to press this view upon you with the earnestness of a conviction which underlies all others.

MARCH 15, 1915 [TO HIS DAUGHTER MRS. SAYRE]

You cannot know, I fear, what it meant to me to have you say that I had in some sort taken your incomparable mother's place when you were here! How little I knew how! and how impossible it was to do more than just let you feel as well as I knew how the infinite tenderness I felt and the longing that was at my heart to make up for what can never be made up for either to you, my sweet daughter, nor to me nor to anyone who ever had a chance to know how sweet and loving and infinitely rewarding she was.

I cannot yet trust myself to speak much of her, even in writing. My heart has somehow been stricken dumb. I felt so dumb when you were here, dear. I did not know how to *say* the things that were in my heart about you and the baby and all the crowding thoughts that made my heart ache with its fullness.

I had to trust you to *see* them; and your dear letter makes me hope that you did. I can talk about most things but I always have been helpless about putting into words the things I feel most deeply, the things that mean most to me; and just now my heart is particularly voiceless.

But I do love you and yours, my dear, more than words can say, and there *is* added to my love now the mother tenderness which I know the depths and beauties of in *her* heart. She was beyond comparison the deepest, truest, noblest lover I ever knew or ever heard those who knew the human heart wish for!

APRIL 1, 1915 [TO MAJOR PULLMAN]
Major Pullman had been appointed chief of police of the District of Columbia.

Maj. Pullman, you are taking up a most important work, and in connection with it I have but one thing to say and that is to urge you to stamp out special privilege in the administration of the laws. I do not know what my driver does that is wrong, but I do know that when a motorcycle policeman gets near enough to see that it is a White House car he disappears from the scene. I want you to tell your men that White House cars must obey the traffic regulations just the same as any other cars. Another thing, I am told that the police permit certain highly placed persons to put their carriages and automobiles ahead of others waiting in the lines at the gates of the White House on the occasion of the large receptions here. I want that stopped.

If there is any creature on earth that I despise it is the man who by reason of his wealth or his high social position seeks to disregard with impunity minor police regulations and the petty ordinances by which society keeps its processes in order.

While I am here I hope the Washington police will treat every man as equal before the law.

APRIL 7, 1915 [TO HENRY M. PINDELL]
It was certainly very thoughtful and considerate of you to ask whether I thought it best at this time for Americans to be going abroad. I see no sufficient reason why they should not, though the

indications are that both sides are feeling just now a little irritated by our consistent and effective neutrality, and I am afraid that Americans are receiving a less and less cordial welcome on the other side of the water, little as they deserve the feeling that seems to be growing against them.

On May 1, 1915, this notice appeared in the newspapers:

> TRAVELLERS *intending to embark on the Atlantic voyage are reminded that a state of war exists between Germany and her allies and Great Britain and her allies; that the zone of war includes the waters adjacent to the British Isles; that in accordance with formal notice given by the Imperial German Government, vessels flying the flag of Great Britain or of any of her allies, are liable to destruction in those waters and that travellers sailing in the war zones on ships of Great Britain or her allies do so at their own risk.*

As a result of this decision of Germany, the Lusitania, *loaded with American passengers, was sunk on May 7, 1915, without warning. The horror of it gripped the nation. Wilson sent Germany a strong note. The reply was evasive and unsatisfactory. From here on out it was just a matter of time until we went to war with Germany.*

MAY 10, 1915 ["TOO PROUD TO FIGHT"]

Wilson addressed several thousand foreign-born citizens at Philadelphia after their naturalization.

This is the only country in the world which experiences this constant and repeated rebirth. Other countries depend upon the multiplication of their own native people. This country is constantly drinking strength out of new sources by the voluntary association with it of great bodies of strong men and forward-looking women out of other lands.

And so by the gift of the free will of independent people it is being constantly renewed from generation to generation by the same process by which it was originally created. It is as if humanity had determined to see to it that this great Nation, founded for the benefit of humanity, should not lack for the allegiance of the people of the world.

You have just taken an oath of allegiance to the United States. Of allegiance to whom? Of allegiance to no one, unless it be God — certainly not of allegiance to those who temporarily represent this great Government.

You have taken an oath of allegiance to a great ideal, to a great body of principles, to a great hope of the human race. You have said, "We are going to America not only to earn a living, not only to seek the things which it was more difficult to obtain where we were born, but to help forward the great enterprises of the human spirit — to let men know that everywhere in the world there are men who will cross strange oceans and go where a speech is spoken which is alien to them if they can but satisfy their quest for what their spirits crave; knowing that whatever the speech there is but one longing and utterance of the human heart, and that is for liberty and justice."

And while you bring all countries with you, you come with a purpose of leaving all other countries behind you — bringing what is best of their spirit, but not looking over your shoulders and seeking to perpetuate what you intended to leave behind in them.

I certainly would not be one even to suggest that a man cease to love the home of his birth and the nation of his origin — these things are very sacred and ought not to be put out of our hearts — but it is one thing to love the place where you were born and it is another thing to dedicate yourself to the place to which you go.

You cannot dedicate yourself to America unless you become in every respect and with every purpose of your will thorough Americans.

You cannot become thorough Americans if you think of yourselves in groups. America does not consist of groups.

A man who thinks of himself as belonging to a particular national group in America has not yet become an American, and the man who goes among you to trade upon your nationality is no worthy son to live under the Stars and Stripes.

My urgent advice to you would be, not only always to think first of America, but always, also, to think first of humanity. You do not love humanity if you seek to divide humanity into jealous camps.

Humanity can be welded together only by love, by sympathy, by justice, not by jealousy and hatred.

I am sorry for the man who seeks to make personal capital out of the passions of his fellowmen. He has lost the touch and ideal of America, for America was created to unite mankind by those passions which lift and not by the passions which separate and debase.

We came to America, either ourselves or in the persons of our ancestors, to better the ideals of men, to make them see finer things than they had seen before, to get rid of the things that divide and to make sure of the things that unite.

It was but an historical accident no doubt that this great country was called the "United States"; yet I am very thankful that it has the word "United" in its title, and the man who seeks to divide man from man, group from group, interest from interest in this great Union is striking at its very heart.

It is a very interesting circumstance to me, in thinking of those of you who have just sworn allegiance to this great Government, that you were drawn across the ocean by some beckoning finger of hope, by some belief, by some vision of a new kind of justice, by some expectation of a better kind of life.

If I have in any degree forgotten what America was intended for, I will thank God if you will remind me. I was born in America. You dreamed dreams of what America was to be, and I hope you brought the dreams with you.

No man that does not see visions will ever realize any high hope or undertake any high enterprise. Just because you brought dreams with you, America is more likely to realize dreams such as you brought. You are enriching us if you came expecting us to be better than we are.

See what that means. It means that Americans must have a consciousness different from the consciousness of every other nation in the world. The example of America must be a special example. The example of America must be the example not merely of peace because it will not fight, but of peace because peace is the healing and elevating influence of the world and strife is not.

There is such a thing as a man being too proud to fight.

There is such a thing as a nation being so right that it does not need to convince others by force that it is right.

You have come into this great Nation voluntarily seeking something that we have to give, and all that we have to give is this: We cannot exempt you from work. No man is exempt from work anywhere in the world. We cannot exempt you from the strife and the heartbreaking burden of the struggle of the day — that is common to mankind everywhere; we cannot exempt you from the loads that you must carry. We can only make them light by the spirit in which they are carried. That is the spirit of hope, it is the spirit of liberty, it is the spirit of justice.

Wilson's enemies and the propagandists jumped on his phrase, "too proud to fight," and made of it a weapon against him. Two things they did not explain: (1) that it applied to the Mexican situation more than to the European, and (2) that in context it did not mean what they implied.

CHAPTER SIXTEEN

"Preparedness Must Be Both Physical and Spiritual"

⧸⧸⧸⧸⧸⧸⧸⧸⧸⧸⧸⧸⧸⧸⧸⧸⧸⧸⧸⧸⧸⧸

Over and over Wilson reiterated what for him was the fundamental — the principal — level of American idealism. "America asks nothing for herself except what she has a right to ask for humanity itself." "Peace dwells in the character and in the heart, and that is where peace is rooted in this blessed country of ours." Yet, hesitantly, he had to come to the conclusion that this country was going to have to prepare for war.

JUNE 2, 1915

In the same way he was forced to realize that something had to be done about the chaos that existed in Mexico.

For more than two years revolutionary conditions have existed in Mexico. The purpose of the revolution was to rid Mexico of men who ignored the constitution of the Republic and used their power in contempt of the rights of its people; and with these purposes the people of the United States instinctively and generously sympathized.

But the leaders of the revolution, in the very hour of their success, have disagreed and turned their arms against one another. There is no proper protection either for her own citizens or for the citizens of other nations resident and at work within her territory. Mexico is starving and without a government.

In these circumstances the people and Government of the United States cannot stand indifferently by and do nothing to serve their neighbor.

They want nothing for themselves in Mexico. Least of all do they desire to settle her affairs for her, or claim any right to do so. But neither do they wish to see utter ruin come upon her, and they deem it their duty as friends and neighbors to lend any aid they properly can to any instrumentality which promises to be effective in bringing about a settlement which will embody the real objects of the revolution — constitutional government and the rights of the people.

Patriotic Mexicans are sick at heart and cry out for peace and for every self-sacrifice that may be necessary to procure it. Their people cry out for food and will presently hate as much as they fear every man, in their country or out of it, who stands between them and their daily bread.

It is time, therefore, that the Government of the United States should frankly state the policy which in these extraordinary circumstances it becomes its duty to adopt. It must presently do what it has not hitherto done or felt at liberty to do, lend its active moral support to some man or group of men, if such may be found, who can rally the suffering people of Mexico to their support in an effort to ignore, if they cannot unite, the warring factions of the country, return to the constitution of the Republic so long in abeyance, and set up a government at Mexico City which the great powers of the world can recognize and deal with, a government with which the program of the revolution will be a business and not merely a platform.

I, therefore, publicly and very solemnly, call upon the leaders of faction in Mexico to act, to act together, and to act promptly for the relief and redemption of their prostrate country. I feel it to be my duty to tell them that, if they cannot accommodate their differences and unite for this great purpose within a very short time, this Government will be constrained to decide what means should be employed by the United States in order to help Mexico save herself and serve her people.

JUNE 5, 1915 [TO SECRETARY OF STATE BRYAN ON THE *Lusitania* QUESTION]

I hope that you realize how hard it goes with me to differ with you in judgment about such grave matters as we are now handling. You always have such weight of reason, as well as such high motives, behind what you urge that it is with deep misgiving that I turn from what you press upon me.

I am inclined to think that we ought to take steps, as you suggest, to prevent our citizens from travelling on ships carrying munitions of war, and I shall seek to find the legal way to do it. I fear that, whatever it may be best to do about that, it is clearly impossible to act before the new note goes to Germany.

I am sorry to say that, study as I may the way to do it without hopelessly weakening our protest, I cannot find a way to embody in our note the principle of long discussion of a very simple state of facts.

Secretary of State William Jennings Bryan believed that citizens of the United States should stay off the high seas and that they travelled at their own risk. He was opposed to the strong stand that Wilson was taking against Germany, fearing that it would bring on war. On June 9, rather than sign the second Lusitania *note, he resigned. He thought by doing so to crystallize public sentiment for peace, but he was wrong. It was Wilson, not Bryan, that the country believed in.*

JULY 14, 1915 [TO COLONEL HOUSE ABOUT THE GERMAN FOREIGN MINISTER]

Perhaps it might be just as well for you to see Bernstorff, if only to make him feel not only that some way out *should* be found but that some way out *must* be found and that his Government owes it to themselves and to the rest of the world to help to find it.

Apparently the Germans *are* modifying their methods; they must be made to feel that they must continue in their new way unless they deliberately wish to prove to us that they are unfriendly and wish war.

JULY 20, 1915 [TO SECRETARY OF THE NAVY DANIELS]

I have been giving, as I am sure you have also, a great deal of thought to the matter of a wise and adequate naval program, to be proposed to the Congress at its next session, and I would like to discuss the whole subject with you at the earliest possible date.

But first we must have professional advice. I would be very much obliged if you would get the best minds in the department to work on the subject. I mean the men who have been most directly in contact with actual modern conditions, who have most thoroughly comprehended the altered conditions of naval warfare, and who best comprehend what the Navy must be in the future in order to stand upon an equality with the most efficient and most practically serviceable. I want their advice, a programme by them formulated in the most definite terms. Whether we can reasonably propose the whole of it to the Congress immediately or not we can determine when we have studied it. The important thing now is to know and know fully what we need. Congress will certainly welcome such advice and follow it to the limit of its opportunity.

It should be a program planned for a consistent and progressive development of this great defensive arm of the nation, and should be of such a kind as to commend itself to every patriotic and practical man.

JULY 20, 1915 [TO DR. M. W. JACOBUS]

The opinion of the country seems to demand two inconsistent things, firmness and the avoidance of war, but I am hoping that perhaps they are not in necessary contradiction and that firmness may bring peace.

JULY 21, 1915 [THIRD *Lusitania* NOTE TO GERMANY]

Illegal and inhuman acts, however justifiable they may be thought to be against an enemy who is believed to have acted in contravention of law and humanity, are manifestly indefensible when they deprive neutrals of their acknowledged rights, particularly when they violate the right of life itself. If a belligerent can not retaliate against an enemy without injuring the lives of neutrals, as well as their property, humanity, as well as justice and a due regard for the dignity of neutral powers, should dictate that the practice be discontinued. If persisted in it would in such circumstances constitute an unpardonable offense against the sovereignty of the neutral nation affected.

The Government of the United States is not unmindful of the extraordinary conditions created by this war or of the radical alterations of circumstances and method of attack produced by the use of instrumentalities of naval warfare which the nations of the world can not have had in view when the existing rules of international law were formulated, and it is ready to make every reasonable allowance for these novel and unexpected aspects of war at sea; but it can not consent to abate any essential or fundamental right of its people because of a mere alteration of circumstance.

The rights of neutrals in time of war are based upon principle, not upon expediency, and the principles are immutable.

It is the duty and obligation of belligerents to find a way to adapt the new circumstances to them.

August 4, 1915 [to Colonel House]

I am sure that the country is honeycombed with German intrigue and infested with German spies. The evidences of these things are multiplying every day.

I do not feel that Bernstorff is dealing frankly with us.

Shall we ever get out of the labyrinth made for us all by this German frightfulness?

August 18, 1915 [to Secretary of War Garrison]

Mr. Breckinridge handed me, as I wrote you, the paper containing an outline of military policy and I have now read it with very studious attention. I am sorry to say that it does not contain what I hoped it would. In view of what you wrote me in your letter, it is evident that you were thinking chiefly while preparing it of making the test of public opinion to which you referred. The paper is, therefore, lacking in the detail which is necessary before I can really form a personal judgment about it.

I want to say that the general idea contained in it interests me very much and seems to me a feasible one, but the method by which the thing could be done, I mean by which the training of the citizen soldiery could be carried out, and also the cost, it is of the first importance that I should know.

The government of the United States was caught in an inexorable wringer: our foreign relations were based on the isolationist theory, which was reflected politically, while economically we were not isolated at all. Politically we could try to be neutral but economically we could not. From the resignation of Bryan, the decisions in Washington fluctuated between what was legal and what was necessary.

When in September, 1915, McAdoo and Lansing convinced Wilson that England must have immediate credit in excess of half a billion dollars the country at that moment actually entered the war. This, plus the evidence of spy activities of Germany in the country, turned the emphasis in Wilson's mind from neutrality to preparedness.

SEPTEMBER 15, 1915 [TO LUCY M. SMITH]

Apparently the Germans do not know how to keep faith with anybody, and we are walking on quicksand.

SEPTEMBER 26, 1915 [TO MARY W. HOYT]

Something very delightful has happened to me which I am not yet at liberty to tell others but which I want you to know among the first. A great happiness and blessing has come to me in the midst of my loneliness. Mrs. Norman Galt, a lovely Washington woman (born in Virginia) whom I first met in April last through Helen, who had become her fast friend, has promised to marry me. When you know her you will know why it was inevitable that I should fall in love with her, for she is wholly delightful and lovable. She is known here for everything that is fine and for nothing that is touched with the small spirit of the society folk of the place. You would think that it was only love that was speaking if I were to tell you what she is like, how endowed and made distinguished in her loveliness, but you will, I am sure, find out for yourself how truly wonderful she is in gifts both of heart and of mind.

SEPTEMBER 28, 1915

Democracy is the most difficult form of government, because it is the form under which you have to persuade the largest number of persons to do anything in particular.

OCTOBER 5, 1915 [MRS. EDITH G. REID]

The last fourteen months have seemed for me, in a world upset, like fourteen years. It is not the same world in which my dear Ellen lived; and one of the very last things she said to me was that she hoped that what has happened now would happen. It seemed to me incredible then, and would, I think, have continued to seem so if I had not been brought in contact with Mrs. Galt. She seemed to come into our life here like a special gift from Heaven, and I have won a sweet companion who will soon make me forget the intolerable loneliness and isolation of the weary months since this terrible war began.

OCTOBER 25, 1915 [TO HIS DAUGHTER, MRS. SAYRE]

Edith is greatly distressed by the foolish (and lying) publicity of which she is being made the object, poor girl, but is fine about it, as about everything else. She is very well indeed, and seems (to me, at least) to grow more radiant and lovely every day. I am sure she would send deepest love if she knew that I was writing today.

NOVEMBER 4, 1915

No matter what military or naval force the United States might develop, statesmen throughout the whole world might rest assured that we were gathering that force, not for attack in any quarter, not for aggression of any kind, not for the satisfaction of any political or international ambition, but merely to make sure of our own security. We have it in mind to be prepared, not for war, but only for defense; and with the thought constantly in our minds that the principles we hold most dear can be achieved by the slow processes of history only in the kindly and wholesome atmosphere of peace, and not by the use of hostile force.

DECEMBER 7, 1915

Wilson gave a definition of Pan-Americanism in an address to Congress.

There was a time in the early days of our own great nation and of the republics fighting their way to independence in Central and

South America when the government of the United States looked upon itself as in some sort the guardian of the republics to the south of her as against any encroachments or efforts at political control from the other side of the water; felt it its duty to play the part even without invitation from them; and I think that we can claim that the task was undertaken with a true and disinterested enthusiasm for the freedom of the Americas and the unmolested self-government of her independent peoples.

But it was always difficult to maintain such a role without offense to the pride of the peoples whose freedom of action we sought to protect, and without provoking serious misconceptions of our motives, and every thoughtful man of affairs must welcome the altered circumstances of the new day in whose light we now stand, when there is no claim of guardianship or thought of wards, but, instead, a full and honorable association as of partners between ourselves and our neighbors, in the interest of all America, north and south.

Our concern for the independence and prosperity of the states of Central and South America is not altered. We retain unabated the spirit that has inspired us throughout the whole life of our government and which was so frankly put into words by President Monroe. We still mean always to make a common cause of national independence and of political liberty in America.

But that purpose is now better understood so far as it concerns ourselves. It is known not to be a selfish purpose. It is known to have in it no thought of taking advantage of any government in this hemisphere or playing its political fortunes for our own benefit. All the governments of America stand, so far as we are concerned, upon a footing of genuine equality and unquestioned independence.

The states of America are not hostile rivals, but co-operating friends, and their growing sense of community of interest, alike in matters political and in matters economic, is likely to give them a new significance as factors in international affairs and in the political history of the world. It presents them as in a very deep and true sense a unit in world affairs, spiritual partners, standing together because thinking together, quick with common sympathies and common ideals. Separated they are subject to all the cross-currents of the confused politics of a world of hostile rivalries; united in spirit and purpose they cannot be disappointed of their peaceful destiny.

This is Pan-Americanism. It has none of the spirit of empire in it. It is the embodiment, the effectual embodiment, of the spirit of law and independence and liberty and mutual service.

Great democracies are not belligerent. They do not seek or desire war. Their thought is of individual liberty and of the free labor that supports life and the uncensored thought that quickens it. Conquest and dominion are not in our reckoning, or agreeable to our principles.

President Wilson was married to Mrs. Galt on December 18, 1915.

Wilson made a swing through the Middle West — then as now the isolationist section of the country — to let them know, before the Presidential campaign got under way, how he was thinking.

JANUARY 27, 1916 [OUR MISSION AS A NATION]

While America is a very great Nation, while America contains every element of fine force and accomplishment, America does not constitute the major part of the world. We live in a world which we did not make, which we can not alter, which we can not think into a different condition from that which actually exists. It would be a hopeless piece of provincialism to suppose that because we think differently from the rest of the world we are at liberty to assume that the rest of the world will permit us to enjoy that thought without disturbance.

We have preferred to be provincial. We have preferred to stand behind protecting devices. And now, whether we will or no, we are thrust out to do on a scale never dreamed of by recent generations in America the business of the world. We can not any longer be a provincial Nation.

If there is one passion more deep-seated in the hearts of our fellow countrymen than another, it is the passion for peace. No nation in the world ever more instinctively turned away from the thought of war than this Nation to which we belong.

There is no spirit of aggrandizement in America. There is no desire on the part of any thoughtful and conscientious American man to take one foot of territory from any other nation in the world.

I myself share to the bottom of my heart that profound love for peace. I have sought to maintain peace against very great and sometimes very unfair odds. I have had many a time to use every power that was in me to prevent such a catastrophe as war coming upon this country. It is not permissible for any man to say that anxiety for the defense of the Nation has in it the least tinge of desire for a power that can be used to bring on war.

But there is something that the American people love better than they love peace.

They love the principles upon which their political life is founded. They are ready at any time to fight for the vindication of their character and of their honor.

They will not at any time seek the contest, but they will at no time cravenly avoid it; because if there is one thing that the individual ought to fight for, and that the Nation ought to fight for, it is the integrity of its own convictions. We can not surrender our convictions.

January 27, 1916 [on world economics]

There is going on in the world under our eyes an economic revolution. No man understands that revolution; no man has the elements of it clearly in his mind. No part of the business of legislation with regard to international trade can be undertaken until we do understand it; and members of Congress are too busy, their duties are too multifarious and distracting to make it possible within a sufficiently short space of time for them to master the change that is coming.

The circumstances of the world to-day are not what they were yesterday, or ever were in any of our yesterdays. And it is not certain what they will be to-morrow.

I can not tell what the international relations of this country will be to-morrow, and I use the word literally; and I would not dare keep silent and let the country suppose that to-morrow was certain to be as bright as to-day.

JANUARY 29, 1916 [ON PACIFISM]

Of course, there are some gentlemen who allow themselves to be deceived by very handsome sentiments. If a man is so in love with peace that he can not imagine any kind of danger, I almost envy him the trance he is in, and so long as he is in the trance he is not going to do anything but enjoy the vision. But such men are not many. America is a hard-headed nation, and America generally wants to see the facts as they come before they get here. And the facts of the world are such that it is my duty to counsel my fellow citizens that preparation for national defense can not any longer be postponed.

JANUARY 29, 1916 [ON CHANGE]

The world will never be the same again after this war is over. The change may be for weal or it may be for woe, but it will be fundamental and tremendous.

JANUARY 31, 1916 [NOT A PEOPLES' WAR]

I sometimes think that it is true that no people ever went to war with another people. Governments have gone to war with one another. Peoples, so far as I remember, have not, and this is a government of the people, and this people is not going to choose war.

But we are not dealing with people; we are dealing with Governments. We are dealing with Governments now engaged in a great struggle, and therefore we do not know what a day or an hour will bring forth.

All that we know is the character of our own duty. We do not want the question of peace and war, or the conduct of war, entrusted too entirely to our Government.

We want war, if it must come, to be something that springs out of the sentiments and principles and actions of the people themselves; and it is on that account that I am counseling the Congress of the United States not to take the advice of those who recommend that we should have, and have very soon, a great standing Army, but, on the contrary, to see to it that the citizens of this country are so trained and that the military equipment is so sufficiently provided for them that when they choose they can take up arms and defend themselves.

JANUARY 31, 1916 [ON CHANGING CONDITIONS]

A year ago it did seem as if America might rest secure without very great anxiety and take it for granted that she would not be drawn into this terrible maelstrom, but those first six months was merely the beginning of the struggle. Another year has been added, and now no man can confidently say whether the United States will be drawn into the struggle or not.

FEBRUARY 1, 1916 [THE PRICE OF PEACE]

There is a price which is too great to pay for peace, and that price can be put in one word. One can not pay the price of self-respect. One can not pay the price of duties abdicated, of glorious opportunities neglected, of character, national character left without vindication and exemplification in action.

America has a character as distinct as the character of any individual amongst us. We read that character in every page of her singular and glorious history. It is written in invisible signs which, nevertheless, our spirits can decipher upon the very folds of the flag which is the emblem of our national life.

What is America expected to do? She is expected to do nothing less than keep law alive while the rest of the world burns.

I pray God that if this contest have no other result, it will at least have the result of creating an international tribunal and producing some sort of joint guarantee of peace on the part of the great nations of the world.

FEBRUARY 24, 1916 [TO SENATOR W. J. STONE, ON APPEASEMENT]

You are right in assuming that I shall do everything in my power to keep the United States out of war. I think the country will feel no uneasiness about my course in that respect. Through many anxious months I have striven for that object, amidst difficulties more manifold than can have been apparent upon the surface; and so far I have succeeded. I do not doubt that I shall continue to succeed. The course which the central European powers have announced their intention of following in the future with regard to undersea warfare seems for the moment to threaten insuperable obstacles, but its apparent meaning is so manifestly inconsistent with explicit assurances recently given us by those powers with regard to their treatment of merchant vessels on the high seas that I must believe that explanations will presently ensue which will put a different aspect upon it. We have no reason to question their good faith or their fidelity to their promises in the past, and I, for one, feel confident that we shall have none in the future.

But in any event our duty is clear. No nation, no group of nations, has the right while war is in progress to alter or disregard the principles which all nations have agreed upon in mitigation of the horrors and sufferings of war; and if the clear rights of American citizens should ever unhappily be abridged or denied by any such action, we should, it seems to me, have in honor no choice as to what our own course should be.

For my own part, I can not consent to any abridgment of the rights of American citizens in any respect. The honor and self-respect of the nation is involved. We covet peace, and shall preserve it at any cost but the loss of honor.

To forbid our people to exercise their rights for fear we might be called upon to vindicate them would be a deep humiliation indeed. It would be an implicit, all but an explicit, acquiescence in the violation of the rights of mankind everywhere and of whatever nation or allegiance. It would be a deliberate abdication of our hitherto proud position as spokesmen even amidst the turmoil of war for the law and the right. It would make everything this Government has attempted and everything that it has achieved during this terrible struggle of nations meaningless and futile.

It is important to reflect that if in this instance we allowed expediency to take the place of principle, the door would inevitably be opened to still further concessions.

Once accept a single abatement of right and many other humiliations would certainly follow, and the whole fine fabric of international law might crumble under our hands piece by piece. What we are contending for in this matter is of the very essence of the things that have made America a sovereign nation. She cannot yield them without conceding her own impotency as a nation and making virtual surrender of her independent position among the nations of the world.

I am speaking, my dear Senator, in deep solemnity, without heat, with a clear consciousness of the high responsibilities of my office, and as your sincere and devoted friend. If we should unhappily differ, we shall differ as friends; but where issues so momentous as these are involved we must, just because we are friends, speak our minds without reservation.

FEBRUARY 26, 1916 [ADDRESS TO THE GRIDIRON CLUB]

I would a great deal rather know what they are talking about around quiet firesides all over this country than what they are talking about in the cloakrooms of Congress. I would a great deal rather know what the men on the trains and by the wayside and in the shops and on the farms are thinking about and yearning for than hear any of the vociferous proclamations of policy which it is so easy to hear and so easy to read by picking up any scrap of printed paper.

There is only one way to hear these things, and that is constantly to go back to the fountains of American action. Those fountains are not to be found in any recently discovered sources.

And the infinite difficulty of public affairs is not to discover the signs of the heavens and the directions of the wind, but to square the things you do by the not simple but complicated standards of justice. Justice has nothing to do with expediency. Justice has nothing to do with any temporary standard whatever. It is rooted and grounded in the fundamental instincts of humanity.

America ought to keep out of this war. She ought to keep out of this war at the sacrifice of everything except this single thing upon which her character and history are founded, her sense of humanity and justice.

If she sacrifices that, she has ceased to be America; she has ceased to entertain and to love the traditions which have made us proud to be Americans, and when we go about seeking safety at the expense of humanity, then I for one will believe that I have always been mistaken in what I have conceived to be the spirit of American history.

MARCH 26, 1916

Wilson issued a press statement on General Pershing's pursuit of Villa.

As has already been announced, the expedition into Mexico was ordered under an agreement with the *de facto* Government of Mexico for the single purpose of taking the bandit Villa, whose forces had actually invaded the territory of the United States, and is in no sense intended as an invasion of that republic or as an infringement of its sovereignty.

In order to avoid the creation of erroneous and dangerous impressions in this way I have called upon the several news agencies to use the utmost care not to give news stories regarding this expedition the color of war, to withhold stories of troop movements and military preparations which might be given that interpretation, and to refrain from publishing unverified rumors of unrest in Mexico.

I feel that it is most desirable to impress upon both our own people and the people of Mexico the fact that the expedition is simply a necessary punitive measure, aimed solely at the elimination of the marauders who raided Columbus and who infest an unprotected district near the border, which they use as a base in making attacks upon the lives and property of our citizens within our own territory.

APRIL 19, 1916 [TO CONGRESS AFTER THE SINKING OF THE S.S. *Sussex*]

In February, 1915, the Imperial German Government announced its intention to treat the waters surrounding Great Britain and

Ireland as embraced within the seat of war and to destroy all merchant ships owned by its enemies that might be found within any part of that portion of the high seas, and that it warned all vessels, of neutral as well as of belligerent ownership, to keep out of the waters it had thus proscribed or else enter them at their peril.

Notwithstanding the earnest protest of our Government, the Imperial German Government at once proceeded to carry out the policy it had announced. It expressed the hope that the dangers involved, at any rate the dangers to neutral vessels, would be reduced to a minimum by the instructions which it had issued to its submarine commanders, and assured the Government of the United States that it would take every possible precaution both to respect the rights of neutrals and to safeguard the lives of non-combatants.

What has actually happened in the year which has since elapsed has shown that those hopes were not justified, those assurances insusceptible of being fulfilled.

The Government of the United States has been very patient. At every stage of this distressing experience of tragedy after tragedy in which its own citizens were involved it has sought to be restrained from any extreme course of action or of protest by a thoughtful consideration of the extraordinary circumstances of this unprecedented war, and actuated in all that it said or did by the sentiments of genuine friendship which the people of the United States have always entertained and continue to entertain towards the German nation. It has been willing to wait until the significance of the facts became absolutely unmistakable and susceptible of but one interpretation.

That point has now unhappily been reached. The facts are susceptible of but one interpretation. The Imperial German Government has been unable to put any limits or restraints upon its warfare against either freight or passenger ships. It has therefore become painfully evident that the position which this Government took at the very outset is inevitable, namely, that the use of submarines for the destruction of an enemy's commerce is of necessity, because of the very character of the vessels employed and the very methods of attack which their employment of course involves, incompatible with the principles of humanity, the long established and incontrovertible rights of neutrals, and the sacred immunities of noncombatants.

I have deemed it my duty, therefore, to say to the Imperial German Government that if it is still its purpose to prosecute relentless and indiscriminate warfare against vessels of commerce by the use of submarines, this Government can have no choice but to sever diplomatic relations with the Government of the German Empire altogether.

This decision I have arrived at with the keenest regret; the possibility of the action contemplated I am sure all thoughtful Americans will look forward to with unaffected reluctance. But we cannot forget that we are in some sort and by the force of circumstances the responsible spokesmen of the rights of humanity, and that we cannot remain silent while those rights seem in process of being swept utterly away in the maelstrom of this terrible war. We owe it to a due regard for our own rights as a nation, to our sense of duty as a representative of the rights of neutrals the world over, and to a just conception of the rights of mankind to take this stand now with the utmost solemnity and firmness.

MAY 21, 1916 [ON "ONE WORLD"]

America has always been a-making and to be made, and while we were in the midst of this process, apparently at the acme and crisis of this process, while this travail of souls and fermentation of elements was at its height, came this great cataclysm of European war, and almost every other nation in the world became involved in tremendous struggle, which was what, my fellow-citizens?

What are the elements in the struggle?

Don't you see that in this European war is involved the very thing that has been going on in America? It is a competition of national standards, of national traditions, and of national political systems.

Europe has grappled in war, as we have grappled in peace, to see what is going to be done with these things when they come into hot contact with one another. For do you now remember that, while these processes were going on in America, some very interesting things were happening?

It was a very big world into which this nation came when it was born, but it is a very little world now. It used to take as many days to go from Washington to Charlotte in those days as it now takes hours.

And, as these processes of intercommunication have been developed and quickened, men of the same nation not only have grown closer neighbors with each other, but men of different nations have grown closer neighbors with each other; and now that we have these invisible tongues that speak by the wireless through the trackless air to the ends of the world, every man can make every other man in the world and his neighbor speak to him upon the moment.

While these processes of fermentation and travail were going on, men were learning about each other, nations were becoming more and more acquainted with each other, nations were becoming more and more interrelated, and intercommunication was being quickened in every possible way, so that now the melting pot is bigger than America.

It is as big as the world. And what you see taking place on the other side of the waters is the tremendous process by which a contest of elements may in God's process be turned into a co-ordination and co-operation of elements.

See what a new age we have come into. I should think that it would quicken the imagination of every man, and quicken the patriotism of every man who cared for America.

MAY 27, 1916 [FIRST STATEMENT ON A LEAGUE OF NATIONS]

It is plain that this war could have come only as it did, suddenly and out of secret councils, without warning to the world, without discussion, without any of the deliberate movements of counsel with which it would seem natural to approach so stupendous a contest.

It is probable that if it had been foreseen just what would happen, just what alliances would be formed, just what forces arrayed against one another, those who brought the great contest on would have been glad to substitute conference for force.

Only when the great nations of the world have reached some sort of agreement as to what they hold to be fundamental to their common interest, and as to some feasible method of acting in concert when any nation or group of nations seeks to disturb those fundamental things, can we feel that civilization is at last in a way of justifying its existence and claiming to be finally established. It is clear that nations must in the future be governed by the same high code of honor that we demand of individuals.

Repeated utterances of the leading statesmen of most of the great nations now engaged in war, have made it plain that their thought has come to this, that the principle of public right must henceforth take precedence over the individual interests of particular nations, and that the nations of the world must in some way band themselves together to see that that right prevails as against any sort of selfish aggression; that henceforth alliance must not be set up against alliance, understanding against understanding, but that there must be a common agreement for a common object, and that at the heart of that common object must lie the inviolable rights of peoples and of mankind.

We believe these fundamental things: First, that every people has a right to choose the sovereignty under which they shall live. Second, that the small states of the world have a right to enjoy the same respect for their sovereignty and for their territorial integrity that great and powerful nations expect and insist upon. And, third, that the world has a right to be free from every disturbance of its peace that has its origin in aggression and disregard of the rights of peoples and nations.

If it should ever be our privilege to suggest or initiate a movement for peace among the nations now at war, I am sure that the people of the United States would wish their Government to move along these lines: First, such a settlement with regard to their own immediate interests as the belligerents may agree upon.

Second, an universal association of the nations to maintain the inviolate security of the highway of the seas for the common and unhindered use of all the nations of the world, and to prevent any war being begun either contrary to treaty covenants or without warning and full submission of the causes to the opinion of the world — a virtual guarantee of territorial integrity and political independence.

June 2, 1916 [to the graduates at Annapolis]

Once and again when youngsters here or at West Point have forgotten themselves and done something that they ought not to do and were about to be disciplined, perhaps severely, for it, I have been appealed to by their friends to excuse them from the penalty.

Knowing that I have spent most of my life at a college they commonly say to me, "You know college boys. You know what they are. They are heedless youngsters very often, and they ought not to be held up to the same standards of responsibility that older men must submit to." And I have always replied: "Yes; I know college boys. But while these youngsters are college boys, they are something more. They are officers of the United States. They are not merely college boys. If they were, I would look at derelictions of duty on their part in another spirit; but any dereliction of duty on the part of a naval officer of the United States may involve the fortunes of a nation and cannot be overlooked."

Do you not see the difference? You can not indulge yourselves in weaknesses. You cannot forget your duty for a moment, because there might come a time when that weak spot in you should affect you in the midst of a great engagement, and then the whole history of the world might be changed by what you did not do or did wrong.

June 14, 1916 [to the graduates at West Point]

You are not militarists because you are military. Militarism does not consist in the existence of an army, not even in the existence of a very great army. Militarism is a spirit. It is a point of view. It is a system. It is a purpose. The purpose of militarism is to use armies for aggression. The spirit of militarism is the opposite of the civilian spirit, the citizen spirit.

In a country where militarism prevails the military man looks down upon the civilian, regards him as inferior, thinks of him as intended for his, the military man's support and use; and just so long as America is America that spirit and point of view is impossible with us. There is as yet in this country, so far as I can discover, no taint of the spirit of militarism.

You are picked out from the citizens of the United States to be that part of the force of the United States which makes its polity safe against interference. You are the part of American citizens who say to those who would interfere, "You must not" and "You shall not." But you are American citizens, and the idea I want to leave with you boys to-day is this: No matter what comes, always remember that first of all you are citizens of the United States before you are officers, and that you are officers because you represent in your particular profession what the citizenship of the United States stands for.

You know that one thing in which our forefathers took pride was this, that the civil power is superior to the military power in the United States. Once and again the people of the United States have so admired some great military man as to make him President of the United States, when he became commander-in-chief of all the forces of the United States, but he was commander-in-chief because he was President, not because he had been trained to arms, and his authority was civil, not military.

JULY 4, 1916 [DEDICATION OF THE FEDERAL LABOR BUILDING]

I am not at liberty to think of any one class of our fellow citizens to the exclusion of any other class, and since I have been asked to make the dedicatory address of this building, I am going to take the liberty of dedicating it to common counsel and a common understanding.

I am going to take the liberty of dedicating it to the thing that I believe in most, the accommodation of the interests of various classes in the community by means of enabling those classes to understand one another and co-operate with one another.

JULY 10, 1916

Charles Lamb, the English writer, made a very delightful remark that I have long treasured in my memory. He stuttered a little bit, and he said of some one who was not present, "I h-h-hate that m-man"; and some one said, "Why, Charles, I didn't know you knew him." "Oh," he said, "I-I-I don't, I-I can't h-hate a m-man I know." That is a profound human remark. You cannot hate a man you know.

JULY 23, 1916 [TO COLONEL HOUSE]

I am, I must admit, about at the end of my patience with Great Britain and the Allies. This black list business is the last straw. I have told Spring Rice so, and he sees the reasons very clearly. Both he and Jusserand think it a stupid blunder. I am seriously considering asking Congress to authorize me to prohibit loans and restrict exportations to the Allies. It is becoming clear to me that there lies latent in this policy the wish to prevent our merchants getting a foothold in markets which Great Britain has hitherto controlled and all but dominated.

AUGUST 11, 1916 [ON THE COUNTY AGENT SYSTEM]

This piece of legislation is one of the most significant and far-reaching measures for the education of adults ever adopted by any Government. It provides for co-operation between the States and the Federal Government. This is a highly important and significant principle. It will permit the placing in each of the 2850 rural counties of the Nation two farm demonstrators and specialists, who will assist the demonstrators in the more difficult problems confronting them.

With preparedness becoming daily more imperative, the Shipping Bill was reintroduced at Wilson's demand. It was passed on August 18, 1916, by a vote of 38 Senators (all Democrats) to 21 (all Republicans).

Ships that would have cost forty dollars a ton in 1914 now cost from one hundred and fifty to three hundred dollars a ton. Later, in the 1920's, the Republican Party laid the great cost of building ships, which were absolutely necessary to win the war, to Democratic inefficiency.

AUGUST 20, 1916 [TO THE HONORABLE JOSHUA ALEXANDER]

I am a little at sea yet just where to turn for non-partisan members of the Tariff Board.

For I want *non*-partisan members if I can find them, rather than bi-partisan.

AUGUST 29, 1916 [TO CONGRESS]

I earnestly recommend the following legislation:

First, immediate provision for the enlargement and administrative reorganization of the Interstate Commerce Commission in order that the Commission may be enabled to deal with the many great and various duties now devolving upon it with a promptness and thoroughness which are with its present constitution and means of action practically impossible.

Second, the establishment of an eight-hour day as the legal basis alike of work and of wages in the employment of all railway employees who are actually engaged in the work of operating trains in interstate transportation.

Third, the authorization of the appointment by the President of a small body of men to observe the actual results in experience of the adoption of the eight-hour day in railway transportation alike for the men and for the railroads; its effects in the matter of operating costs, in the application of the existing practices and agreements to the new conditions, and in all other practical aspects, with the provision that the investigators shall report their conclusions to the Congress at the earliest possible date, but without recommendation as to legislative action; in order that the public may learn from an unprejudiced source just what actual developments have ensued.

Fourth, explicit approval by the Congress of the consideration by the Interstate Commerce Commission of an increase of freight rates to meet such additional expenditures by the railroads as may have been rendered necessary by the adoption of the eight-hour day and which have not been offset by administrative readjustments and economies, should the facts disclosed justify the increase.

Fifth, an amendment of the existing federal statute which provides for the mediation, conciliation, and arbitration of such controversies as the present by adding to it a provision that in case the methods of accommodation now provided for should fail, a full public investigation of the merits of every such dispute shall be instituted and completed before a strike or lockout may lawfully be attempted.

And, sixth, the lodgement in the hands of the Executive of the power, in case of military necessity, to take control of such portions and such rolling stock of the railways of the country as may be required for military use and to operate them for military purposes, with authority to draft into the military service of the United States such train crews and administrative officials as the circumstances require for their safe and efficient use.

This last suggestion I make because we cannot in any circumstances suffer the nation to be hampered in the essential matter of national defense. At the present moment circumstances render this duty particularly obvious.

Wilson felt it of highest importance that the workers' living standards be maintained in spite of the great pressure for adequate national defense. Later, after the declaration of war with Germany, he wrote Samuel Gompers:

With all my heart I want them [*the workers*] to feel that their devotion to country is in no wise a betrayal of principle, and that in serving America today they are serving their cause no less faithfully than in the past. I myself have had sympathy with the fears of the workers of the United States; for the tendency of war is toward reaction, and too often military necessities have been made an excuse for the destruction of laboriously erected industrial and social standards.

These fears, happily, have proved to be baseless. With quickened sympathies and appreciation, with a new sense of the invasive and insidious dangers of oppression, our people have not only held every inch of ground that has been won by years of struggle, but have added to the gains of the Twentieth Century along every line of human betterment. Questions of wages and hours of labor and industrial readjustment have found a solution which gives to the toiler a new dignity and a new sense of social and economic security. I beg you to feel that my support has not been lacking and that the Government has not failed at any point in granting every just request advanced by you and your associates in the name of the American worker.

No one who is not blind can fail to see that the battle line of democracy for America stretches today from the fields of Flanders to every house and workshop where toiling, upward striving men and women are counting the treasures of right and justice and liberty which are being threatened by our present enemies.

It has not been a matter of surprise to me that the leaders in certain groups have sought to ignore our grievances against the men who have equally misled the German people. Their insistence that a nation whose rights have been grossly violated, whose citizens have been foully murdered under their own flag, whose neighbors have been invited to join in making conquest of its territory, whose patience in pressing the claims of justice and humanity has been met with the most shameful policy of truculence and treachery; their insistence that a nation so outraged does not know its own mind, that it has no comprehensible reason for defending itself, or for joining with all its might in maintaining a free future for itself and its ideals, is of a piece with their deafness to the oft-repeated statement of our national purpose.

Is it, perhaps, that these forces of antagonism have not yet learned to know the voice of that America we love and serve? It may well be that those among us who stand ready to forward the plans of aggression bred in secret do not understand the language of democracy when it proclaims the purposes of war in terms of a peace for the peoples that shall be untroubled by those to whom men are but the pawns in their struggle for power and gain. But true Americans, those who toil here for home and the hope of better things, whose lifted eyes have caught the vision of a liberated world, have said that of the policy of blood and iron there shall be an end and that equal justice which is the heart of democracy shall rule in its stead.

May not those who toil and those who have made common cause of the larger hope for the masses of mankind take renewed heart as they think on these days when America has taken its stand for the rights of humanity and the fellowship of social and international justice?

CHAPTER SEVENTEEN

The Difference between a Republican and a Democrat

❯❯❯❮❮❮❯❯❯❮❮❮❯❯❯❮❮❮❯❯❯❮❮❮❯❯❯❮❮❮❯❯❯❮❮❮❯❯❯❮❮❮❯❯❯❮❮❮❯❯❯❮❮❮❯❯❯❮❮❮❯❯❯❮❮❮

The Democratic Party renominated Woodrow Wilson and the Republican Party nominated Chief Justice Charles Evans Hughes as the candidates for the Presidency.

SEPTEMBER 2, 1916

In his acceptance speech President Wilson laid out a blueprint for the United States, if it were to take its place successfully in the world of the future. This speech could well be read by all those who are interested in the "democratic" future of the world.

The Republican party was put out of power because of failure, practical failure and moral failure; because it had served special interests and not the country at large; because, under the leadership of its preferred and established guides, of those who still make its choices, it had lost touch with the thoughts and the needs of the Nation and was living in a past age and under a fixed illusion, the illusion of greatness.

It had framed tariff laws based upon a fear of foreign trade, a fundamental doubt as to American skill, enterprise, and capacity, and a very tender regard for the profitable privileges of those who had gained control of domestic markets and domestic credits; and yet had enacted antitrust laws which hampered the very things they meant to foster, which were stiff and inelastic, and in part unintelligible.

It had permitted the country throughout the long period of its control to stagger from one financial crisis to another under the operation of a national banking law of its own framing which made stringency and panic certain and the control of the larger business operations of the country by the bankers of a few reserve centers inevitable; had made as if it meant to reform the law but had faint-heartedly failed in the attempt, because it could not bring itself to do the one thing necessary to make the reform genuine and effectual, namely, break up the control of small groups of bankers.

It had been oblivious, or indifferent, to the fact that the farmers, upon whom the country depends for its food and in the last analysis for its prosperity, were without standing in the matter of commercial credit, without the protection of standards in their market transactions, and without systematic knowledge of the markets themselves; that the laborers of the country carried their labor as a mere commodity to market, were subject to restraint by novel and drastic process in the courts, were without assurance of compensation for industrial accidents, without federal assistance in accommodating labor disputes, and without national aid or advice in finding the places and the industries in which their labor was most needed. The country had no national system of road construction and development.

Little intelligent attention was paid to the army, and not enough to the navy.

The other republics of America distrusted us, because they found that we thought first of the profits of American investors and only as an afterthought of impartial justice and helpful friendship.

So things stood when the Democratic Party came into power. How do they stand now? Alike in the domestic field and in the wide field of the commerce of the world, American business and life and industry have been set free to move as they never moved before.

The tariff has been revised, not on the principle of repelling foreign trade, but upon the principle of encouraging it, upon something like a footing of equality with our own in respect of the terms of competition, and a Tariff Board has been created whose function it will be to keep the relations of American with foreign business and industry under constant observation, for the guidance alike of our business men and of our Congress. American energies are now directed towards the markets of the world.

The laws against trusts have been clarified by definition, with a view to making it plain that they were not directed against big business but only against unfair business and the pretense of competition where there was none; and a Trade Commission has been created with powers of guidance and accommodation which have relieved business men of unfounded fears and set them upon the road of hopeful and confident enterprise.

By the Federal Reserve Act the supply of currency at the disposal of active business has been rendered elastic, taking its volume, not from a fixed body of investment securities, but from the liquid assets of daily trade; and these assets are assessed and accepted, not by distant groups of bankers in control of unavailable reserves, but by bankers at the many centers of local exchange who are in touch with local conditions everywhere.

Effective measures have been taken for the re-creation of an American merchant marine and the revival of the American carrying trade indispensable to our emancipation from the control which foreigners have so long exercised over the opportunities, the routes, and the methods of our commerce with other countries.

The Interstate Commerce Commission has been reorganized to enable it to perform its great and important functions more promptly and more efficiently. We have created, extended and improved the service of the parcels post.

The Republican leaders, apparently, know of no means of assisting business but "protection." How to stimulate it and put it upon a new footing of energy and enterprise they have not suggested.

For the farmers of the country we have virtually created commercial credit, by means of the Federal Reserve Act and the Rural Credits Act. They now have the standing of other business men in the money market. We have successfully regulated speculation in "futures" and established standards in the marketing of grains. By an intelligent Warehouse Act we have assisted them in making standard crops available as never before both for systematic marketing and as a security for loans from the banks. We have greatly added to the work of neighborhood demonstration on the farm itself of improved methods of cultivation, and, through the intelligent extension of the functions of the Department of Agriculture, have made it possible for the farmer to learn systematically where his best markets are and how to get at them.

The workingmen of America have been given a veritable emancipation, by the legal recognition of a man's labor as part of his life, and not a mere marketable commodity; by exempting labor organizations from processes of the courts which treated their members like fractional parts of mobs and not like accessible and responsible individuals; by releasing our seamen from involuntary servitude; by making adequate provision for compensation for industrial accidents; by providing suitable machinery for mediation and conciliation in industrial disputes; and by putting the Federal Department of Labor at the disposal of the workingman when in search of work.

We have effected the emancipation of the children of the country by releasing them from hurtful labor. We have instituted a system of national aid in the building of highroads such as the country has been feeling after for a century.

We have sought to equalize taxation by means of an equitable income tax. We have taken the steps that ought to have been taken at the outset to open up the resources of Alaska. We have provided for national defense upon a scale never before seriously proposed upon the responsibility of an entire political party. We have driven the tariff lobby from cover and obliged it to substitute solid arguments for private influence.

This extraordinary recital must sound like a platform, a list of sanguine promises; but it is not. It is a record of promises made four years ago and now actually redeemed in constructive legislation.

These things must profoundly disturb the thoughts and confound the plans of those who have made themselves believe that the Democratic Party neither understood nor was ready to assist the business of the country in the great enterprises which it is its evident and inevitable destiny to undertake and carry through. The breaking up of the lobby must especially disconcert them; for it was through the lobby that they sought and were sure they had found the heart of things. The game of privilege can be played successfully by no other means.

This record must equally astonish those who feared that the Democratic Party had not opened its heart to comprehend the demands of social justice. We have in four years come very near to carrying out the platform of the Progressive Party as well as our own; for we also are progressives.

There is one circumstance connected with this program which ought to be very plainly stated. It was resisted at every step by the interests which the Republican Party had catered to and fostered at the expense of the country, and these same interests are now earnestly praying for a reaction which will save their privileges — for the restoration of their sworn friends to power before it is too late to recover what they have lost.

They fought with particular desperation and infinite resourcefulness the reform of the banking and currency system, knowing that to be the citadel of their control; and most anxiously are they hoping and planning for the amendment of the Federal Reserve Act by the concentration of control in a single bank which the old familiar group of bankers can keep under their eye and direction.

But while the "big men" who used to write the tariffs and command the assistance of the Treasury have been hostile — all but a few with vision — the average business man knows that he has been delivered, and that the fear that was once every day in his heart that the men who controlled credit and directed enterprise from the committee rooms of Congress would crush him, is there no more, and will not return — unless the party that consulted only the "big men" should return to power — the party of masterly inactivity and cunning resourcefulness in standing pat to resist change.

The Republican Party is just the party that *cannot* meet the new conditions of a new age. *It does not know the way and it does not wish new conditions.*

It tried to break away from the old leaders and could not. They still select its candidates and dictate its policy, still resist change, still hanker after the old conditions, still know no methods of encouraging business but the old methods. When it changes its leaders and its purposes and brings its ideas to date it will have the right to ask the American people to give it power again; but not until then. A new age, an age of revolutionary change, needs new purposes and new ideas.

In foreign affairs we have been guided by principles clearly conceived and consistently lived up to. Perhaps they have not been fully comprehended because they have hitherto governed international affairs only in theory, not in practice. They are simple, obvious, easily stated, and fundamental to American ideals.

The rights of our own citizens of course became involved: that was inevitable. Where they did, this was our guiding principle: that property rights can be vindicated by claims for damages when the war is over, and no modern nation can decline to arbitrate such claims; but the fundamental rights of humanity cannot be. The loss of life is irreparable.

Neither can direct violations of a nation's sovereignty await vindication in suits for damages.

The nation that violates these essential rights must expect to be checked and called to account by direct challenge and resistance. It at once makes the quarrel in part our own.

These are plain principles and we have never lost sight of them or departed from them, whatever the stress or the perplexity of circumstance or the provocation to hasty resentment. The record is clear and consistent throughout and stands distinct and definite for anyone to judge who wishes to know the truth about it.

We have professed to believe, and we do believe, that the people of small and weak states have the right to expect to be dealt with exactly as the people of big and powerful states would be. We have acted upon that principle in dealing with the people of Mexico.

Our recent pursuit of bandits into Mexican territory was no violation of that principle. It was a plain case of the violation of our own sovereignty which could not wait to be vindicated by damages and for which there was no other remedy. The authorities of Mexico were powerless to prevent it.

Many serious wrongs against the property, many irreparable wrongs against the persons, of Americans have been committed within the territory of Mexico herself during this confused revolution, wrongs which could not be effectually checked so long as there was no constituted power in Mexico which was in a position to check them.

We could not act directly in that matter ourselves without denying Mexicans the right to any revolution at all which disturbed us and making the emancipation of her own people await our own interest and convenience.

For it is their emancipation that they are seeking — blindly, it may be, and as yet ineffectually, but with profound and passionate purpose and within their unquestionable right, apply what true American principle you will — any principle that an American would publicly avow. The people of Mexico have not been suffered to own their own country or direct their own institutions. Outsiders, men out of other nations and with interests too often alien to their own, have dictated what their privileges and opportunities should be and who should control their land, their lives, and their resources — some of them Americans, pressing for things they could never have got in their own country.

The Mexican people are entitled to attempt their liberty from such influences; and so long as I have anything to do with the action of our great Government I shall do everything in my power to prevent anyone standing in their way.

I know that this is hard for some persons to understand; but it is not hard for the plain people of the United States to understand. It is hard doctrine only for those who wish to get something for themselves out of Mexico.

I have heard no one who was free from such influences propose interference by the United States with the internal affairs of Mexico. Certainly no friend of the Mexican people has proposed it.

I here again vow it. I am more interested in the fortunes of oppressed men and pitiful women and children than in any property rights whatever. Mistakes I have no doubt made in this perplexing business, but not in purpose or object.

More is involved than the immediate destinies of Mexico and the relations of the United States with a distressed and distracted people.

All America looks on. Test is now being made of us whether we be sincere lovers of popular liberty or not and are indeed to be trusted to respect national sovereignty among our weaker neighbours. We have undertaken these many years to play big brother to the republics of this hemisphere. This is the day of our test whether we mean, or have ever meant, to play that part for our own benefit wholly or also for theirs.

The republics of America have in the last three years been drawing together in a new spirit of accommodation, mutual understanding, and cordial co-operation. Much of the politics of the world in the years to come will depend upon their relationships with one another. It is a barren and provincial statesmanship that loses sight of such things.

The future, the immediate future, will bring us squarely face to face with many great and exacting problems which will search us through and through whether we be able and ready to play the part in the world that we mean to play.

It will not bring us into their presence slowly, gently, with ceremonious introduction, but suddenly and at once, the moment the war in Europe is over. They will be new problems, most of them; many will be old problems in a new setting and with new elements which we have never dealt with or reckoned the force and meaning of before. They will require for their solution new thinking, fresh courage and resourcefulness, and in some matters radical reconsiderations of policy. We must be ready to mobilize our resources alike of brains and of materials.

Look first at what it will be necessary that the nations of the world should do to make the days to come tolerable and fit to live and work in; and then look at our part in what is to follow and our own duty of preparation. For we must be prepared both in resources and in policy.

There must be a just and settled peace, and we here in America must contribute the full force of our enthusiasm and of our authority as a nation to the organization of that peace upon world-wide foundations that cannot easily be shaken.

No nation should be forced to take sides in any quarrel in which its own honor and integrity and the fortunes of its own people are not involved; but no nation can any longer remain neutral as against any wilful disturbance of the peace of the world. The effects of war can no longer be confined to the areas of battle. No nation stands wholly apart in interest when the life and interests of all nations are thrown into confusion and peril. If hopeful and generous enterprise is to be renewed, if the healing and helpful arts of life are indeed to be revived when peace comes again, a new atmosphere of justice and friendship must be generated by means the world has never tried before. The nations of the world must unite in joint guarantees that whatever is done to disturb the whole world's life must first be tested in the court of the whole world's opinion before it is attempted.

These are the new foundations the world must build for itself, and we must play our part in the reconstruction, generously and without too much thought of our separate interests. We must make ourselves ready to play it intelligently, vigorously and well.

We must see to it that the people in our insular possessions are treated in their own lands as we would treat them here, and make the rule of the United States mean the same thing everywhere — the same justice, the same consideration for the essential rights of men.

Besides contributing our ungrudging moral and practical support to the establishment of peace throughout the world we must actively and intelligently prepare ourselves to do our full service in the trade and industry which are to sustain and develop the life of the nations in the days to come.

We can no longer indulge our traditional provincialism. We are to play a leading part in the world drama whether we wish it or not. We shall lend, not borrow; act for ourselves, not imitate or follow; organize and initiate, not peep about merely to see where we may get in.

At home also we must see to it that the men who plan and develop and direct our business enterprises shall enjoy definite and settled conditions of law, a policy accommodated to the freest progress. We have set the just and necessary limits. We have put all kinds of unfair competition under the ban and penalty of the law.

We ought both to husband and to develop our natural resources, our mines, our forests, our water power.

We must hasten and quicken the spirit and efficiency of labor throughout our whole industrial system by everywhere and in all occupations doing justice to the laborer, not only by paying a living wage but also by making all the conditions that surround labor what they ought to be. And we must do more than justice. We must safeguard life and promote health and safety in every occupation in which they are threatened or imperilled. That is more than justice, and better, because it is humanity and economy.

Thus shall we stand ready to meet the future as circumstances and international policy effect their unfolding, whether the changes come slowly or come fast and without preface.

NOVEMBER 5, 1916 [TO SECRETARY OF STATE ROBERT LANSING]

There is a matter which has occupied my thoughts throughout the campaign and which I want to lay before you before the election, while I can discuss it without any touch of feeling as to the result.

Again and again the question has arisen in my mind, What would it be my duty to do were Mr. Hughes to be elected? Four months would elapse before he could take charge of the affairs of the government, and during those four months I would be without such moral backing from the nation as would be necessary to steady and control our relations with other governments. I would be known to be the rejected, not the accredited, spokesman of the country; and yet the accredited spokesman would be without legal authority to speak for the nation. Such a situation would be fraught with the gravest dangers. The direction of the foreign policy of the government would in effect have been taken out of my hands and yet its new definition would be impossible until March.

I feel that it would be my duty to relieve the country of the perils of such a situation at once. The course I have in mind is dependent upon the consent and co-operation of the Vice President; but, if I could gain his consent to the plan, I would ask your permission to invite Mr. Hughes to become Secretary of State and would then join the Vice President in resigning, and thus open to Mr. Hughes the immediate succession to the presidency.

All my life long I have advocated some such responsible government for the United States as other constitutional systems afford as of course, and as such action on my part would inaugurate, at least by example. Responsible government means government by those whom the people trust, and trust at the time of decision and action. The whole country has long perceived, without knowing how to remedy, the extreme disadvantage of having to live for four months after an election under a party whose guidance had been rejected at the polls. Here is the remedy, at any rate so far as the Executive is concerned. In ordinary times it would perhaps not be necessary to apply it. But it seems to me that in the existing circumstances it would be imperatively necessary. The choice of policy in respect of our foreign relations rests with the Executive. No such critical circumstances in regard to our foreign policy have ever before existed. It would be my duty to step aside so that there would be no doubt in any quarter how that policy was to be directed, towards what objects and by what means. I would have no right to risk the peace of the nation by remaining in office after I had lost my authority.

I hope and believe that your own judgment will run with mine in this critical matter.

In the early hours of Election Day night it looked as though Hughes had been elected. Wilson told those about him the story of the Confederate veteran who had returned to his farm to find the buildings burned, the stock killed or run off or stolen, the fences down. He glanced down at his bare and bleeding feet and at an arm in a sling.

"I'm glad I fought," he said aloud, "I'm proud of the part I played. I have no regrets. But I'll be damned if I ever love another country."

By morning, however, late returns showed that Wilson had just barely squeezed in. He had lost most of his majorities in both the House and the Senate.

DECEMBER 12, 1916 [TO GARRETT DROPPERS]

The campaign was indeed one of the most virulent and bitter and, I must believe, one of the most unfair on the part of the Republican opposition that the country has ever seen, but I think that very circumstance worked to my advantage. I think the country resented the methods used, and that a very strong resentment was felt which was characterized by strong and generous feeling.

The results show themselves more truly in the popular vote than in the electoral vote, and I am heartened by the feeling that it can no longer be said that I represent a minority of the nation.

This reference is to the fact that in the election of 1912 he did not get a majority of popular votes over President Taft and Theodore Roosevelt.

PART V

When a World Comes to Itself

CHAPTER EIGHTEEN

"The World Must Be Made Safe for Democracy"

❯❯❯❮❮❮❯❯❯❮❮❮❯❯❯❮❮❮❯❯❯❮❮❮❯❯❯❮❮❮❯❯❯❮❮❮❯❯❯❮❮❮❯❯❯❮❮❮❯❯❯❮❮❮❯❯❯❮❮❮❯❯❯❮❮❮

On January 9, 1917, unknown to President Wilson, the German high command embarked on a campaign of unrestricted warfare. Before he learned about this, Wilson delivered to the Senate his "Peace without Victory" speech, in which he set forth his ideas of what would constitute an enduring peace for the world. In this speech his statesmanship probably reached its highest peak.

JANUARY 22, 1917 [TO THE SENATE, ON "PEACE WITHOUT VICTORY"]

On the eighteenth of December last I addressed an identical note to the governments of the nations now at war requesting them to state, more definitely than they had yet been stated by either group of belligerents, the terms upon which they would deem it possible to make peace. I spoke on behalf of humanity and of the rights of all neutral nations like our own, many of whose most vital interests the war puts in constant jeopardy.

The Central Powers united in a reply which stated merely that they were ready to meet their antagonists in conference to discuss terms of peace. The Entente Powers have replied much more definitely and have stated, in general terms, indeed, but with sufficient definiteness to imply details, the arrangements, guarantees, and acts of reparation which they deem to be the indispensable conditions of a satisfactory settlement.

We are that much nearer a definite discussion of the peace which shall end the present war. We are that much nearer the discussion of the international concert which must thereafter hold the world at peace. In every discussion of the peace that must end this war it is taken for granted that that peace must be followed by some definite concert of power which will make it virtually impossible that any such catastrophe should ever overwhelm us again. Every lover of mankind, every sane and thoughtful man must take that for granted.

I have sought this opportunity to address you because I thought that I owed it to you, as the counsel associated with me in the final determination of our international obligations, *to disclose to you without reserve* the thought and purpose that have been taking form in my mind in regard to the duty of our Government in the days to come when it will be necessary to lay afresh and upon a new plan the foundations of peace among the nations.

It is inconceivable that the people of the United States should play no part in that great enterprise. To take part in such a service will be the opportunity for which they have sought to prepare themselves by the very principles and purposes of their polity and the approved practices of their Government ever since the days when they set up a new nation in the high and honorable hope that it might in all that it was and did, show mankind the way to liberty. They cannot in honor withhold the service to which they are now about to be challenged. They do not wish to withhold it. But they owe it to themselves and to the other nations of the world to state the conditions under which they will feel free to render it.

That service is nothing less than this, to add their authority and their power to the authority and force of other nations to guarantee peace and justice throughout the world. Such a settlement cannot now be long postponed. It is right that before it comes this Government should frankly formulate the conditions upon which it would feel justified in asking our people to approve its formal and solemn adherence to a League for Peace. I am here to attempt to state those conditions.

The present war must first be ended; but we owe it to candor and to a just regard for the opinion of mankind to say that, so far as our participation in guarantees of future peace is concerned, it makes a great deal of difference in what way and upon what terms it is ended. The treaties and agreements which bring it to an end must embody terms which will create a peace that will win the approval of mankind, not merely a peace that will serve the several interests and immediate aims of the nations engaged.

We shall have no voice in determining what those terms shall be, but we shall, I feel sure, have a voice in determining whether they shall be made lasting or not by the guarantees of a universal covenant, and our judgment upon what is fundamental and essential as a condition precedent to permanency should be spoken now, not afterwards when it may be too late.

No covenant of co-operative peace that does not include the peoples of the New World can suffice to keep the future safe against war; and yet there is only one sort of peace that the peoples of America could join in guaranteeing. The elements of that peace must be elements that engage the confidence and satisfy the principles of the American governments, elements consistent with their political faith and with the practical convictions which the peoples of America have once for all embraced and undertaken to defend.

It will be absolutely necessary that a force be created as a guarantor of the permanency of the settlement so much greater than the force of any nation now engaged or any alliance hitherto formed or projected that no nation, no probable combination of nations could face or withstand it. If the peace presently to be made is to endure, it must be a peace made secure by the organized major force of mankind.

The question upon which the whole future peace and policy of the world depends is this: Is the present war a struggle for a just and secure peace, or only for a new balance of power? If it be only a struggle for a new balance of power, who will guarantee, who can guarantee the stable equilibrium of the new arrangement? Only a tranquil Europe can be a stable Europe. There must be, not a balance of power, but a community of power; not organized rivalries, but an organized common peace.

Fortunately we have received very explicit assurances on this point. The statesmen of both of the groups of nations now arrayed against one another have said, in terms that could not be misinterpreted, that it was no part of the purpose they had in mind to crush their antagonists.

They imply, first of all, that it must be a peace without victory. It is not pleasant to say this. I beg that I may be permitted to put my own interpretation upon it and that it may be understood that no other interpretation was in my thought. I am seeking only to face realities and to face them without soft concealments.

Victory would mean peace forced upon the loser, a victor's terms imposed upon the vanquished. It would be accepted in humiliation, under duress, at an intolerable sacrifice, and would leave a sting, a resentment, a bitter memory upon which terms of peace would rest, not permanently, but only as upon quicksand.

Only a peace between equals can last. Only a peace the very principle of which is equality and a common participation in a common benefit. The right state of mind, the right feeling between nations, is as necessary for a lasting peace as is the just settlement of vexed questions of territory or of racial and national allegiance.

The equality of nations upon which peace must be founded if it is to last must be an equality of rights; the guarantees exchanged must neither recognize nor imply a difference between big nations and small, between those that are powerful and those that are weak. Right must be based upon the common strength, not upon the individual strength, of the nations upon whose concert peace will depend. Equality of territory or of resources there of course cannot be; nor any other sort of equality not gained in the ordinary peaceful and legitimate development of the peoples themselves. But no one asks or expects anything more than an equality of rights. Mankind is looking now for freedom of life, not for equipoises of power.

And there is a deeper thing involved than even equality of rights among organized nations. No peace can last, or ought to last, which does not recognize and accept the principle that governments derive all their just powers from the consent of the governed, and that no right anywhere exists to hand peoples about from sovereignty to sovereignty as if they were property.

That henceforth inviolable security of life, of worship, and of industrial and social development should be guaranteed to all peoples who have lived hitherto under the power of governments devoted to a faith and purpose hostile to their own.

I speak of this, not because of any desire to exalt an abstract political principle which has always been held very dear by those who have sought to build up liberty in America, but for the same reason that I have spoken of the other conditions of peace which seem to me clearly indispensable — because I wish frankly to uncover realities. Any peace which does not recognize and accept this principle will inevitably be upset. It will not rest upon the affections or the convictions of mankind. The ferment of spirit of whole populations will fight subtly and constantly against it, and all the world will sympathize. The world can be at peace only if its life is stable, and there can be no stability where the will is in rebellion, where there is not tranquillity of spirit and a sense of justice, of freedom, and of right.

So far as practicable, moreover, every great people now struggling towards a full development of its resources and of its powers should be assured a direct outlet to the great highways of the sea. Where this cannot be done by the cession of territory, it can no doubt be done by the neutralization of direct rights of way under the general guarantee which will assure the peace itself. With a right comity of arrangement no nation need be shut away from free access to the open paths of the world's commerce.

And the paths of the sea must alike in law and in fact be free. No doubt a somewhat radical reconsideration of many of the rules of international practice hitherto thought to be established may be necessary in order to make the seas indeed free and common in practically all circumstances for the use of mankind, but the motive for such changes is convincing and compelling. There can be no trust or intimacy between the peoples of the world without them. The free, constant, unthreatened intercourse of nations is an essential part of the process of peace and of development. It need not be difficult either to define or to secure the freedom of the seas if the governments of the world sincerely desire to come to an agreement concerning it.

It is a problem closely connected with the limitation of naval armaments and the co-operation of the navies of the world in keeping the seas at once free and safe. And the question of limiting naval armaments opens the wider and perhaps more difficult question of the limitation of armies and of all programs of military preparation. Difficult and delicate as these questions are, they must be faced with the utmost candor and decided in a spirit of real accommodation if peace is to come with healing in its wings, and come to stay. Peace cannot be had without concessions and sacrifice. There can be no sense of safety and equality among the nations if great preponderating armaments are henceforth to continue here and there to be built up and maintained. The statesmen of the world must plan for peace and nations must adjust and accommodate their policy to it as they have planned for war and made ready for pitiless contest and rivalry. The question of armaments, whether on land or sea, is the most immediately and intensely practical question connected with the future fortunes of nations and of mankind.

I have spoken upon these great matters without reserve and with the utmost explicitness because it has seemed to me to be necessary if the world's yearning desire for peace was anywhere to find free voice and utterance.

Perhaps I am the only person in high authority amongst all the peoples of the world who is at liberty to speak and hold nothing back. I am speaking as an individual, and yet I am speaking also, of course, as the responsible head of a government, and I feel confident that I have said what the people of the United States would wish me to say.

May I not add that I hope and believe that I am in effect speaking for liberals and friends of humanity in every nation and of every program of liberty? I would fain believe that I am speaking for the silent mass of mankind everywhere who have as yet had no place or opportunity to speak their real hearts out concerning the death and ruin they see to have come already upon the persons and the homes they hold most dear.

And in holding out the expectation that the people and Government of the United States will join the other civilized nations of the world in guaranteeing the permanence of peace upon such terms as I have named I speak with the greater boldness and confidence because it is clear to every man who can think that there is in this promise no breach in either our traditions or our policy as a nation, but a fulfilment, rather, of all that we have professed or striven for.

I am proposing, as it were, that the nations should with one accord adopt the doctrine of President Monroe as the doctrine of the world: that no nation should seek to extend its polity over any other nation or people, but that every people should be left free to determine its own polity, its own way of development, unhindered, unthreatened, unafraid, the little along with the great and powerful.

I am proposing that all nations henceforth avoid entangling alliances which would draw them into competitions of power; catch them in a net of intrigue and selfish rivalry, and disturb their own affairs with influences intruded from without. There is no entangling alliance in a concert of power. When all unite to act in the same sense and with the same purpose all act in the common interest and are free to live their own lives under a common protection.

I am proposing government by the consent of the governed; that freedom of the seas which in international conference after conference representatives of the United States have urged with the eloquence of those who are the convinced disciples of liberty; and that moderation of armaments which makes of armies and navies a power for order merely, not an instrument of aggression or of selfish violence.

These are American principles, American policies. We could stand for no others. And they are also the principles and policies of forward-looking men and women everywhere, of every modern nation, of every enlightened community. They are the principles of mankind and must prevail.

Germany relentlessly pursued her threat of unrestricted submarine warfare. As a result, on February 3, 1917, the United States broke off diplomatic relations with her. At the same time Wilson asked for authority to arm merchant ships.

A little group in the Senate undertook, through filibustering and delaying tactics, to stop Wilson. This brought forth a famous statement from him.

MARCH 4, 1917 ["A LITTLE GROUP OF WILLFUL MEN"]

The termination of the last session of the Sixty-fourth Congress by constitutional limitation disclosed a situation unparalleled in the history of the country, perhaps unparalleled in the history of any modern Government.

In the immediate presence of a crisis fraught with more subtle and far-reaching possibilities of national danger than any other the Government has known within the whole history of its international relations, the Congress has been unable to act either to safeguard the country or to vindicate the elementary rights of its citizens.

More than 500 of the 531 members of the two houses were ready and anxious to act; the House of Representatives had acted, by an overwhelming majority; but the Senate was unable to act because a little group of eleven Senators had determined that it should not.

The Senate has no rules by which debate can be limited or brought to an end, no rules by which dilatory tactics of any kind can be prevented. A single member can stand in the way of action, if he have but the physical endurance. The result in this case is a complete paralysis alike of the legislative and of the executive branches of the Government.

This inability of the Senate to act has rendered some of the most necessary legislation of the session impossible at a time when the need of it was most pressing and most evident.

It would not cure the difficulty to call the Sixty-fifth Congress in extraordinary session. The paralysis of the Senate would remain.

The purpose and the spirit of action are not lacking now. The Congress is more definitely united in thought and purpose at this moment, I venture to say, than it has been within the memory of any men now in its membership. There is not only the most united patriotic purpose, but the objects members have in view are perfectly clear and definite.

But the Senate cannot act unless its leaders can obtain unanimous consent. Its majority is powerless, helpless. In the midst of a crisis of extraordinary peril, when only definite and decided action can make the nation safe or shield it from war itself by the aggression of others, action is impossible.

Although, as a matter of fact, the Nation and the representatives of the Nation stand back of the Executive with unprecedented unanimity and spirit, the impression made abroad will, of course, be that it is not so and that other Governments may act as they please without fear that this Government can do anything at all. We cannot explain. The explanation is incredible. The Senate of the United States is the only legislative body in the world which cannot act when its majority is ready for action.

A little group of willful men, representing no opinion but their own, have rendered the great Government of the United States helpless and contemptible.

The remedy? There is but one remedy. The only remedy is that the rules of the Senate shall be so altered that it can act. The country can be relied upon to draw the moral. I believe that the Senate can be relied on to supply the means of action and save the country from disaster.

On March 15, 1917, Czar Nicholas II of Russia abdicated and a provisional government was formed. Another great world threat was in the making.

APRIL 2, 1917 [MESSAGE TO THE CONGRESS FOR A DECLARATION OF WAR]

International law had its origin in the attempt to set up some law which would be respected and observed upon the seas, where no nation had right of dominion and where lay the free highways of the world. By painful stage after stage has that law been built up, with meager enough results, indeed, after all was accomplished that could be accomplished, but always with a clear view, at least, of what the heart and conscience of mankind demanded.

This minimum of right the German Government has swept aside under the plea of retaliation and necessity and because it had no weapons which it could use at sea except these which it is impossible to employ as it is employing them without throwing to the winds all scruples of humanity or of respect for the understandings that were supposed to underlie the intercourse of the world.

I am not now thinking of the loss of property involved, immense and serious as that is, but only of the wanton and wholesale destruction of the lives of noncombatants, men, women, and children, engaged in pursuits which have always, even in the darkest periods of modern history, been deemed innocent and legitimate.

Property can be paid for; the lives of peaceful and innocent people cannot be. The present German submarine warfare against commerce is a warfare against mankind. The challenge is to all mankind. Each nation must decide for itself how it will meet it.

Our motive will not be revenge or the victorious assertion of the physical might of the nation, but only the vindication of right, of human right, of which we are only a single champion.

There is one choice we cannot make, we are incapable of making; we will not choose the path of submission and suffer the most sacred rights of our Nation and our people to be ignored or violated. The wrongs against which we now array ourselves are no common wrongs; they cut to the very roots of human life.

I advise that the Congress declare the recent course of the Imperial German Government to be in fact nothing less than war against the government and people of the United States; that it formally accept the status of belligerent which has thus been thrust upon it; and that it take immediate steps not only to put the country in a more thorough state of defense but also to exert all its power and employ all its resources to bring the Government of the German Empire to terms and end the war.

Let us be very clear, and make very clear to all the world what our motives and our objects are.

Our object is to vindicate the principles of peace and justice in the life of the world as against selfish and autocratic power and to set up amongst the really free and self-governed peoples of the world such a concert of purpose and of action as will henceforth insure the observance of those principles.

Neutrality is no longer feasible or desirable where the peace of the world is involved and the freedom of its peoples, and the menace to that peace and freedom lies in the existence of autocratic governments backed by organized force which is controlled wholly by their will, not by the will of their people. We have seen the last of neutrality in such circumstances.

We are at the beginning of an age in which it will be insisted that the same standards of conduct and of responsibility for wrong done shall be observed among nations and their governments that are observed among the individual citizens of civilized states.

We have no quarrel with the German people. We have no feeling towards them but one of sympathy and friendship. It was not upon their impulse that their government acted in entering this war. It was not with their previous knowledge or approval. It was a war determined upon as wars used to be determined upon in the old, unhappy days when peoples were nowhere consulted by their rulers and wars were provoked and waged in the interest of dynasties or of little groups of ambitious men who were accustomed to use their fellow men as pawns and tools.

Self-governed nations do not fill their neighbor states with spies or set the course of intrigue to bring about some critical posture of affairs which will give them an opportunity to strike and make conquest.

Such designs can be successfully worked out only under cover and where no one has the right to ask questions. Cunningly contrived plans of deception or aggression, carried, it may be, from generation to generation, can be worked out and kept from the light only within the privacy of courts or behind the carefully guarded confidences of a narrow and privileged class. They are happily impossible where public opinion commands and insists upon full information concerning all the nation's affairs.

A steadfast concert for peace can never be maintained except by a partnership of democratic nations.

No autocratic government could be trusted to keep faith within it or observe its covenants. It must be a league of honor, a partnership of opinion.

Intrigue would eat its vitals away; the plottings of inner circles who could plan what they would and render account to no one would be a corruption seated at its very heart. Only free peoples can hold their purpose and their honor steady to a common end and prefer the interests of mankind to any narrow interest of their own.

One of the things that has served to convince us that the Prussian autocracy was not and could never be our friend is that from the very outset of the present war it has filled our unsuspecting communities and even our offices of government with spies and set criminal intrigues everywhere afoot against our national unity of counsel, our peace within and without, our industries and our commerce.

Indeed, it is now evident that its spies were here even before the war began; and it is unhappily not a matter of conjecture but a fact proved in our courts of justice that the intrigues which have more than once come perilously near to disturbing the peace and dislocating the industries of the country have been carried on at the instigation, with the support, and even under the personal direction of official agents of the Imperial Government accredited to the Government of the United States.

But they have played their part in serving to convince us at last that that Government entertains no real friendship for us and means to act against our peace and security at its convenience.

We are accepting this challenge of hostile purpose because we know that in such a Government, following such methods, we can never have a friend; and that in the presence of its organized power, always lying in wait to accomplish we know not what purpose, there can be no assured security for the democratic Governments of the world.

We are glad, now that we see the facts with no veil of false pretense about them, to fight thus for the ultimate peace of the world and for the liberation of its peoples, the German peoples included: for the rights of nations great and small and the privilege of men everywhere to choose their way of life and of obedience.

The world must be made safe for democracy.

Its peace must be planted upon the tested foundations of political liberty. We have no selfish ends to serve. We desire no conquest, no dominion. We seek no indemnities for ourselves, no material compensation for the sacrifices we shall freely make. We are but one of the champions of the rights of mankind. We shall be satisfied when those rights have been made as secure as the faith and the freedom of nations can make them.

It is a distressing and oppressive duty which I have performed in thus addressing you. There are, it may be, many months of fiery trial and sacrifice ahead of us. It is a fearful thing to lead this great peaceful people into war, into the most terrible and disastrous of all wars, civilization itself seeming to be in the balance.

But the right is more precious than peace, and we shall fight for the things which we have always carried nearest our hearts — for democracy, for the right of those who submit to authority to have a voice in their own Governments, for the rights and liberties of small nations, for a universal dominion of right by such a concert of free peoples as shall bring peace and safety to all nations and make the world itself at last free.

To such a task we can dedicate our lives and our fortunes, everything that we are and everything that we have, with the pride of those who know that the day has come when America is privileged to spend her blood and her might for the principles that gave her birth and happiness and the peace which she has treasured. God helping her, she can do no other.

For the first time in an appearance before a joint session of both Houses, Wilson got the wild and enthusiastic applause of almost every member on the floor and from the gallery. He had not slept the night before. Later, as he sat in the cabinet room, pale as a ghost, he said, "Think what it was they were applauding. My message today was a message of death for our young men. How strange it seems to applaud that."

CHAPTER NINETEEN

Making the World Safe for Democracy

✦✦✦✦✦✦✦✦✦✦✦✦✦✦✦✦✦✦✦✦✦✦✦✦

To announce that "the world must be made safe for democracy," and making good that announcement, were, obviously, separated by multitudinous and challenging difficulties. Only a few phases of World War I can be traced here. These, however, set forth rather well President Wilson's thinking.

APRIL 6, 1917 [TO OTTO H. KAHN]

It would not be wise to express an opinion in regard to this matter, and yet personally I should hate to see them stop German opera. I have no doubt that I can trust to the good sense and moderation of the directors of the Metropolitan Opera Company not to take any extreme or unnecessary action.

APRIL 12, 1917

The suggestion of a commission to Russia has come to me from a number of quarters and I am inclined to think that it would be a good plan to send one, and send it practically at once.

The important, perhaps the all-important, thing is the personnel. Men of large view, tested discretion, and a sympathetic appreciation of just what it is they have been sent over for are the sort we need; and is it necessary, besides, that they should *look* the part?

We must find the right men, and they must not all be Democrats — need not any of them be Democrats — but should all be genuinely enthusiastic for the success of the Russian revolution.

APRIL 19, 1917 [SELECTIVE SERVICE VERSUS VOLUNTEER SYSTEM]

I took occasion the other day in an address to the people of the country to point out the many forms of patriotic service that were open to them and to emphasize the fact that the military part of the service was by no means the only part, and perhaps, all things considered, not the most vital part. Our object is a mobilization of all the productive and active forces of the nation and their development to the highest point of cooperation and efficiency, and the idea of the selective draft is that those should be chosen for service in the Army who can be most readily spared from the prosecution of the other activities which the country must engage in and to which it must devote a great deal of its best energy and capacity.

The volunteer system does not do this. When men choose themselves, they sometimes choose without due regard to their other responsibilities. Men may come from the farms or from the mines or from the factories or centers of business who ought not to come but ought to stand back of the armies in the field and see that they get everything that they need and that the people of the country are sustained in the meantime.

The principle of the selective draft, in short, has at its heart this idea: that there is a universal obligation to serve and that a public authority should choose those upon whom the obligation of military service shall rest, and also in a sense choose those who shall do the rest of the nation's work. The bill if adopted will do more, I believe, than any other single instrumentality to create the impression of universal service in the Army and out of it, and if properly administered will be a great source of stimulation.

Those who feel that we are turning away altogether from the voluntary principle seem to forget that some 600,000 men will be needed to fill the ranks of the Regular Army and the National Guard and that a very great field of individual enthusiasm lies there wide open.

APRIL 25, 1917 [TO ARTHUR BRISBANE]

I can imagine no greater disservice to the country than to establish a system of censorship that would deny to the people of a free republic like our own their indisputable right to criticise their own public officials. While exercising the great powers of the office I hold, I would regret in a crisis like the one through which we are now passing to lose the benefit of patriotic and intelligent criticism.

In these trying times one can feel certain only of his motives, which he must strive to purge of selfishness of every kind, and wait with patience for the judgment of a calmer day to vindicate the wisdom of the course he has tried conscientiously to follow.

APRIL 28, 1917

Rabbi Stephen S. Wise urged that Wilson not appoint Elihu Root to the Russian Commission. "Why," Rabbi Wise asked, "should a man be singled out for this great opportunity of service to a fellow-democracy in the making who is not of your mind, who is not a sharer of your own spirit touching the fundamental issues of democracy?"

Before your letter about Mr. Root came, I had already asked him to serve as the head of the commission we are about to send to Russia. Before doing so I convinced myself that he was genuinely and heartily in sympathy with the revolution in Russia, and his experience is such, his tact so great, and his appreciation of the object of the commission so clear that I cannot but feel that he will prove to have been an admirable choice.

This is one bit of advice that Wilson should have heeded. Perhaps it influenced him greatly later when he did not take men of a like ilk to the Peace Conference. He had had experience. For Root proved to be, as Rabbi Wise had predicted, not in sympathy with the revolution.

MAY 3, 1917 [TO EDWARD BOK]

It was very kind of you to send me the advance sheets of Mr. Christopher Morley's sketch, "The Man." All the physical part of it — I mean his really very beautiful descriptions of where I was and how I acted and how I looked — is fiction. I wish that I did act with such dramatic propriety, but it is all very finely conceived and I have no objection to being so represented.

Seriously speaking, I feel myself very much Mr. Morley's debtor for his very sympathetic and illuminating treatment of the matter.

MAY 4, 1917 [TO MRS. GEORGE BASS]

I have not for a moment lost sight of the danger of the breaking down of the standards of labor, the risk of a relaxation of the enforcement of the Child Labor Law, or the preservation in general of the social structure during hostilities. On the contrary, I think that the Draft Act affords me an unusual power to see that the unfortunate things these ladies dread do not occur, because the idea of the draft is not only the drawing of men into the military service of the Government, but the virtual assigning of men to the necessary labor of the country. Its central idea was to disturb the industrial and social structure of the country just as little as possible.

MAY 5, 1917 [TO BRAXTON D. GIBSON]

I do not know that I can give you the best advice about attending the meeting of the League to Enforce Peace, but I may say that I think that the activities of the League are based upon a very much too definite programme which I myself have been very careful not to subscribe to. The general idea of the League I have publicly endorsed in an address at one of those banquets given by the League, but further than that I cannot go and I think it would be very unwise to go at the present time. The agitation conducted by the League has not always been wise, but in view of my concurrence with the general idea they have advocated, I have never felt at liberty to criticise them.

MAY 15, 1917 [ON LABOR]

I have been very much alarmed at the apparent inclination of the legislatures of one or two of our States to set aside even temporarily the laws which have safeguarded the standards of labor and of life.

I think nothing would be more deplorable than that. We are trying to fight in a cause which means the lifting of the standards of life, and we can fight in that cause best by voluntary cooperation.

We are fighting for democracy in a larger sense than can be expressed in any political terms. There are many forms of democratic government, and we are not fighting for any particular form; but we are fighting for the essential part of it all, namely, that we are all equally interested in our social and political life and all have a right to a voice in the Government under which we live; and that when men and women are equally admitted to those rights we have the best safeguard of justice and of peace that the world affords. There is no other safeguard.

Let any group of men, whatever their original intentions, attempt to dictate to their fellow men what their political fortunes shall be, and the result is injustice, and hardship, and wrong of the deepest sort.

MAY 18, 1917

Upon Wilson's demand, the Draft Bill was passed, which required all persons between the ages of twenty-one and thirty to register. Wilson said:

The whole Nation must be a team in which each man shall play the part for which he is best fitted.

The significance of this cannot be overstated. It is a new thing in our history and a landmark in our progress. It is a new manner of accepting and vitalizing our duty to give ourselves with thoughtful devotion to the common purpose of us all. It is in no sense a conscription of the unwilling; it is, rather, selection from a nation which has volunteered in mass. It is no more a choosing of those who shall march with the colors than it is a selection of those who shall serve an equally necessary and devoted purpose in the industries that lie behind the battle line.

MAY 19, 1917

I have asked Mr. Herbert Hoover to undertake the all-important task of food administration. He has expressed his willingness to do so on condition that he is to receive no payment for his services and that the whole of the force under him, exclusive of clerical assistance, shall be employed so far as possible upon the same volunteer basis. He has expressed his confidence that this difficult matter of food administration can be successfully accomplished through the voluntary cooperation and direction of legitimate distributors of foodstuffs and with the help of the women of the country.

Although it is absolutely necessary that unquestionable powers shall be placed in my hands in order to insure the success of this administration of the food supplies of the country, I am confident that the exercise of those powers will be necessary only in the few cases where some small and selfish minority proves unwilling to put the Nation's interests above personal advantage and that the whole country will heartily support Mr. Hoover's efforts by supplying the necessary volunteer agencies throughout the country for the intelligent control of food consumption and securing the cooperation of the most capable leaders of the very interests most directly affected, that the exercise of the powers deputed to him will rest very successfully upon the good will and cooperation of the people themselves, and that the ordinary economic machinery of the country will be left substantially undisturbed.

MAY 22, 1917 [ON CENSORSHIP]

I have been very much surprised to find several of the public prints stating that the administration had abandoned the position which it so distinctly took, and still holds, that authority to exercise censorship over the press is absolutely necessary to the public safety. It, of course, has not been abandoned, because the reasons still exist why such authority is necessary for the protection of the Nation.

I have every confidence that the great majority of the newspapers of the country will observe a patriotic reticence about everything whose publication could be of injury, but in every country there are some persons in a position to do mischief in this field who cannot be relied upon and whose interests or desires will lead to actions on their part highly dangerous to the Nation in the midst of a war. I want to say again that it seems to me imperative that powers of this sort should be granted.

I am willing to consider any reasonable solution of the censorship question. With ninety-nine out of every hundred papers the question would not arise, but there are some papers and some news agencies which we simply cannot trust and I feel it absolutely essential for the safety of the country that I should have some power in the premises.

The commission sent to Russia, headed by Elihu Root, arrived in Petrograd June 13, 1917.

JUNE 13, 1917 [ON CAPITAL AND LABOR]

It should be definitely understood that the administration is not engaged in directing or suggesting the organization of either capital or labor, except in so far as may be necessary to coordinate their energies for the promotion of the public welfare.

It is very generally acknowledged that our laws and the long established policy of our Government recognize the right of workingmen to organize unions if they so desire, just as we recognize the right of capital to organize co-partnerships and corporations. In so organizing each is exercising a natural and legal right. When, negotiating with each other in the exercise of these rights, they come to a disagreement concerning the terms of employment, which threatens to cause a stoppage of work, the rest of the public is interested in an adjustment of their differences, because the conflict may interfere with the supplies needed for the sustenance of the people, or the safety of our institutions.

Congress has consequently created mediation agencies which may be utilized to bring about a mutually satisfactory adjustment of disputes of this character.

JULY 3, 1917 [TO ADMIRAL WILLIAM S. SIMS]

From the beginning of the war I have been surprised by nothing so much as the failure of the British Admiralty to use Great Britain's great naval superiority in any effective way. In the presence of the present submarine emergency they are helpless to the point of panic. Every plan we suggest they reject for some reason of prudence.

In my view this is not a time for prudence but for boldness even at the risk of great losses. In most of your dispatches you have very properly advised us of the sort of aid and cooperation desired from us by the Admiralty. The trouble is that their plans and methods do not seem to us effective. I would be very much obliged to you if you would report to me, confidentially of course, exactly what the Admiralty have been doing and what they have accomplished and add to the report your own comments and suggestions based upon independent study of the whole situation without regard to the judgments already arrived at on that side of the water. In particular I am not at all satisfied with the conclusions of the Admiralty with regard to the convoying of groups of merchantmen.

I do not see how the necessary military supplies and supplies of food and fuel oil are to be delivered at British ports in any other way than under convoy. There will presently not be ships enough or tankers enough and our ship-building plans may not begin to yield important results in less than eighteen months.

The convoy system, which played such a large part in winning the First World War, came out of President Wilson's insistence that better protection be given to merchantmen. When asked for his suggestion on how this could be done he told Sir William Wiseman of the British Navy that "lanes should be formed, strongly guarded by destroyers, through which the merchantmen could pass."

JULY 12, 1917 [ON PROFITS]

A just price must, of course, be paid for everything the Government buys. By a just price I mean a price which will sustain the industries concerned in a high state of efficiency, provide a living for those who conduct them, enable them to pay good wages, and make possible expansions of their enterprises which will from time to time become necessary as the stupendous undertakings of this great war develop.

We could not wisely or reasonably do less than pay such prices.

They are necessary for the maintenance and development of industry; and the maintenance and development of industry are necessary for the great task we have in hand. We ought not to put the acceptance of such prices on the ground of patriotism.

Patriotism has nothing to do with profits in a case like this. Patriotism and profits ought never in the present circumstances to be mentioned together.

It is perfectly proper to discuss profits as a matter of business, with a view to maintaining the integrity of capital and the efficiency of labor; but it would be absurd to discuss them as a motive for helping to serve and save our country. Patriotism leaves profits out of the question.

In these days of our supreme trial, when we are sending hundreds of thousands of our young men across the seas to serve a great cause, no true man who stays behind to work for them and sustain them by his labor will ask himself what he is personally going to make out of that labor.

No true patriot will permit himself to take toll of their heroism in money or seek to grow rich by the shedding of their blood. When they are giving their lives will he not give at least his money?

I hear it insisted that more than a just price, more than a price that will sustain our industries, must be paid; that it is necessary to pay very liberal and unusual profits in order to "stimulate production"; that nothing but pecuniary rewards will do it — rewards paid in money, not in the mere liberation of the world.

I take it for granted that those who argue thus do not stop to think what that means.

Do they mean that you must be paid, must be bribed, to make your contribution, a contribution that costs you neither a drop of blood nor a tear, when the whole world is in travail and men everywhere depend upon and call to you to bring them out of bondage and make the world a fit place to live in again, amidst peace and justice?

Do they mean that you will exact a price, drive a bargain, with the men who are enduring the agony of this war on the battlefield, in the trenches, amidst the lurking dangers of the sea, or with the bereaved women and the pitiful children, before you will come forward to do your duty and give some part of your life, in easy, peaceful fashion, for the things we are fighting for, the things we have pledged our fortunes, our lives, our sacred honor to vindicate and defend — liberty and justice and fair dealing and the peace of nations? It is inconceivable.

JULY 17, 1917 [TO SECRETARY OF WAR NEWTON D. BAKER ON THE WAR INDUSTRIES BOARD]

My suggestion is that the three persons to whom will be entrusted the direction of purchases of raw materials, the purchases of finished products, and the arrangement of priorities of purchase and of shipment, shall themselves be members of the War Industries Board, together with representatives of the War and Navy Departments; that the War Industries Board serve as a clearing house for the determination of the immediate needs of the Government and the sequence of those needs; and that the three officials I have named shall in association with Mr. Hoover in the matter of the purchase of foodstuffs be the executive agency through which all purchases are arranged for. It seems to me that in this way we shall get rid of what might be in danger of being a complicated piece of machinery without in any way interfering with the independence and energy of the three officials mentioned.

JULY 21, 1917 [TO COLONEL HOUSE]

England and France *have not the same views with regard to peace that we have* by any means. When the war is over we can force them to our way of thinking, because by that time they will, among other things, be financially in our hands; but we cannot force them now, and any attempt to speak for them or to speak our common mind would bring on disagreements which would inevitably come to the surface in public and rob the whole thing of its effect. I saw this all too plainly in a conversation with Viviani. If there is to be an interchange of views at all, it ought to be between us and the liberals in Germany, with no one else brought in. Our real peace terms — those upon which we shall undoubtedly insist — are not now acceptable to either France or Italy (leaving Great Britain for the moment out of consideration).

JULY 23, 1917
A resolution pending in Congress provided for a "Joint Committee in Congress on Expenditures in the Conduct of the War."

If enacted into law, it would render my task of conducting the war practically impossible. I cannot believe that those who proposed this section scrutinized it with care or analyzed the effects which its operation would necessarily have. The constant supervision of executive action which it contemplates would amount to nothing less than an assumption on the part of the legislative body of the executive work of the administration.

There is a very ominous precedent in our history which shows how such a supervision would operate. I refer to the committee on the conduct of the war constituted by the Congress during the administration of Mr. Lincoln. It was the cause of constant and distressing harassment and rendered Mr. Lincoln's task all but impossible.

I am not in any way questioning what might be the motives or the purpose of the members of such a committee: I am ready to assume that they would wish to cooperate in the most patriotic spirit, but cooperation of that kind is not practicable in the circumstances. The responsibility rests upon the administration. There are abundant existing means of investigation and of the effective enforcement of that responsibility. I sincerely hope that upon the reconsideration of this matter both Houses of Congress will see that my objections rest upon indisputable grounds and that I could only interpret the final adoption as arising from a lack of confidence in myself.

AUGUST 11, 1917 [ADDRESS TO NAVY OFFICERS]
This is an unprecedented war and, therefore, it is a war in one sense for amateurs. Nobody ever before conducted a war like this and therefore nobody can pretend to be a professional in a war like

this. Here are two great navies, not to speak of the others associated with us, our own and the British, outnumbering by a very great margin the navy to which we are opposed, and yet casting about for a way in which to use our superiority and our strength, because of the novelty of the instruments used, because of the unprecedented character of the war, because nobody ever before fought a war like this, in the way that this is being fought at sea — or on land either for that matter.

The experienced soldier — experienced in previous wars — is a back number so far as his experience is concerned; not so far as his intelligence is concerned. His experience does not count, because he never fought a war as this is being fought, and therefore he is an amateur along with the rest of us. Now, somebody has got to think this war out. Somebody has got to think out the way not only to fight the submarine, but to do something different from what we are doing.

We are hunting hornets all over the farm and letting the nest alone. None of us knows how to go to the nest and crush it, and yet I despair of hunting for hornets all over the sea when I know where the nest is and know that the nest is breeding hornets as fast as I can find them. I am willing for my part to sacrifice half the navy Great Britain and we together have to crush that nest, because if we crush it, the war is won.

I have come here to say that I do not care where it comes from, I do not care whether it comes from the youngest officer or the oldest, but I want the officers of this Navy to have the distinction of saying how this war is going to be won.

The Secretary of the Navy and I have just been talking over plans for putting the planning machinery of the Navy at the disposal of the brains of the Navy and not stopping to ask what rank that brains has, because, as I have said before and want to repeat, so far as experience in this kind of war is concerned we are all of the same rank.

I am not saying that I do not expect the Admirals to tell us what to do, but I am saying that I want the youngest and most modest youngster in the service to tell us what we ought to do if he knows what it is. I am willing to make any sacrifice for that. I mean any sacrifice of time or anything else. I am ready to put myself at the disposal of any officer in the Navy who thinks he knows how to run this war. I will not undertake to tell you whether he does or not, because I know I cannot, but I will undertake to put him in communication with those who can find out whether his idea will work or not. I have the authority to do that and I will do it with the greatest pleasure.

I cannot say it too often to any audience, we are fighting a thing, not a people. The most extraordinary circumstance of modern history is the way in which the German people have been subordinated to the German system of authority, and how they have accepted their thinking from authority as well as their action from authority.

Now, we do not intend to let that method of action and of thinking be imposed upon the rest of the world.

I wish that I could think and had the brains to think in the terms of marine warfare, because I would feel then that I was figuring out the future history of the political freedom of mankind.

Every time we have suggested anything to the British Admiralty the reply has come back that virtually amounted to this, that it had never been done that way, and I felt like saying, "Well, nothing was ever done so systematically as nothing is being done now. Therefore, I should like to see something unusual happen, something that was never done before; and inasmuch as the things that are being done to you were never done before, don't you think it is worth while to try something that was never done before against those who are doing them to you?"

There is no other way to win, and the whole principle of this war is the kind of thing that ought to hearten and stimulate America. America has always boasted that she could find men to do anything.

She is the prize amateur nation of the world. Germany is the prize professional nation of the world.

Now, when it comes to doing new things and doing them well, I will back the amateur against the professional every time, because the professional does it out of the book and the amateur does it with his eyes open upon a new world and with a new set of circumstances. He knows so little about it that he is fool enough to try the right thing.

The men that do not know the danger are the rashest men, and I have several times ventured to make this suggestion to the men about me in both arms of the service: Please leave out of your vocabulary altogether the word "prudent."

Do not stop to think about what is prudent for a moment. Do the thing that is audacious to the utmost point of risk and daring, because that is exactly the thing that the other side does not understand, and you will win by the audacity of method when you cannot win by circumspection and prudence. I think that there are willing ears to hear this in the American Navy and the American Army because that is the kind of folks we are. We get tired of the old ways and covet the new ones.

You are doing your job admirably, the job that you have been taught to do; now let us do something that we were never taught to do and do it just as well as we are doing the older and more habitual things, and do not let anybody ever put one thought of discouragement into your minds.

I do not know what is the matter with the newspapers of the United States! I suppose they have to vary the tune from time to time just to relieve their minds, but every now and then a wave of the most absurd discouragement and pessimism goes through the country and we hear nothing except of the unusual advantages and equipment and sagacity and preparation and all the other wonderful things of the German Army and Navy.

My comment is always the very familiar comment, "Rats!" They are working under infinite disadvantages. They not only have no more brains than we have, but they have a different and less serviceable kind of brains than we have, if we will use the brains we have got. I am not discouraged for a moment, particularly because we have not even begun and, without saying anything in disparagement of those with whom we are associated in the war, I do expect things to begin when we begin. If they do not, American history will have changed its course; the American Army and Navy will have changed their character. There will have to come a new tradition into a service which does not do new and audacious and successful things.

AUGUST, 1917 [ON THE FLYLEAVES OF BIBLES GIVEN TO SERVICE MEN]

The Bible is the word of life. I beg that you will read it and find this out for yourselves — read, not little snatches here and there, but long passages that will really be the road to the heart of it.

You will find it full of real men and women not only, but also of things you have wondered about and been troubled about all your life, as men have been always; and the more you read the more it will become plain to you what things are worth while and what are not, what things make men happy — loyalty, right dealings, speaking the truth, readiness to give everything for what they think their duty, and, most of all, the wish that they may have the real approval of the Christ, who gave everything for them — and the things that are guaranteed to make men unhappy — selfishness, cowardice, greed, and everything that is low and mean.

When you have read the Bible you will know that it is the Word of God, because you will have found it the key to your own heart, your own happiness, and your own duty.

AUGUST 30, 1917 [TO SAMUEL GOMPERS]

I myself have had sympathy with the fears of the workers of the United States; for the tendency of war is toward reaction, and too often military necessities have been made an excuse for the destruction of laboriously erected industrial and social standards.

No one who is not blind can fail to see that the battle line of democracy for America stretches today from the fields of Flanders to every house and workshop where toiling, upward-striving men and women are counting the treasures of right and justice and liberty which are being threatened by our present enemies.

SEPTEMBER 2, 1917 [TO COLONEL HOUSE]

I am beginning to think that we ought to go systematically to work to ascertain as fully and precisely as possible just what the several parties to this war on our side of it will be inclined to insist upon as part of the final peace arrangements, in order that we may formulate our own position either for or against them and begin to gather the influences we wish to employ — or, at least, ascertain what influences we can use: in brief, prepare our case with a full knowledge of the position of all the litigants.

OCTOBER 25, 1917 [ON WOMAN SUFFRAGE]

The whole world is witnessing a struggle between two ideals of government. It is a struggle which goes deeper and touches more of the foundations of the organized life of men than any struggle that has ever taken place before, and no settlement of the questions that lie on the surface can satisfy a situation which requires that the questions which lie underneath and at the foundation should also be settled and settled right.

I am free to say that I think the question of woman suffrage is one of those questions which lie at the foundation.

In October the Bolshevists took over in Russia. On November 7, 1917, Kerenski escaped from Petrograd with a statement to the American ambassador that he expected the "whole affair to be liquidated in five days." At ten o'clock Lenin proclaimed that the provisional government had been overthrown.

From this date until March 16, 1918, when the Treaty of Brest-Litovsk was ratified, the affairs of Russia moved in two main courses: the consolidation of control of the Bolshevists, and the initiation of peace negotiations with Germany.

The question which confronted the Allies was how to prevent Russia from falling into the hands of the Central Powers.

NOVEMBER 12, 1917 [ON AMERICANISM]

Let us show ourselves Americans by showing that we do not want to go off in separate camps or groups by ourselves, but that we want to cooperate with all other classes and all other groups in the common enterprise which is to release the spirits of the world from bondage.

I would be willing to set that up as the final test of an American. That is the meaning of democracy. I have been very much distressed by some of the things that have happened recently. The mob spirit is displaying itself here and there in this country. I have no sympathy with what some men are saying, but I have no sympathy with the men who take their punishment into their own hands; and I want to say to every man who does join such a mob that I do not recognize him as worthy of the free institutions of the United States.

There are some organizations in this country whose object is anarchy and the destruction of law, but I would not meet their efforts *by making myself partner in destroying the law.* I despise and hate their purposes as much as any man, but I respect the ancient processes of justice; and I would be too proud not to see them done justice, however wrong they were.

NOVEMBER 13, 1917 [TO REPRESENTATIVE FRANK CLARK]
I have not lost faith in the Russian outcome by any means. Russia, like France in a past century, will no doubt have to go through deep waters but she will come out upon firm land on the other side and her great people, for they are a great people, will in my opinion take their proper place in the world.

NOVEMBER 15, 1917 [TO COLONEL HOUSE]
Take the whip hand. We not only accede to the plan for a unified conduct of the war but insist upon it. It is not practicable for us to be represented *in the same way* as the other governments on the civil side, but we will be on the military.

NOVEMBER 15, 1917 [TO GENERAL JOHN J. PERSHING]
It is urged that:
1. The most intense energy should be put into developing America's fighting forces for active service during the coming summer. Winning the war is vital to our future, and if humanly possible it ought to be done in 1918. There is no telling what might happen if we defer our utmost exertion until 1919.
2. All available sources of supply of artillery and ammunition

should be investigated and developed, having in mind Japan's resources in this regard.

3. Finally, every possible ton of shipping should be secured with the least delay for use in carrying our armies to France.

NOVEMBER 19, 1917 [TO COLONEL HOUSE]

Am distressed to differ with McCormick but inasmuch as we are fighting a war of principle I do not feel that I can consent to demand of Norway what we would not in similar circumstances allow any government to demand of us, namely the cessation of exports of her own products to any place she can send them. I am convinced that our only legitimate position is that we will not supply the deficiencies which she thus creates for herself if the exports are to our enemies.

NOVEMBER 22, 1917 [TO DOUGLAS FAIRBANKS]

George Creel was kind enough to hand me yesterday a copy of your "Laugh and Live" which you were thoughtful enough to send me, and I want to send you this line of sincere appreciation. If laughter can keep me alive, I am apt to live, because I fortunately come of a race that had laughter implanted in them.

The Allied Supreme War Council held its initial session on December 1, 1917, at Versailles, France — Great Britain, Italy, France and the United States being represented.

On the same date Trotsky ordered the removal of all diplomats who were not in sympathy with the Soviet regime.

DECEMBER 3, 1917 [TO COLONEL HOUSE — A CABLEGRAM]

Sorry impossible to omit foreign affairs from address to Congress. Reticence on my part at this juncture would be misunderstood and resented and do much harm.

DECEMBER 4, 1917 [TO CONGRESS]

Let there be no misunderstanding. Our present and immediate task is to win the war, and nothing shall turn us aside from it until it is accomplished. Every power and resource we possess, whether of men, of money, or of materials, is being devoted and will continue to be devoted to that purpose until it is achieved. Those who desire to bring peace about before that purpose is achieved I counsel to carry their advice elsewhere. We will not entertain it.

We shall regard the war as won only when the German people say to us, through properly accredited representatives, that they are ready to agree to a settlement based upon justice and the reparation of the wrongs their rulers have done.

The worst that can happen to the detriment of the German people is this, that if they should still, after the war is over, continue to be obliged to live under ambitious and intriguing masters interested to disturb the peace of the world, men or classes of men whom the other peoples of the world could not trust, it might be impossible to admit them to the partnership of nations which must henceforth guarantee the world's peace. That partnership *must be a partnership of peoples,* not a mere partnership of governments.

The thought of the plain people here and everywhere throughout the world, the people who enjoy no privilege and have very simple and unsophisticated standards of right and wrong, is the air all governments must henceforth breathe if they would live. It is in the full disclosing light of that thought that all policies must be conceived and executed in this midday hour of the world's life.

German rulers have been able to upset the peace of the world only because the German people were not suffered under their tutelage to share the comradeship of the other peoples of the world either in thought or in purpose. They were allowed to have no opinion of their own which might be set up as a rule of conduct for those who exercised authority over them.

All these things have been true from the very beginning of this stupendous war; and I cannot help thinking that if they had been made plain at the very outset the sympathy and enthusiasm of the Russian people might have been once for all enlisted on the side of the Allies, suspicion and distrust swept away, and a real and lasting union of purpose effected.

Had they believed these things at the very moment of their revolution and had they been confirmed in that belief since, the sad reverses which have recently marked the progress of their affairs toward an ordered and stable government of free men might have been avoided.

The Russian people have been poisoned by the very same falsehoods that have kept the German people in the dark, and the poison has been administered by the very same hands. The only possible antidote is the truth. It cannot be uttered too plainly or too often.

DECEMBER 17, 1917 [TO WILLIAM JENNINGS BRYAN]

My attention has been called to a book in which the author states by clear implication that I demanded your resignation as Secretary of State. You may quote me as saying that I did not ask for your resignation or desire it, as anyone can learn from my note accepting your resignation.

When President Wilson could get no real co-operation from the Allies on his idea for a lasting peace, he simply used his old, time-tested method of appealing to the people of the world over the heads of their rulers. He announced his plan for a world peace.

JANUARY 8, 1918 [THE FOURTEEN POINTS, IN AN ADDRESS TO CONGRESS]

The Central Empires have again attempted to acquaint the world with their objects in the war and have again challenged their adversaries to say what their objects are and what sort of settlement they would deem just and satisfactory.

There is no good reason why that challenge should not be responded to, and responded to with the utmost candor.

It will be our wish and purpose that the processes of peace, when they are begun, shall be absolutely open and that they shall involve and permit henceforth no secret understandings of any kind. The day of conquest and aggrandizement is gone by; so is also the day of secret covenants entered into in the interest of particular governments and likely at some unlooked-for moment to upset the peace of the world. It is this happy fact, now clear to the view of every public man whose thoughts do not still linger in an age that is dead and gone, which makes it possible for every nation whose purposes are consistent with justice and the peace of the world to avow now or at any other time the objects it has in view.

We entered this war because violations of right had occurred which touched us to the quick and made the life of our own people impossible unless they were corrected and the world secured once for all against their recurrence. What we demand in this war is that the world be made safe for every peace-loving nation which, like our own, wishes to live its own life, determine its own institutions, be assured of justice and fair dealing by the other peoples of the world as against force and selfish aggression. All the peoples of the world are in effect partners in this interest, and for our own part we see very clearly that unless justice be done to others it will not be done to us. The program of the world's peace, therefore, is our program; and that program, the only possible program, as we see it, is this:

I. Open covenants of peace, openly arrived at, after which there shall be no private international understandings of any kind but diplomacy shall proceed always frankly and in the public view.

II. Absolute freedom of navigation upon the seas, outside territorial waters, alike in peace and in war, except as the seas may be closed in whole or in part by international action for the enforcement of international covenants.

III. The removal, so far as possible, of all economic barriers and the establishment of an equality of trade conditions among all the nations consenting to the peace and associating themselves for its maintenance.

IV. Adequate guarantees given and taken that national armaments will be reduced to the lowest point consistent with domestic safety.

V. A free, open-minded, and absolutely impartial adjustment of all colonial claims, based upon a strict observance of the principle that in determining all such questions of sovereignty the interests of the populations concerned must have equal weight with the equitable claims of the government whose title is to be determined.

VI. The evacuation of all Russian territory and such a settlement of all questions affecting Russia as will secure the best and freest cooperation of the other nations of the world in obtaining for her an unhampered and unembarrassed opportunity for the independent determination of her own political development and national policy and assure her of a sincere welcome into the society of free nations under institutions of her own choosing; and, more than a welcome, assistance also of every kind that she may need and may herself desire.

VII. Belgium, the whole world will agree, must be evacuated and restored, without any attempt to limit the sovereignty which she enjoys in common with all other free nations.

VIII. All French territory should be freed and the invaded portions restored, and the wrong done to France by Prussia in 1871 in the matter of Alsace-Lorraine, which has unsettled the peace of the world for nearly fifty years, should be righted, in order that peace may once more be made secure in the interest of all.

IX. A readjustment of the frontiers of Italy should be effected along clearly recognizable lines of nationality.

X. The peoples of Austria-Hungary, whose place among the nations we wish to see safeguarded and assured, should be accorded the freest opportunity of autonomous development.

XI. Rumania, Serbia, and Montenegro should be evacuated; occupied territories restored; Serbia accorded free and secure access to the sea; and the relations of the several Balkan states to one another determined by friendly counsel along historically established lines of allegiance and nationality; and international guarantees of the political and economic independence and territorial integrity of the several Balkan states should be entered into.

XII. The Turkish portions of the present Ottoman Empire should be assured a secure sovereignty, but the other nationalities which are now under Turkish rule should be assured an undoubted security of life and an absolutely unmolested opportunity of autonomous development, and the Dardanelles should be permanently opened as a free passage to the ships and commerce of all nations under international guarantees.

XIII. An independent Polish state should be erected which should include the territories inhabited by indisputably Polish populations, which should be assured a free and secure access to the sea, and whose political and economic independence and territorial integrity should be guaranteed by international covenant.

XIV. A general association of nations must be formed under specific covenants for the purpose of affording mutual guarantees of political independence and territorial integrity to great and small states alike.

For such arrangements and covenants we are willing to fight and to continue to fight until they are achieved; but only because we wish the right to prevail and desire a just and stable peace such as can be secured only by removing the chief provocation of war, which this program does remove.

We have no jealousy of German greatness, and there is nothing in this program that impairs it. We grudge her no achievement or distinction of learning or of pacific enterprise such as have made her record very bright and very enviable. We do not wish to injure her or to block in any way her legitimate influence or power. We do not wish to fight her either with arms or with hostile arrangements of trade if she is willing to associate herself with us and the other peace-loving nations of the world in covenants of justice and law and fair dealing. We wish her only to accept a place of equality among the peoples of the world — the new world in which we now live — instead of a place of mastery.

Neither do we presume to suggest to her any alteration or modification of her institutions. But it is necessary, we must frankly say, and necessary as a preliminary to any intelligent dealings with her on our part, that we should know whom her spokesmen speak for when they speak to us, whether for the Reichstag majority or for the military party and the men whose creed is imperial domination.

JANUARY 26, 1918 [TO CYRUS H. McCORMICK]

Of course, I have given a great deal of thought to the question of universal military service and have by no means turned away from it in the sense of rejecting it, but it is clear to me and it is clear to many who have studied our present military problem that it would be unwise, and indeed impracticable, to institute such training now. We have not the officers with which to undertake it and we have not the equipment, and the additional financial strain would be too great; besides which, its immediate institution would seriously interfere with the more immediate task we have of preparing and sending an Army across the seas.

My feeling is that it is impossible to forecast now what the condition of the world will be, and therefore our own military task and duty, when the war is over. When we do see the conditions which follow the war, I hope and believe that we shall know what to do, and it may be that we shall have to undertake some such great plan.

JANUARY 31, 1918 [TO SECRETARY OF WAR BAKER]

We are having hard luck with our military attachés at Petrograd, are we not? I should think that being sent to Petrograd would drive most men to drink, but anyone who is so driven is the very man who cannot be trusted to do the real job there, am I not right?

FEBRUARY 6, 1918 [TO SENATOR JOHN SHARP WILLIAMS]

I do not know that I have ever had a more tiresome struggle with quicksand that I am having in trying to do the right thing in respect to our dealings with Russia.

FEBRUARY 26, 1918 [TO SECRETARY OF THE TREASURY McADOO]

I am mighty sorry but I can't let you have Baruch for the Finance Corporation. He has trained now in the War Industries Board until he is thoroughly conversant with the activities of it from top to bottom, and as soon as I can do so without risking new issues on the Hill I am going to appoint him chairman of that board.

MARCH 4, 1918

Bernard Baruch was appointed as chairman of the War Industries Board, the functions of which were to be:

(1) The creation of new facilities and the disclosing, if necessary the opening up, of new or additional sources of supply;

(2) The conversion of existing facilities, where necessary, to new uses;

(3) The studious conservation of resources and facilities by scientific, commercial, and industrial economies;

(4) Advice to the several purchasing agencies of the Government with regard to the prices to be paid;

(5) The determination, wherever necessary, of priorities of production and of delivery and of the proportions of any given article to be made immediately accessible to the several purchasing agencies when the supply of that article is insufficient, either temporarily or permanently;

(6) The making of purchases for the Allies.

MARCH 12, 1918 [ON OPEN DIPLOMACY]

When I pronounced for open diplomacy I meant not that there should be no private discussions of delicate matters, but that no secret agreement of any sort should be entered into and that all international relations, when fixed, should be open, aboveboard, and explicit.

MARCH 22, 1918

Senator Morris Sheppard proposed, if the President approved, to introduce a bill for complete wartime prohibition.

My feeling is that the introduction and discussion of such a bill might operate seriously to disturb and delay the necessary business of the session, and that I should very much deplore.

Besides it would undoubtedly introduce a new element of disturbance in the labor situation which I should dread, because I would know of no way in which it could be quieted. I have received delegations of working men who, apparently speaking with the utmost sincerity, have declared that they would regard it as a genuine hardship if they were deprived of their beer, for example. There is no arguing with feelings of that sort, and just because there is no arguing with them there would be no way of handling them in this time of crisis.

On March 26, 1918, Marshal Foch of France was made supreme commander of the Allied armies. This action was taken only after Germany nearly won the war by driving a wedge between the British and French armies.

APRIL 18, 1918 [TO S. R. BERTRON]

There are many difficulties in the way of my seeing the newspaper men, the chief being that I am dependent in every interview upon the discretion and good will of the least discreet and friendly member of the conference, and that has made it very difficult for me to talk as frankly as I should like to talk with the general body of correspondents down here, but it is not a matter which I have finally closed my mind about by any means.

Unlike FDR, President Wilson could not josh and joke with the newspapermen while not telling them things they wanted to know but should not for various reasons.

MAY 27, 1918

The profiteering that cannot be got at by the restraints of conscience and love of country can be got at by taxation.

There is such profiteering now and the information with regard to it is available and indisputable.

MAY 27, 1918 [TO SECRETARY OF WAR BAKER]

There is no subject which deserves more immediate or earnest consideration than the subject of the physical reconstruction of disabled soldiers. It is desirable that plans with regard to this important matter should be formed at once, and I welcome every instrumentality which is being used to bring about the proper consideration and execution of such plans.

JUNE 3, 1918

The Supreme Court declared the Child Labor Law unconstitutional, with a dissenting opinion read by Justice Holmes and concurred in by Justices Brandeis, Clarke and McKenna. A few days later Secretary Albert S. Burleson stayed after a cabinet meeting for a private conference.

*"Burleson," said the President, "I want a Child Labor Law that
will stand. How can I get it?"*

*"I'll tell you," replied Burleson, "but if I were in Congress, I
should vote against it. I am not in sympathy with you on it, but
I'll help you."*

The problem was not settled until the FDR administration.

JUNE 11, 1918 [TO CHARLES R. CRANE]

Of course, I will try to see Professor Masaryk. I had been planning to have a joint conference with him and one or two others in
order to work out a scheme for the relief of Russia, and I am very
glad indeed to know when Professor Masaryk will be here.

JUNE 14, 1918 [TO HERBERT HOOVER]

I think that the reasons you give for your plan to go abroad and
consult with the Food Administrators of France, England and Italy
are entirely conclusive, and I believe that your visit to the other side
will probably result in a better situation all around with regard to
food supplies. My best wishes will certainly follow you.

*By July 1, 1918, 1,019,000 men had embarked for France, wrote
Secretary Baker to the President — double the number that critics
of eight months before had said we should have by midsummer,
1918.*

JULY 4, 1918 [THE FOUR POINT SPEECH]

The plot is written plain upon every scene and every act of the
supreme tragedy. On the one hand stand the peoples of the world —
not only the peoples actually engaged, but many others also who
suffer under mastery but cannot act; peoples of many races and in
every part of the world — the people of stricken Russia still, among
the rest, though they are for the moment unorganized and helpless.

Opposed to them, masters of many armies, stand an isolated,
friendless group of governments who speak no common purpose
but only selfish ambitions of their own by which none can profit
but themselves, and whose peoples are fuel in their hands; governments which fear their people and yet are for the time their
sovereign lords, making every choice for them and disposing of

their lives and fortunes as they will, as well as of the lives and fortunes of every people who fall under their power — governments clothed with the strange trappings and the primitive authority of an age that is altogether alien and hostile to our own.

The Past and the Present are in deadly grapple and the peoples of the world are being done to death between them.

There can be but one issue. The settlement must be final. There can be no compromise. No halfway decision would be tolerable. No halfway decision is conceivable. These are the ends for which the associated peoples of the world are fighting and which must be conceded them before there can be peace:

I. The destruction of every arbitrary power anywhere that can separately, secretly, and of its single choice disturb the peace of the world; or, if it cannot be presently destroyed, at the least its reduction to virtual impotence.

II. The settlement of every question, whether of territory, or sovereignty, of economic arrangement, or of political relationship, upon the basis of the free acceptance of that settlement by the people immediately concerned, and not upon the basis of the material interest or advantage of any other nation or people which may desire a different settlement for the sake of its own exterior influence or mastery.

III. The consent of all nations to be governed in their conduct towards each other by the same principles of honor and of respect for the common law of civilized society that govern the individual citizens of all modern states in their relations with one another; to the end that all promises and covenants may be sacredly observed, no private plots or conspiracies hatched, no selfish injuries wrought with impunity, and a mutual trust established upon the handsome foundation of a mutual respect for right.

IV. The establishment of an organization of peace which shall make it certain that the combined power of free nations will check every invasion of right and serve to make peace and justice the more secure by affording a definite tribunal of opinion to which all must submit and by which every international readjustment that cannot be amicably agreed upon by the peoples directly concerned shall be sanctioned.

These great objects can be put into a single sentence. What we seek is the reign of law, based upon the consent of the governed and sustained by the organized opinion of mankind.

These great ends cannot be achieved by debating and seeking to reconcile and accommodate what statesmen may wish, with their projects for balances of power and of national opportunity. They can be realized only by the determination of what the thinking peoples of the world desire, with their longing hope for justice and for social freedom and opportunity.

On July 5, 1918, Oscar T. Crosby, recently home from Europe, called in the evening. "Mr. President," he said, "perhaps it is known to you already, but if not, may I say that your League of Nations plans are not taken seriously by the heads of state in Europe? Mr. Lloyd George has laughed at the proposed League in my presence, and Monsieur Clemenceau has sneered at it."

"Yes," replied the President, "I know that Europe is still governed by the same reactionary forces which controlled this country until a few years ago. But I am satisfied that if necessary I can reach the peoples of Europe over the heads of their rulers."

In July, 1918, Franklin D. Roosevelt, Assistant Secretary of the Navy, conferred with Wilson about the merits of Al Smith for candidate for Governor of New York. "I should be entirely satisfied with Smith's nomination," Wilson said. "He seems to be a man who has responded in an extraordinary manner to the awakening forces of a new day and the compulsion of changing circumstances. He seems to have noteworthy support from organizations and individuals who are working in one way or another for the improvement of government."

Roosevelt pointed out that Smith was a Catholic. "The day to take political consideration of that has gone by," Wilson said. "People are every day reading the casualty lists of American boys of every creed."

JULY 17, 1918 [ON RUSSIA]

It is the clear and fixed judgment of the Government of the Ur
States, arrived at after repeated and very searching reconsidera
of the whole situation in Russia, that military intervention t
would injure her rather than help her, and that it would be c
advantage in the prosecution of our main design, to win the
against Germany. It can not, therefore, take part in such i
vention or sanction it in principle. For helping the Czecho-Slo
[*stranded in Siberia*] there is immediate necessity and suffi
justification. Recent developments have made it evident that
is in the interest of what the Russian people themselves de
and the Government of the United States is glad to contribute
small force at its disposal for that purpose. It yields, also, to
judgment of the Supreme Command in the matter of establis
a small force at Murmansk, to guard the military stores at Kola
to make it safe for Russian forces to come together in orgar
bodies in the north. But it can go no further. It is not in a po:
to take part in organized intervention in adequate force from e
Vladivostok or Murmansk and Archangel.

It hopes to carry out the plans for safeguarding the rear c
Czecho-Slovaks operating from Vladivostok in a way that will
it and keep it in close cooperation with a small military force
its own from Japan, and if necessary from the other Allies, a
proposes to ask all associated in this course of action to un.
assuring the people of Russia in the most public and solemn
ner that none of the governments uniting in action either in Si
or in northern Russia contemplates any interference of any
with the political sovereignty of Russia, any intervention in
internal affairs, or any impairment of her territorial integrity
now or hereafter, but that each of the associated powers ha
single object of affording such aid as shall be acceptable, anc
such aid as shall be acceptable, to the Russian people in the
deavor to regain control of their own affairs, their own ter
and their own destiny.

It is the hope and purpose of the Government of the U

States to take advantage of the earliest opportunity to send to Siberia a commission in order in some systematic manner to relieve the immediate economic necessities of the people there.

August 8, 1918 [to George Creel]

I am sorry to disappoint the National War Savings Committee, but I know that Mrs. Wilson would not be willing to make any statement such as they suggest. Her chief anxiety is to keep out of the papers, and she has confined herself, and I am sure will confine herself, to those things with which she has been obliged to form a sort of official connection.

August 14, 1918 [to Russell B. Harrison]

The Secretary of War and I agree that we are under something more than a logical necessity in the matter of the classification of Russia as a belligerent. Where shall we classify her if not in the list of belligerents? When she had a stable government she declared war against the Central Empires and became one of the principal and one of the earliest participants in the war. After the revolution, the Government of the United States recognized the revolutionary government and received its Ambassador here. We have recognized no subsequent government in Russia, and if we were now to classify her as a neutral, we would necessarily base that classification upon the Brest Litovsk Treaty, which we have never recognized as binding and which we cannot recognize as binding without accepting the Lenin-Trotsky Government.

August 26, 1918

Mrs. Jessie Eldridge Southwick wrote with great indignation of reports that it was "well known" that the President had bargained with Wall Street to bring on the war; that Mrs. Wilson was German in sympathy; and so on. The President answered:

It was certainly very kind of you to write me . . . and I am grateful that you should be so much concerned about slanders which are being circulated to my disadvantage.

But I feel confident that you can dismiss the slanders which you were kind enough to tell me about without the least concern as to the harm they may do, because they are so entirely false in every particular that they can do, I believe, no harm. I have found that lies take care of themselves. They are so inconsistent with each other, of necessity, and are so colored with all sorts of impossible allegations that they break down of their own absurdity. These particular lies are almost grotesque in their falseness.

I am quite aware that efforts of this sort are constantly being made to discredit me, with what motive I find it difficult to conjecture, but I have steeled my heart to endure them because, although it is very distressing to be so maligned, my own conscience so entirely acquits me that I cannot bring myself to take the malignancy too seriously.

August 30, 1918

Professor Edward S. Corwin of Princeton had written that he would like a hand in the preparation of the history of America's participation in the war, which he understood was to be prepared by the government.

I do not think that this is the time to write the executive and legislative history of the war. That history will be accessible for a great many years, and more accessible in the future than it is now, in the official documents, and I have always had the feeling that an official "Remembrancer" never could do the same work that a historian could do at a later time.

August 30, 1918 [to Royal Meeker]

I have read with sympathy your letter of yesterday, but the trouble is that I have not the legal power to regulate and control the prices and qualities of textiles and clothing in the same way that the Food Administrator regulates and controls the qualities and prices of food stuffs. The powers of the Food Administrator were specifically conferred by Congress, but no such powers have been conferred upon the Executive with regard to textiles and clothing. I wish with all my heart they had been. Just now, it seems rather futile, at the end of a hurried session, to attempt to bring this matter to action in the Congress.

AUGUST 31, 1918 [TO FRANK P. GLASS]

I must admit that I am at a loss to understand the desire of the British authorities to have group after group of Americans go over to England, but I am glad, if they are choosing, that they choose men of discretion like yourself, because the usefulness of such a group is exactly equal to the discretion of the least discreet member of it, and some of our fellow-citizens have by no means been expressing the views of the United States in what they have said on the other side.

AUGUST 31, 1918 [TO RABBI STEPHEN S. WISE]

I have watched with deep and sincere interest the reconstructive work which the Weizmann Commission has done in Palestine at the instance of the British Government, and I welcome an opportunity to express the satisfaction I have felt in the progress of the Zionist movement in the United States and in the Allied Countries since the declaration by Mr. Balfour on behalf of the British Government, of Great Britain's approval of the establishment in Palestine of a national home for the Jewish people, and his promise that the British Government would use its best endeavors to facilitate the achievement of that object, with the understanding that nothing would be done to prejudice the civil and religious rights of non-Jewish people in Palestine or the rights and political status enjoyed by Jews in other countries.

I think that all Americans will be deeply moved by the report that even in this time of stress the Weizmann Commission has been able to lay the foundation of the Hebrew University at Jerusalem, with the promise that that bears of spiritual rebirth.

SEPTEMBER 5, 1918 [TO ACTING SECRETARY OF WAR BENEDICT CROWELL]

I am told that the War Department is, through its intelligence officers, in some way interesting itself in the matter of propaganda abroad, and I would be very much obliged if you would make inquiry and find how far this is true and what is being attempted, because it is my wish to keep the matter of propaganda entirely in my own hands and I had not known that any other agencies than those I had set up were attempting to interest themselves in it. I regard nothing as more delicate or more intimately associated with the policy of the administration than propaganda, and if any agency of the Army is attempting to organize propaganda of any sort or to take a hand in controlling it, I would be very much obliged if you would "call them off." You will know how to do it kindly and without intimating any criticism on my part, but only my sense of the absolute necessity of my directing that whole matter.

SEPTEMBER 10, 1918 [TO THOMAS G. MASARYK]

It reassures me to know that you think that I have followed the right course in my earnest endeavor to be of as much service as possible to the Czecho-Slovak peoples, and I want you to know how much the Secretary of State and I have valued the counsel and guidance which you have given us. It will always be a matter of profound gratitude to me if it should turn out that we have been able to render a service which will redound to the permanent advantage and happiness of the great group of peoples whom you represent.

SEPTEMBER 13, 1918 [TO ACTING SECRETARY OF WAR CROWELL]

I have little enough sympathy with the conscientious objector, but I am sure we all want to avoid unnecessary harshness and injustice of any sort.

SEPTEMBER 16, 1918

The President wrote to Postmaster General Burleson, in regard to censorship of an issue of The World Tomorrow.

I know the principal writer for this paper, Norman Thomas. He was once a pupil of mine at Princeton. I have just had a talk with Nevin Sayre about the whole matter of the holding up of this particular issue and have urged views upon him which I hope and believe will alter the policy and, to some extent, the point of view of men like Thomas; but I write this only to suggest that you treat these men with all possible consideration, for I know they are absolutely sincere and I would not like to see this publication held up unless there is a very clear case indeed.

SEPTEMBER 19, 1918

General Graves telegraphed from Siberia: "French and English are, undoubtedly, trying to get the Allied forces committed to some act which will result in the establishment of an Eastern front."

Wilson was in complete sympathy with the Russian Revolution as long as he thought that it was taking that country towards a democratic government.

On the other hand, regardless of the way the revolution went for the moment, he was not going to be pressured into starting an Eastern front, manned by Americans, until he saw much farther down the road. During early fall, 1918, the pressure upon him from other countries for expeditions into all parts of Russia became so great that he, in a conference with Secretary of the State Lansing and General Peyton C. March, Chief of Staff, made a flat announcement that no more troops would be sent to Russia.

CHAPTER TWENTY

Over the Heads of the Rulers

❯❯❯❮❮❮❯❯❯❮❮❮❯❯❯❮❮❮❯❯❯❮❮❮❯❯❯❮❮❮❯❯❯❮❮❮❯❯❯❮❮❮❯❯❯❮❮❮❯❯❯❮❮❮❯❯❯❮❮❮

SEPTEMBER 27, 1918 [ADDRESS IN NEW YORK]

On this date President Wilson, feeling that the Central Powers were cracking up, delivered an address which was aimed at widening the breach between the rulers and the people by giving the "particulars" of a permanent peace.

Everyone who wants to know what Wilson believed when the war ended, and when he went to Paris to try to make such a peace a reality instead of a chimera, should read this address.

The war has lasted more than four years and the whole world has been drawn into it. The common will of mankind has been substituted for the particular purposes of individual states.

The issues of the war are these:

Shall the military power of any nation or group of nations be suffered to determine the fortunes of peoples over whom they have no right to rule except the right of force?

Shall strong nations be free to wrong weak nations and make them subject to their purpose and interest?

Shall peoples be ruled and dominated, even in their own internal affairs, by arbitrary and irresponsible force or by their own will and choice?

Shall there be a common standard of right and privilege for all peoples and nations or shall the strong do as they will and the weak suffer without redress?

No man, no group of men, chose these to be the issues of the struggle. They *are* the issues of it; and they must be settled — by no arrangement or compromise or adjustment of interests, but definitely and once for all and with a full and unequivocal acceptance of the principle that the interest of the weakest is as sacred as the interest of the strongest.

This is what we mean when we speak of a permanent peace, if we speak sincerely, intelligently, and with a real knowledge and comprehension of the matter we deal with.

It is of capital importance that we should also be explicitly agreed that no peace shall be obtained by any kind of compromise or abatement of the principles we have avowed as the principles for which we are fighting. There should exist no doubt about that. I am, therefore, going to take the liberty of speaking with the utmost frankness about the practical implications that are involved in it.

If it be in deed and in truth the common object of the Governments associated against Germany and of the nations whom they govern, as I believe it to be, to achieve by the coming settlements a secure and lasting peace, it will be necessary that all who sit down at the peace table shall come ready and willing to pay the price, the only price, that will procure it; and ready and willing, also, to create in some virile fashion the only instrumentality by which it can be made certain that the agreements of the peace will be honored and fulfilled.

That price is impartial justice in every item of the settlement, no matter whose interest is crossed, and not only impartial justice, but also the satisfaction of the several peoples whose fortunes are dealt with. That indispensable instrumentality is a League of Nations formed under covenants that will be efficacious.

Without such an instrumentality, by which the peace of the world can be guaranteed, peace will rest in part upon the word of outlaws and only upon that word. For Germany will have to redeem her character, not by what happens at the peace table, but by what follows.

And, as I see it, the constitution of that League of Nations and the clear definition of its objects must be a part, is in a sense the most essential part, of the peace settlement itself. *It cannot be formed now.* If formed now, it would be merely a new alliance confined to the nations associated against a common enemy. *It is not likely that it could be formed after the settlement.* It is necessary to guarantee the peace; and the peace cannot be guaranteed as an afterthought.

The reason, to speak in plain terms again, why it must be guaranteed is that there will be parties to the peace whose promises have proved untrustworthy, and means must be found in connection with the peace settlement itself to remove that source of insecurity.

But these general terms do not disclose the whole matter. Some details are needed to make them sound less like a thesis and more like a practical program. These, then, are some of the particulars, and I state them with the greater confidence because I can state them authoritatively as representing this Government's interpretation of its own duty with regard to peace:

First, the impartial justice meted out must involve no discrimination between those to whom we wish to be just and those to whom we do not wish to be just. It must be a justice that plays no favorites and knows no standard but the equal rights of the several peoples concerned;

Second, no special or separate interest of any single nation or any group of nations can be made the basis of any part of the settlement which is not consistent with the common interest of all;

Third, there can be no leagues or alliances or special covenants and understandings within the general and common family of the League of Nations.

Fourth, and more specifically, there can be no special, selfish economic combinations within the League and no employment of any form of economic boycott or exclusion except as the power of economic penalty by exclusion from the markets of the world may be vested in the League of Nations itself as a means of discipline and control.

Fifth, all international agreements and treaties of every kind must be made known in their entirety to the rest of the world.

Special alliances and economic rivalries and hostilities have been the prolific source in the modern world of the plans and passions that produce war. It would be an insincere as well as insecure peace that did not exclude them in definite and binding terms.

In the same sentence in which I say that the United States will enter into no special arrangements or understandings with particular nations let me say also that the United States is prepared to assume its full share of responsibility for the maintenance of the common covenants and understandings upon which peace must henceforth rest.

We still read Washington's immortal warning against "entangling alliances" with full comprehension and an answering purpose. But only special and limited alliances entangle; and we recognize and accept the duty of a new day in which we are permitted to hope for a general alliance which will avoid entanglements and clear the air of the world for common understandings and the maintenance of common rights.

As I have said, neither I nor any other man in governmental authority created or gave form to the issues of this war. I have simply responded to them with such vision as I could command.

But I have responded gladly and with a resolution that has grown warmer and more confident as the issues have grown clearer and clearer.

It is now plain that they are issues which no man can pervert unless it be willfully.

I am bound to fight for them, and happy to fight for them as time and circumstance have revealed them to me as to all the world. Our enthusiasm for them grows more and more irresistible as they stand out in more and more vivid and unmistakable outline.

It is the peculiarity of this great war that while statesmen have seemed to cast about for definitions of their purpose and have sometimes seemed to shift their ground and their point of view, the thought of the mass of men, whom statesmen are supposed to instruct and lead, has grown more and more unclouded; more and more certain of what it is that they are fighting for.

National purposes have fallen more and more into the background and the common purpose of enlightened mankind has taken their place. The counsels of plain men have become on all hands more simple and straightforward and more unified than the counsels of sophisticated men of affairs, who still retain the impression that they are playing a game of power and playing for high stakes. That is why I have said that this is a peoples' war, not a statesmen's. *Statesmen must follow the clarified common thought or be broken.*

I take that to be the significance of the fact that assemblies and associations of many kinds made up of plain workaday people have demanded, almost every time they came together, and are still demanding, that the leaders of their Governments declare to them plainly what it is, exactly what it is, that they were seeking in this war, and what they think the items of the final settlement should be. They are not yet satisfied with what they have been told.

They still seem to fear that they are getting what they ask for only in statesmen's terms — only in the terms of territorial arrangements and divisions of power, and not in terms of broad-visioned justice and mercy and peace and the satisfaction of those deep-seated longings of oppressed and distracted men and women and enslaved peoples that seem to them the only things worth fighting a war for that engulfs the world. Perhaps statesmen have not always recognized this changed aspect of the whole world of policy and action. Perhaps they have not always spoken in direct reply to the questions asked because they did not know how searching those questions were and what sort of answers they demanded.

Unity of purpose and of counsel are as imperatively necessary in this war as was unity of command in the battlefield; and with perfect unity of purpose and counsel will come assurance of complete victory. It can be had in no other way. "Peace drives" can be effectively neutralized and silenced only by showing that every victory of the nations associated against Germany brings the nations nearer the sort of peace which will bring security and reassurance to all peoples and make the recurrence of another such struggle of pitiless force and bloodshed forever impossible, and that nothing else can.

Germany is constantly intimating the "terms" she will accept;

and always finds that the world does not want terms. It wishes the final triumph of justice and fair dealing.

In October the "fireworks" began. On October 6, 1918, came the first German note asking for an armistice on the terms outlined by Wilson in his message to Congress, January 8, 1918, and in his speech on September 27, 1918. Samuel Gompers, speaking for the American Federation of Labor, opposed an armistice. Senator Henry Cabot Lodge wrote Theodore Roosevelt: "I am living in constant anxiety now of a sudden plunge of the Administration for a negotiated peace. At this point, if we make an armistice we have lost the war and we shall leave Germany about where she started. I am sure the American people want a complete victory and an unconditional surrender." Theodore Roosevelt joined the thundering by saying, "I most earnestly hope that the Senate of the United States and all other persons competent to speak for the American people will emphatically repudiate the so-called fourteen points and the various similar utterances of the President. To do as the President has done in this case becomes dangerously near to being treacherous diplomacy."

OCTOBER 8, 1918 [WILSON'S REPLY TO THE GERMAN NOTE]

The President feels bound to say with regard to the suggestion of an armistice that he would not feel at liberty to propose a cessation of arms to the Governments with which the Government of the United States is associated against the Central Powers so long as the armies of those powers are upon their soil. The good faith of any discussion would manifestly depend upon the consent of the Central Powers immediately to withdraw their forces everywhere from invaded territory.

OCTOBER 14, 1918

Wilson's message to Germany clarifying what asking for an armistice must mean:

It must be clearly understood that the process of evacuation and the conditions of an armistice are matters which must be left to the judgment and advice of the military advisers of the Government of the United States and the Allied Governments, and the President feels it his duty to say that no arrangement can be accepted by the Government of the United States which does not provide absolutely satisfactory safeguards and guarantees of the maintenance of the present military supremacy of the armies of the United States and of the Allies in the field.

The President feels that it is also his duty to add that neither the Government of the United States nor, he is quite sure, the Governments with which the Government of the United States is associated as a belligerent will consent to consider an armistice so long as the armed forces of Germany continue the illegal and inhumane practices which they still persist in.

At the very time that the German Government approaches the Government of the United States with proposals of peace its submarines are engaged in sinking passenger ships at sea, and not the ships alone, but the very boats in which their passengers and crews seek to make their way to safety; and in their present enforced withdrawal from Flanders and France the German armies are pursuing a course of wanton destruction which has always been regarded as in direct violation of the rules and practices of civilized warfare. Cities and villages, if not destroyed, are being stripped of all they contain not only, but often of their very inhabitants. The nations associated against Germany cannot be expected to agree to a cessation of arms while acts of inhumanity, spoliation, and desolation are being continued which they justly look upon with horror and with burning hearts.

It is necessary that the President should call the attention of the Government of Germany to the language and plain intent of one of the terms of peace which the German Government has now accepted. It is contained in the address of the President delivered at Mount Vernon on the Fourth of July last. It is as follows: "The destruction of every arbitrary power anywhere that can separately, secretly, and of its single choice disturb the peace of the world; or, if it cannot be presently destroyed, at least its reduction to virtual impotency." The power which has hitherto controlled the German Nation is of the sort here described. It is within the choice of the German Nation to alter it. The President's words just quoted naturally constitute a condition precedent to peace, if peace is to come by the action of the German people themselves. The President feels bound to say that the whole process of peace will, in his judgment, depend upon the definiteness and the satisfactory character of the guarantees which can be given in this fundamental matter. It is indispensable that the Governments associated against Germany should know beyond a peradventure with whom they are dealing.

Another crisis was facing Wilson. The off-year elections were at hand, and what happened at them might determine whether the sort of peace Wilson wanted would be approved by the membership in Congress — particularly the Senate.

Members of the Democratic party were pressuring him to make a statement to the country asking that a Democratic Congress be returned.

At the same time the delicate negotiations with Germany were causing all kinds of trouble, particularly from most of the Republican members of Congress, who were using every bit of argument to try to get control of Congress and to lay the groundwork for getting control of the Presidency again.

OCTOBER 22, 1918 [TO SECRETARY OF WAR BAKER]

I am very glad to have your letter of this morning reporting that more than two million American soldiers have sailed from the ports of this country to participate in the war overseas. I am sure that this will be a matter of deep gratification and reassurance to the country and that everyone will join me in congratulating the War and Navy Departments upon the steady accomplishment in this all-important application of force to the liberation of the world.

OCTOBER 22, 1918 [TO SENATOR G. M. HITCHCOCK]

In reply to your letter of October 21st, let me say that it seems to me really not worth while to answer the Republican attacks on

Article 3 of the peace terms I suggested in my address of January 8th. The words I used are perfectly clear to any honest mind.

They leave every nation free to determine its own economic policy, except in the one particular that its policy must be the same for all other nations and not be compounded of hostile discriminations between one nation and another, such weapons of discrimination being left to the joint action of the nations for the purpose of disciplining those who will not submit to the general programme of justice and equality.

It would be impossible to follow up all the perversions and misrepresentations that some of the Republicans are now indulging in, and my own judgment is that we can safely leave the matter to the good sense of our fellow-countrymen who can read English.

OCTOBER 23, 1918 [WILSON'S ULTIMATUM TO GERMANY]

Feeling that the whole peace of the world depends now on plain speaking and straightforward action, the President deems it his duty to say, without any attempt to soften what may seem harsh words, that the nations of the world do not and cannot trust the word of those who have hitherto been the masters of German policy, and to point out once more that in concluding peace and attempting to undo the infinite injuries and injustices of this war the Government of the United States cannot deal with any but veritable representatives of the German people who have been assured of a genuine constitutional standing as the real rulers of Germany. If it must deal with the military masters and the monarchical autocrats of Germany now, or if it is likely to have to deal with them later in regard to the international obligations of the German Empire, it must demand, not peace negotiations, but surrender. Nothing can be gained by leaving this essential thing unsaid.

OCTOBER 24, 1918

Mrs. Wilson went into the President's study and found him just getting up from his typewriter. He had in his hand his appeal for a Democratic Congress and he read it to her.

"I would not send it out," she said. "It is not a dignified thing to do."

"That is what I thought at first," he replied, "but it is too late now. I have told them I would do it."

It is said that this may have lost Wilson the control of Congress. Great howls went up. Yet Theodore Roosevelt, who, with Senator Lodge, howled the loudest, sent out telegrams to Senators Lodge, Poindexter and Hiram Johnson: "Let us dictate peace by the hammering guns and not chat about peace to the accompaniment of the clicking of typewriters."

Perhaps Newton D. Baker summed the matter up better than anyone: "It was wrong for a Democrat to ask the people to vote for him — that that right was the private prerogative of Republicans!"

The election at hand was, in its vital import, perhaps the most important ever held in the world. If a Democratic Congress had been returned, the League might not have been ultimately doomed.

OCTOBER 25, 1918 [APPEAL FOR A DEMOCRATIC CONGRESS]

The Congressional elections are at hand. They occur in the most critical period our country has ever faced or is likely to face in our time. If you have approved of my leadership and wish me to continue to be your unembarrassed spokesman in affairs at home and abroad, I earnestly beg that you will express yourselves unmistakably to that effect by returning a Democratic majority to both the Senate and the House of Representatives.

I am your servant and will accept your judgment without cavil, but my power to administer the great trust assigned me by the Constitution would be seriously impaired should your judgment be adverse, and I must frankly tell you so because so many critical issues depend upon your verdict. No scruple of taste must in grim times like these be allowed to stand in the way of speaking the plain truth.

I have no thought of suggesting that any political party is paramount in matters of patriotism. I feel too keenly the sacrifices which have been made in this war by all our citizens, irrespective of party affiliations, to harbor such an idea. I mean only that the difficulties and delicacies of our present task are of a sort that makes it imperatively necessary that the Nation should give its undivided support to the Government under a unified leadership, and that a Republican Congress would divide the leadership.

The leaders of the minority in the present Congress have unquestionably been pro-war, but they have been anti-administration. At almost every turn, since we entered the war, they have sought to take the choice of policy and the conduct of the war out of my hands and put it under the control of instrumentalities of their own choosing.

This is no time either for divided counsel or for divided leadership. Unity of command is as necessary now in civil action as it is upon the field of battle.

If the control of the House and Senate should be taken away from the party now in power an opposing majority could assume control of legislation and oblige all action to be taken amidst contest and obstruction.

The return of a Republican majority to either House of the Congress would, moreover, certainly be interpreted on the other side of the water as a repudiation of my leadership. Spokesmen of the Republican Party are urging you to elect a Republican Congress in order to back up and support the President, but even if they should in this way impose upon some credulous voters on this side of the water, they would impose on no one on the other side.

It is well understood there as well as here that the Republican leaders desire not so much to support the President as to control him. The peoples of the allied countries with whom we are associated against Germany are quite familiar with the significance of elections. They would find it very difficult to believe that the voters of the United States had chosen to support their President by electing to the Congress a majority controlled by those who are not in fact in sympathy with the attitude and action of the administration.

I need not tell you that I am asking your support not for my own sake or for the sake of a political party, but for the sake of the

Nation itself, in order that its inward unity of purpose may be evident to all the world. In ordinary times I would not feel at liberty to make such an appeal to you. In ordinary times divided counsels can be endured without permanent hurt to the country. But these are not ordinary times. If in these critical days it is your wish to sustain me with undivided minds, I beg that you will say so in a way which it will not be possible to misunderstand either here at home or among our associates on the other side of the sea. I submit my difficulties and my hopes to you.

OCTOBER 28, 1918 [TO COLONEL HOUSE]

My deliberate judgment is that our whole weight should be thrown for an armistice which will prevent a renewal of hostilities by Germany but which will be as moderate and reasonable as possible within those limits because it is certain that too much success or security on the part of the Allies will make a genuine peace settlement exceedingly difficult, if not impossible. The position of Haig and Milner and Petain as reported by our commander-in-chief is therefore safer than Foch's. See Baker's despatch of today to commander-in-chief. Foresight is wiser than immediate advantage.

OCTOBER 28, 1918 [TO COLONEL HOUSE]

Much as I should enjoy Paris I think neutral place of meeting much wiser care being taken not to choose a place where either German or English influence would be strong. My preference is for Lausanne.

OCTOBER 29, 1918 [TO COLONEL HOUSE]

Can be no real difficulty about peace terms and interpretation of fourteen points if the Entente statesmen will be perfectly frank with us and have no selfish aims of their own which would in any case alienate us from them altogether. It is the fourteen points that Germany has accepted. England cannot dispense with our friendship in the future and the other Allies cannot without our assistance get their rights as against England. If it is the purpose of the Allied statesmen to nullify my influence force the purpose boldly to the surface and let me speak of it to all the world as I shall. League of nations underlies freedom of the seas and every other part of peace programme so far as I am concerned. I am ready to repudiate any selfish program openly, but assume that the Allies cannot honorably turn the present discussions into a peace conference without me.

Certainly England, France and Italy did not relish an ending of the war on Wilson's terms. But there was little they could do. He had gotten the power of peoples everywhere behind him — except in the United States. Here the old reactionary Republicans under Roosevelt and Lodge were beating down everything that he had built up and paving the way for another World War. Unfortunately, at the time, the people did not listen to Herbert Hoover, who urged "united support for the President. There can be no party policies. It is vital that we have a solid front and sustained leadership. I am for President Wilson's leadership not only in the conduct of the war but also in the negotiations of peace, and afterward in the direction of America's burden in the rehabilitation of the world."

OCTOBER 31, 1918 [TO COLONEL HOUSE]

I fully and sympathetically recognize the exceptional position and necessities of Great Britain with regard to the use of the seas for defense both at home and throughout the Empire and also realize that freedom of the seas needs careful definition and is full of questions upon which there is need of the freest discussion and the most liberal interchange of views, but I am not clear that the Allies definitely accept the principle of freedom of the seas and mean to reserve only the free discussion of definitions and limitations. Please insist that that be made clear before I decide whether to accept the reply or go again to Congress who confidentially will have no sympathy whatever with spending American lives for British naval control.

Freedom of the seas will not have to be discussed with Germany if we agree among ourselves beforehand but will be if we do not. Blockade is one of the many things which will require immediate redefinition in view of the many new circumstances of warfare developed by this war. There is no danger of its being abolished.

NOVEMBER 3, 1918 [TO COLONEL HOUSE]

I suggest that if the English cannot rely on our friendship and good faith and accept the principle of freedom of the seas, you urge that they can count on the certainty of our using our present great equipment to build up the strongest navy our resources permit as our people have long desired.

In spite of Wilson's appeal to return a Democratic Congress (or because of it) the Republicans won both houses in Congress. Tough days were ahead for Wilson — and the world. William Howard Taft wrote in the Philadelphia Public Ledger: *"The people will hold the Republican majorities to a strict accountability for the way in which they use their power." A rejection of the treaty would not be countenanced "for any but the gravest reasons."*

CHAPTER TWENTY-ONE

Making Democracy Safe for the World

❯❯❰❰❮❯❯❰❰❮❯❯❰❰❮❯❯❰❰❮❯❯❰❰❮❯❯❰❰❮❯❯❰❰❮❯❯❰❰❮❯❯❰❰❮❯❯❰❰❮❯❯❰❰❮❯❯❰❰❮

Nᴏᴠᴇᴍʙᴇʀ 11, 1918 [ᴛᴏ Cᴏɴɢʀᴇss]

The German authorities who have, at the invitation of the Supreme War Council, been in communication with Marshal Foch
have accepted and signed the terms of armistice which he was
authorized and instructed to communicate to them.

The war thus comes to an end; for, having accepted these terms
of armistice, it will be impossible for the German command to
renew it.

It is not now possible to assess the consequences of this great consummation. We know only that this tragical war, whose consuming
flames swept from one nation to another until all the world was on
fire, is at an end and that it was the privilege of our own people to
enter it at its most critical juncture in such fashion and in such force
as to contribute in a way of which we are all deeply proud to the
great result.

We know, too, that the object of the war is attained; the object
upon which all free men had set their hearts; and attained with a
sweeping completeness which even now we do not realize. Armed
imperialism such as the men conceived who were but yesterday the
masters of Germany is at an end, its illicit ambitions engulfed in
black disaster.

Who will now seek to revive it? The arbitrary power of the military caste of Germany which once could secretly and of its own
single choice disturb the peace of the world is discredited and destroyed. And more than that — much more than that — has been accomplished.

The great nations which associated themselves to destroy it have now definitely united in the common purpose to set up such a peace as will satisfy the longing of the whole world for disinterested justice, embodied in settlements which are based upon something much better and much more lasting than the selfish competitive interests of powerful states.

The humane temper and intention of the victorious Governments has already been manifested in a very practical way. Their representatives in the Supreme War Council at Versailles have by unanimous resolution assured the peoples of the Central Empires that everything that is possible in the circumstances will be done to supply them with food and relieve the distressing want that is in so many places threatening their very lives; and steps are to be taken immediately to organize these efforts at relief in the same systematic manner that they were organized in the case of Belgium. By the use of the idle tonnage of the Central Empires it ought presently to be possible to lift the fear of utter misery from their oppressed populations and set their minds and energies free for the great and hazardous tasks of political reconstruction which now face them on every hand.

Hunger does not breed reform; it breeds madness and all the ugly distempers that make an ordered life impossible.

For with the fall of the ancient governments which rested like an incubus upon the peoples of the Central Empires has come political change not merely, but revolution. There is here matter for no small anxiety and misgiving. When peace is made, upon whose promises and engagements besides our own is it to rest?

Let us be perfectly frank with ourselves and admit that these questions cannot be satisfactorily answered now or at once.

But the moral is not that there is little hope of an early answer that will suffice. It is only that we must be patient and helpful and mindful above all of the great hope and confidence that lie at the heart of what is taking place.

Excesses accomplish nothing. Unhappy Russia has furnished abundant recent proof of that. Disorder immediately defeats itself. If excesses should occur, if disorder should for a time raise its head, a sober second thought will follow and a day of constructive action, if we help and do not hinder.

The present and all that it holds belong to the nations and the peoples who preserve their self-control and the orderly processes of their governments; the future to those who prove themselves the true friends of mankind.

To conquer with arms is to make only a temporary conquest; to conquer the world by earning its esteem is to make permanent conquest.

I am confident that the nations that have learned the discipline of freedom and that have settled with self-possession to its ordered practice are now about to make conquest of the world by the sheer power of example and of friendly helpfulness.

The peoples who have but just come out from under the yoke of arbitrary government and who are now coming at last into their freedom will never find the treasures of liberty they are in search of if they look for them by the light of the torch. They will find that every pathway that is stained with the blood of their own brothers leads to the wilderness, not to the seat of their hope. They are now face to face with their initial test.

We must hold the light steady until they find themselves.

And in the meantime, if it be possible, we must establish a peace that will justly define their place among the nations, remove all fear of their neighbors and of their former masters, and enable them to live in security and contentment when they have set their own affairs in order. I, for one, do not doubt their purpose or their capacity. There are some happy signs that they know and will choose the way of self-control and peaceful accommodation. If they do, we shall put our aid at their disposal in every way that we can. If they do not, we must await with patience and sympathy the awakening and recovery that will assuredly come at last.

NOVEMBER 16, 1918 [TO COLONEL HOUSE]

I infer that French and English leaders desire to exclude me from the Conference for fear I might there lead the weaker nations against them. If I were to come to the seat of the Conference and remain outside I would be merely the centre of a sort of sublimated lobby. All weak parties would resort to me and there would be exactly the same jealousy that was excited by the Germans addressing themselves exclusively to me. I play the same part in our government that the prime ministers play in theirs. The fact that I am head of the state is of no practical consequence. No point of dignity must prevent our obtaining the results we have set our hearts upon and must have. It is universally expected and generally desired here that I should attend the conference, but I believe that no one would wish me to sit by and try to steer from the outside. I am thrown into complete confusion by the change of program. The program proposed for me by Clemenceau, George, Reading, and the rest seems to me a way of pocketing me. I hope you will be very shy of their advice and give me your own independent judgment after reconsideration.

NOVEMBER 18, 1918 [TO SECRETARY OF STATE LANSING]

Please express to the French and British authorities our hope and expectation that they will entirely remove the present political censorship upon American press dispatches. Now that the argument of military necessity no longer obtains, there can be no good reason why the character of the political information supplied to our people should be determined by the British and French Governments, and there is danger of a very serious revulsion of feeling on this side of the water, if such a censorship is continued. I hope that you will press the matter very earnestly and very promptly.

NOVEMBER 20, 1918 [TO SENATOR HENRY L. MYERS]

I think I need not tell you my own cordial feeling towards Mr. Bryan. I should have entire confidence in his principles and in his influence at the conference, but I feel that it is our duty to keep in mind, particularly at this time when all the world is a bit abnormal in its acute sensibilities, the reactions of the public mind of the several countries concerned. Mr. Bryan is softhearted, and the world just now is very hard-hearted. It would render a very large and influential body of our public opinion very uneasy if they thought that

peace was to be approached in the spirit which they would attribute
to Mr. Bryan. I think it highly important to hold opinion steady and
calm, and for that reason I do not think that it would be wise to
include Mr. Bryan among the commissioners, much as it would
personally gratify me to do so.

NOVEMBER 22, 1918 [TO FRANK W. MORRISON]

I have received a great many messages besides your own very
interesting and persuasive message with regard to appointing a representative of labor on the Peace Commission, and have of course
given the matter the most serious consideration.

I have at the same time received equally strong appeals to appoint
a representative of the agricultural interests of the country, a representative of the socialistic bodies of the country, a representative of
the women of the country, and many other similar suggestions. I
am not putting all of these upon a par. I am merely illustrating the
fact that many special bodies and interests of our complex nation
have felt, and felt very naturally, a desire to have special spokesmen
among the peace delegates.

I must say, however, that my own feeling is that the peace delegates should represent no portion of our people in particular, but
the country as a whole, and that it was unwise to make any selection
on the ground that the man selected represented a particular group
or interest, for after all each interest is, or should be, related to the
whole, and no proper representative of the country could fail to
have in mind the great and all-pervasive interest of labor or of any
other great body of humanity.

NOVEMBER 25, 1918

*The question of the appointment of Elihu Root to the peace dele-
gation had been raised.*

Of course I realize the force of the recommendation which Mr.
William McAdoo urges, but I could not think of appointing Mr.
Root, because I have had more opportunities than he has had of
knowing just how hopeless a reactionary he is. I think his appointment would discourage every liberal element in the world.

NOVEMBER 27, 1918 [TO BERNARD M. BARUCH]

I hope you have felt how entirely you have won my confidence not only, but my affection, and how I have learned to value your counsel and your assistance. It has been a delightful experience to know you and to work with you, and I have learned to have the highest admiration for your ability and your character.

But your letter sounds too much like a goodbye. I do not mean to let you go yet if I can help it, because there is much remaining to be done, and I do not like to feel that I am going away and leaving it to be done by inexperienced hands. We will have a talk about this.

NOVEMBER 28, 1918 [ADDRESS TO CONGRESS]

The past is secure, but the future is doubtful, and there are so many questions intimately associated with justice that are to be solved at the peace table and by the commissions which no doubt will be arranged for at the peace table, that I feel in one sense as if our work of justice had just begun.

And the embarrassment in that connection is this. It is one thing to give a people its right of self-determination, but it is another to enter into its internal affairs and get satisfactory guarantees of the use it will make of its independence and its power, because that, in a way, involves a kind of supervision which is hateful to the people concerned and difficult to those who undertake it.

There cannot be any peace with a constantly recurring sense of injustice. And therefore we have this challenge to put to the peoples who will be concerned with the settlement.

Do you, or do you not, truly desire permanent peace, and are you ready to pay the price — the only price — which will secure it?

It will be awkward for them to answer that question except in the affirmative, and impossible for them to answer it genuinely in the affirmative unless they intend that every race shall have justice. So that I think the probability is that the more plainly we speak — I do not mean the more harshly — but the more plainly and candidly we speak, the more probable it will be that we shall arrive at a just settlement.

DECEMBER 2, 1918 [ADDRESS TO CONGRESS]

I welcome this occasion to announce to the Congress my purpose to join in Paris the representatives of the governments with which we have been associated in the war against the Central Empires for the purpose of discussing with them the main features of the treaty of peace. I realize the great inconveniences that will attend my leaving the country, particularly at this time, but the conclusion that it was my paramount duty to go has been forced upon me by considerations which I hope will seem as conclusive to you as they have seemed to me.

The peace settlements which are now to be agreed upon are of transcendent importance both to us and to the rest of the world, and I know of no business or interest which should take precedence of them.

I shall be in close touch with you and with affairs on this side of the water, and you will know all that I do. At my request, the French and English Governments have absolutely removed the censorship of cable news which until within a fortnight they had maintained and there is now no censorship whatever exercised at this end except upon attempted trade communications with enemy countries.

May I not hope that in the delicate tasks I shall have to perform on the other side of the sea, in my efforts truly and faithfully to interpret the principles and purposes of the country we love, I may have the encouragement and the added strength of your united support?

I realize the magnitude and difficulty of the duty I am undertaking; I am poignantly aware of its grave responsibilities. I can have no private thought or purpose of my own in performing such an errand. I go to give the best that is in me to the common settlements which I must now assist in arriving at in conference with the other working heads of the associated Governments.

I shall count upon your friendly countenance and encouragement. I shall make my absence as brief as possible and shall hope to return with the happy assurance that it has been possible to translate into action the great ideals for which America has striven.

On December 4, 1918, Wilson sailed for Europe to attend the Peace Conference. As the George Washington *crossed the Atlantic, in many ways going from the New World to the Old, it was symbolical of the ushering in of a new age in world history.*

Wilson's words had caught the imagination of the world, even of the German people. They had been more powerful in ending the war than Foch's soldiers. The cause of the Allies had been lifted out of naked imperialism to a spiritual level.

And with his ability to tell what he thought, believed and hoped, perhaps more powerfully than anyone who ever lived, Wilson was now faced with the task of trying to translate these things into action.

He was not fooled as to the difficulty of the task. Many an hour he strode alone on the deck of the George Washington *— thinking, thinking, thinking.*

As the boat neared Europe, Wilson called the American delegation together in his cabin and pointed out to them that, as the only "disinterested" group at the Conference, it was up to them to "follow the opinions of mankind and to express the will of the people rather than that of their leaders at the Conference," and that their decisions must rest upon this opinion of mankind and "not upon the previous determinations and diplomatic schemes of the assembled representatives." Above all there must be an organization, a League of Nations, to give both security and elasticity to the settlements, and to make easier alterations in them after the violent passions engendered by the war had subsided.

"Tell me what is right," he told his experts, "and I'll fight for it. Give me a guaranteed position." About a League of Nations he said, "If it won't work, it must be made to work." Through a League it was necessary to work for a new order, "agreeably if we can, disagreeably if we must."

Wilson knew what was needed. There were two great central ideas to his program, both American in their origin. First, the right of "self-determination" of peoples, which is nothing more than that government must rest upon the "consent of the governed." Second, the ob-

ligation to co-operate in a world association for mutual aid and protection and for the elimination of wars. This is simply the extension of liberty beyond the individual to the group. He had said on July 4, 1918:

These great objects can be put in a single sentence. What we seek is the reign of law, based upon the consent of the governed and sustained by the organized opinion of mankind.

In essence this is the same thing that Lincoln had said in his "government of the people, by the people, for the people." Wilson had gone on:

People are not to be bartered about from sovereignty to sovereignty — as if they were mere chattels and pawns of a game.

Every territorial settlement involved in this war must be made in the interest and for the benefit of the populations concerned.

Self-determination is an imperative principle of action which statesmen will henceforth ignore at their peril.

Wilson arrived at Paris on December 14, 1918. In the next few weeks he toured Europe, making speeches in which he set forth his ideas. Back on May 18, 1918, he had said:

If you could catch some of these voices that speak of the utter longing of the oppressed and helpless peoples all over the world and hear something like the "Battle Hymn of the Republic," hear the feet of the great hosts of liberty going to set them free, to set their minds free, to set their children free, then you would know what comes into the hearts of those who are trying to contribute all the brains and power they have to this great enterprise of liberty.

That is what Wilson wanted, that is what he thought the United States of America wanted — and the people, the great majority of them, in their hearts, did and do. It was simply passing on to a nation the same chance that an individual has — to be noble rather than great. It was a vision of great states seeking not their own self-ag-

grandizement, but serving humanity, and a new international relationship founded upon that spirit.

It was wanting to give to Germany and all conquered peoples what the United States has recently given to Japan in the treaty with her.

This idea that a great nation is a servant rather than a master of mankind is at the exact polar opposite of the notion of national greatness to subject other nations — a notion that came to complete fruition in Hitlerism.

Thus it was that Wilson thought of America — not in terms of a great political power, nor of a rich nation, but in terms of moral leadership and service to humanity. He had said back on April 2, 1917:

We have no selfish ends to serve. We desire no conquest, no dominion. We seek no indemnities for ourselves, no material compensation for the sacrifices we shall freely make. We are but one of the champions of mankind. We shall be satisfied when those rights have been made as secure as the faith and the freedom of nations can make them.

Opposed to this was a totally different world that was controlled by traditions of many centuries' making. It was used to diplomacy in which there was a lot of genteel talk, but back of which were secret treaties, private understandings, trades and jockeying. Nobody trusted anybody. The Bolshevists when they took over the government of Russia published all of the secret treaties in which Russia had participated. This really brought to light what had been going on behind the scenes. Wilson felt that the United States was not bound by these treaties.

The Peace Conference did not assemble until January 12, 1919. In the meantime Europe, suffering from war weariness had a chance to get rid of its idealistic feelings and revert to greediness. The leaders saw to that. Lloyd George was re-elected to the premiership on a campaign built around the slogan "Be tough on Germany." Winston Churchill said that he "believed in" the League of Nations but it was no substitute for the British fleet and that none of Germany's colonies would go back to Germany.

At about the same time Senator Henry Cabot Lodge was saying in the United States that Germany should be made to pay up to the absolute level of her ability and "the United States must have its proper and proportional share."

Clemenceau was giving lip service to the League but telling the French Chamber of Deputies that France must have a peace which would forever keep Germany crushed.

DECEMBER 29, 1918 [ON MORAL FORCE]

It is moral force that is irresistible. It is moral force as much as physical that has defeated the effort to subdue the world. Words have cut as deep as the sword. The knowledge that wrong was being attempted has aroused the nations. They have gone out like men upon a crusade. No other cause could have drawn so many nations together.

DECEMBER 30, 1918 [ADDRESS AT LONDON]

It is very interesting that the Lord Mayor should have referred in his address to a vital circumstance in our friendship. He referred to the fact that our men and your men had fought side by side in the great battles in France, but there was more than that in it. *For the first time, upon such a scale at any rate, they fought under a common commander.* That is the advance which we have made over previous times, and what I have been particularly interested in has been the generosity of spirit with which that unity of command has been assented to. It takes a real man to subordinate himself. It takes a real soldier to know that unity of command is the secret of success, and that unity of command did swing the power of the nations into a mighty force. I think we all must have felt the new momentum which got into all the armies so soon as they became a single army, and we felt that we had overcome one of the most serious obstacles in the strength of the enemy, that he had unity of command and could strike where he would with a common plan and we could not.

And with that unity of command there rose the unity of spirit.

The minute we consented to cooperate our hearts were drawn together in the cooperation. So, from the military side we have given ourselves an example for the years to come; not that in the years to come we must submit to a unity of command, but it does seem to me that in the years to come we must plan a unity of purpose, and in that unity of purpose we shall find that great recompense, the strengthening of our spirits in everything that we do.

There is nothing so hampering and nothing so demeaning as jealousy. It is a canker. It is a canker in the heart not only, but it is a canker in the counting-room; it is a canker throughout all the processes of civilization. Having now seen that we can fight shoulder to shoulder, we will continue to advance shoulder to shoulder, and I think that you will find that the people of the United States are not the least eager of the parties.

I remember hearing a story of a warning which one of your Australian soldiers gave to one of ours. Our soldiers were considered by the older men a bit rash when they went in. I understand that even the Australians said that our men were a "bit rough," and on one occasion a friendly Australian said to one of our men, "Man, a barrage is not a thing meant to lean up against." They were a little bit inclined to lean up against the barrage, and yet I must confide to you that I was a bit proud of them for it. They had come over to get at the enemy, and they did not know why they should delay.

And now that there is no common enemy except distrust and marring of plans, we can all feel the same eagerness in the new comradeship, and can feel that there is a common enterprise for it. For, after all, though we boast of the material sides of our civilization, they are merely meant to support the spiritual side.

We are not men because we have skill of hand, but we are men because we have elevation of spirit. It is in the spirit that we live and not in the task of the day.

A friend of mine said very truly that when peace is conducted in the spirit of war, there will be no war; when business is done with the point of view of the soldier, that he is serving his country, then business will be as histrionic as war. And I believe that from generation to generation conceptions of that sort are getting more and more currency and that men are beginning to see, not perhaps a golden age, but at any rate an age which is brightening from decade to decade and may lead us some time to an elevation from which we can see the things for which the heart of mankind has longed.

Never before in the history of the world, I believe, has there been such a keen international consciousness as there is now. Men all over the world know that they have been embarrassed by national antagonisms and that the interest of each is the interest of all, and that men as men are the objects of government and international arrangements. There is a great voice of humanity abroad in the world just now *which he who cannot hear is deaf.* There is a great compulsion of the common conscience now in existence which if any statesman resist he has gained the most unenviable eminence in history.

We are not obeying the mandates of parties or of politics. We are obeying the mandates of humanity. That is the reason why it seems to me that the things that are most often in our minds are the least significant.

I am not hopeful that the individual items of the settlements which we are about to attempt will be altogether satisfactory. One has but to apply his mind to any one of the questions of boundary and of altered sovereignty and of racial aspiration to do something more than conjecture that there is no man and no body of men who know just how it ought to be settled. Yet if we are to make unsatisfactory settlements, we must see to it that they are rendered more and more satisfactory by the subsequent adjustments which are made possible.

So that we must provide a machinery of readjustment in order that we may have a machinery of good will and of friendship.

Friendship must have a machinery. If I cannot correspond with you, if I cannot learn your mind, if I cannot co-operate with you, I cannot be your friend, and if the world is to remain a body of friends it must have the means of friendship, the means of constant friendly intercourse, the means of constant watchfulness over the common interest — not making it necessary to make a great effort upon some great occasion and confer with one another, but have an easy and constant method of conference, so that troubles may be taken when they are little and not allowed to grow until they are big.

It is the wish to come together that is more than half of the process. This is a doctrine which ought to be easy of comprehension in a great commercial center like this. You cannot trade with men who suspect you. You cannot establish commercial and industrial relations with those who do not trust you. Good will is the forerunner of trade, and trade is the great amicable instrument of the world on that account.

JANUARY 3, 1919 [ON THE WAY TO CONQUER]

I have been reflecting in these recent days about a colossal blunder that has just been made — the blunder of force by the Central Empires. If Germany had waited a single generation, she would have had a commercial empire of the world. She was not willing to conquer by skill, by enterprise, by commercial success. She must needs attempt to conquer by arms, and the world will always acclaim the fact that it is impossible to conquer it by arms; that the only thing that conquers it is the sort of service which can be rendered in trade, in intercourse, in friendship, and that there is no conquering power which can suppress the freedom of the human spirit.

The distinguishing fact of this war is that great empires have gone to pieces, and the characteristic of those empires was that they held different peoples reluctantly together under the coercion of force and the guidance of intrigue. The great difficulty among such States as those of the Balkans has been that they were always accessible to secret influence; that they were always being penetrated by intrigue of one sort or another; and that north of them lay disturbed populations which were held together, not by sympathy and friendship, but by the coercive force of a military power.

Now the intrigue is checked and the bands are broken, and what are we going to do to provide a new cement to hold these people together?

They have not been accustomed to being independent. They must now be independent. I am sure that you recognize the principle as I do that it is not our privilege to say what sort of government they shall set up, but we are friends of these people and it is our duty as their friends to see to it that some kind of protection is thrown around them, something supplied which will hold them together. There is only one thing that holds nations together, if you exclude force, and that is friendship and good will. The only thing that binds men together is friendship and by the same token the only thing that binds nations together is friendship.

Therefore, our task at Paris is *to organize the friendship of the world,* to see to it that all the moral forces that make for right and justice and liberty are united and are given a vital organization to which the peoples of the world will readily and gladly respond.

In other words, our task is no less colossal than this, to set up a new international psychology, to have a new atmosphere.

JANUARY 13, 1919 [TO CONGRESS]

I cannot too earnestly or solemnly urge upon the Congress the appropriation for which Mr. Hoover has asked for the administration of food relief. Food relief is now the key to the whole European situation and to the solutions of peace.

Bolshevism is steadily advancing westward, is poisoning Germany. It cannot be stopped by force, but it can be stopped by food; and all the leaders with whom I am in conference agree that concerted action in this matter is of immediate and vital importance. The money will not be spent for food for Germany itself, because Germany can buy its food; but it will be spent for financing the movement of food to our real friends in Poland and to the people of the liberated units of the Austro-Hungarian Empire and to our associates in the Balkans. I do not see how we can find definite powers with whom to conclude peace unless this means of stemming the tide of anarchism be employed.

CHAPTER TWENTY-TWO

The Machinery for Making the World Safe

Even before the Peace Conference got under way, it was evident that most of the nations were there to get their handout. "President Wilson could help give the nations an instrumentality for expressing their good will," wrote Ray Stannard Baker, "but he could not give them good will."

In getting their spoils, the leaders of the nations wanted to be at it in the time-honored way. A group of diplomats, each representing a selfish interest, in accordance with this way, would meet in secret and by trades and combinations come at last to a settlement. Then they would give out to the public high-sounding pronouncements and hope to maintain the conclusions that they had arrived at by treaties, sometimes secret, and by balances of power based on military might.

Opposed to this, Wilson wanted to start with general principles of right and justice and have the principles applied in the settlements not by diplomats but by experts — geographers, ethnologists, economists — who would try to help in arriving at a just decision. This was the sort of staff that he took to Paris. He had been preparing for this since the United States entered the war.

Probably one of the most difficult problems that faced the conference was that of news censorship. Wilson wanted everything possible in the open and turned over to the press. The French wanted complete censorship. No clear-cut decision was made on this, and a leakage (probably deliberate) to the French press gave most of the news that came out of the conference a French slant. In this particu-

lar case Wilson probably made his chief mistake. By not being able to appeal to the people over the heads of the diplomats with whom he was dealing, he lost his most effective weapon.

From the very start his chief insistence was that the League of Nations should be a part of the treaty. When his opponents found that they could not sway him on this, they tried to circumvent him by getting the spoils first and then accepting the League later. In the end England and France and Japan got most of the spoils that they asked for because Wilson, harried in the conference and back in the United States, had to yield, hoping that the League of Nations, later, might correct the inequities.

This chapter will only attempt to give Wilson's viewpoints on some of the major issues. These will illustrate by analogy, it is hoped, his attitude on the entire question of peace.

JANUARY 18, 1919

Marshal Foch suggested that an American army be sent through Poland and on into Russia to crush Bolshevism. Wilson refused on the ground that "it was unwise to take action in a military form before the Powers were agreed upon a course of action for checking Bolshevism as a social and political danger."

Most power politicians have not yet realized the wisdom of his reply.

JANUARY 22, 1919 [WILSON WARNED THE CONFERENCE]

I am seeking only to face realities. Victory would mean peace forced upon the loser, a victor's terms imposed upon the vanquished. It would be accepted in humiliation, under duress, at an intolerable sacrifice, and would leave a sting, a resentment, a bitter memory upon which terms of peace would rest, not permanently, but only as upon quicksand.

JANUARY 25, 1919 [ADDRESS TO THE PEACE CONFERENCE]

We have assembled for two purposes, to make the present settlements which have been rendered necessary by this war, and also to secure the peace of the world, not only by the present settlements, but by the arrangements we shall make at this conference for its maintenance.

The League of Nations seems to me to be necessary for both of these purposes. There are many complicated questions connected with the present settlements which perhaps cannot be successfully worked out to an ultimate issue by the decisions we shall arrive at here. I can easily conceive that many of these settlements will need subsequent reconsideration, that many of the decisions we make shall need subsequent alteration in some degree; for, if I may judge by my own study of some of these questions, they are not susceptible of confident judgments at present.

It is, therefore, necessary that we should set up some machinery by which the work of this conference should be rendered complete.

Settlements may be temporary, but the action of the nations in the interest of peace and justice must be permanent. *We can set up permanent processes. We may not be able to set up permanent decisions.* Therefore, it seems to me that we must take, so far as we can, a picture of the world into our minds.

Is it not a startling circumstance, for one thing, that the great discoveries of science, that the quiet studies of men in laboratories, that the thoughtful developments which have taken place in quiet lecture rooms, have now been turned to the destruction of civilization?

The powers of destruction have not so much multiplied as gained facility. The enemy whom we have just overcome had at his seats of learning some of the principal centers of scientific study and discovery, and he used them in order to make destruction sudden and complete; and only the watchful, continuous cooperation of men can see to it that science as well as armed men is kept within the harness of civilization.

In coming into this war the United States never for a moment thought that she was intervening in the politics of Europe or the politics of Asia or the politics of any part of the world. Her thought was that all the world had not become conscious that there was a single cause which turned upon the issues of this war. That was the cause of justice and of liberty for men of every kind and place.

Therefore, the United States should feel that its part in this war had been played in vain if there ensued upon it merely a body of European settlements. It would feel that it could not take part in guaranteeing those European settlements unless that guarantee involved the continuous superintendence of the peace of the world by the associated nations of the world.

Therefore, it seems to me that we must concert our best judgment in order to make this League of Nations a vital thing — not merely a formal thing, not an occasional thing, not a thing sometimes called into life to meet an exigency, but always functioning in watchful attendance upon the interests of the nations — and that its continuity should be a vital continuity; that it should have functions that are continuing functions and that do not permit an intermission of its watchfulness and of its labor; that it should be the eye of the nations to keep watch upon the common interest, an eye that does not slumber, an eye that is everywhere watchful and attentive.

And if we do not make it vital, what shall we do?

We shall disappoint the expectations of the peoples. The fortunes of mankind are now in the hands of the plain people of the whole world. Satisfy them, and you have justified their confidence not only, but established peace. Fail to satisfy them, and no arrangement that you can make will either set up or steady the peace of the world.

JANUARY 27, 1919 [ON MANDATES]

Of course the big move by the victors was to divide up the colonial possessions of Germany. Wilson tried to head this off by turning over various "backward" peoples as "mandates" or wards who, when the time was right, should be given their freedom.

The basis of this idea was the feeling which had sprung up all over the world against further annexation. Yet, if the Colonies were not to be returned to Germany (as all agreed), some other basis must be found to develop them and to take care of the inhabitants of these backward territories. It was with this object that the idea of administration through mandatories acting on behalf of the

League of Nations arose. Some institution must be found to carry out the ideas all had in mind, namely, the development of the country for the benefit of those already in it and for the advantage of those who would live there later.

The purpose was to serve the people in undeveloped parts, to safeguard them against abuses such as had occurred under German administrations. Further, where people and territories were undeveloped, to assure their development so that, when the time came, their interests, as they saw them, might qualify them to express a wish as to their ultimate relations — perhaps lead them to desire their union with the mandatory power.

In the first place, the League of Nations would lay down certain general principles in the mandate, namely, that districts be administered primarily with a view to the betterment of the conditions of the inhabitants. Secondly, that there should be no discrimination against members of the League of Nations so as to restrict economic access to the resources of the districts. All countries would pay the same duties, all would have the same right of access.

JANUARY 28, 1919 [ON DIRECT ANNEXATION]

The world would say that the Great Powers first portioned out the helpless parts of the world, and then formed a League of Nations. The crude fact would be that each of these parts of the world had been assigned to one of the Great Powers. The world would not accept such action: it would make the League of Nations impossible and they [all countries] would have to return to the system of competitive armaments, with accumulating debts and the burden of great armies.

When it became definite that Wilson was not going to give in, the opponents shifted their method of attack. The French began an attack on Wilson in the newspapers. They began to comment on his "impractical idealism." The various prime ministers of the British dominions attacked him also. In a measure he stopped the direct attack in the French press but he could not stop the indirect one.

From about February 1, more and more important problems were assigned to the experts for investigation and recommendation, and it soon became the practice, where the experts were in agreement, to accept their findings without further comment. Probably three quarters, perhaps a larger proportion, of the treaty provisions were settled in this way.

The trouble was that the major problems of the peace were not turned over to experts — the great powers prevented it.

But progress was made. More important, the wall of the old method was breached.

Wilson believed in great force as much as Clemenceau. But his approach was different. "Where the great force lies," he said, "there must be the sanction of peace." But his great message to the world was that this power should be used for the service, not the oppression, of humanity; for the benefit of the world, not the interests of particular states; in the performance of duties, not the assertion of rights. He thought it "excellent to have a giant's strength but tyrannous to use it like a giant."

February 3, 1919

No problem confronting the Conference was thornier than that of armaments. France, with Germany just across an invisible line, wasn't willing to give up her arms. She wanted a huge international army, staffed by French officers, to protect her.

Wilson had included disarmament among his Fourteen Points. He included it as absolutely basic in all of his drafts for a Covenant for the League of Nations. He said of France:

Hers was the immediate peril. Hers was the constant dread. I do not need to point out to you that east of you in Europe the future is full of questions. Beyond the Rhine, across Germany, across Poland, across Russia, across Asia, there are questions unanswered. France stands in the presence of these threatening and unanswered questions — *threatening because unanswered* — stands waiting for the solution of matters which touch her directly, intimately and constantly, and if she must stand alone, what must she do?

The trouble was that France saw safety only in arms; Wilson saw it in co-operation of nations "which will make it unnecessary, in the future, to maintain those crushing armaments which make the peoples suffer almost as much in peace as they suffered in war."

France wanted to cripple Germany permanently — militarily, politically and economically. But above all she wanted "safety" — not knowing that you cannot get it as she was trying. In reply to her demands Wilson said:

We must do everything that is possible to ensure the safety of the world. I know how France has suffered, and I know that she wishes to obtain the best guarantees possible before she enters the League, and everything that we can do in this direction we shall do, but we cannot accept proposals which are in direct contradiction to our Constitution. The only method by which we can achieve this end lies in our having confidence in the good faith of the nations who belong to the League. There must be between them a cordial agreement and good will.

In the end Germany was disarmed. As to the Allies' disarming, there were provisions for future inquiry by the League of Nations, but this was a long way off.

FEBRUARY 8, 1919 [ON SELF-DETERMINATION]

The point of view of the United States of America was indifferent to the claims both of Great Britain and France over peoples unless those peoples wanted them. One of the fundamental principles to which the United States of America adhered was the consent of the governed. This was ingrained in the thought of the United States of America.

In addition to self-determination, Wilson wanted a settlement based on facts, not secret diplomacy. He suggested that commissions be sent to the various countries to find out what the people there wanted and to come back and report to the conference. These commissions were to be composed of an equal number of French, British, Italian and American representatives. Wilson got the best men he

*could. The French and British, while agreeing "in principle," stalled
and finally refused to appoint members of the commissions.*

They had grave doubts as to what the reports would be.

FEBRUARY 14, 1919

*Wilson sent a cablegram to the Foreign Relations Committee of
the Senate and the Foreign Affairs Committee of the House:*

Last night the committee of the conference charged with the duty
of drafting a constitution for a League of Nations concluded its
work.

The committee which drafted these articles was fairly representative of the world.

Each article was passed only after the most careful examination by
each member of the committee. There is a good and sufficient reason
for the phraseology and substance of each article. I request that I be
permitted to go over with you article by article the constitution before this part of the work of the conference is made the subject of
debate of Congress. With this in view I request that you dine with
me at the White House as soon after I arrive in the United States as
my engagements permit.

FEBRUARY 14, 1919 [ADDRESS TO THE PEACE CONFERENCE ON THE
LEAGUE OF NATIONS]

Now, as to the character of the document, I think you will see at
once that it is, after all, very simple, and in nothing so simple as in
the structure which it suggests for the League of Nations — a body
of delegates, an executive council, and a permanent secretariat.

When it came to the question of determining the character of the
representation in the body of delegates, we were all aware of a feeling which is current throughout the world. Inasmuch as I am stating
it in the presence of official representatives of the various Governments here present, including myself, I may say that there is a universal feeling that the world cannot rest satisfied with merely official
guidance.

There reached us through many channels the feeling that if the
deliberative body of the League was merely to be a body of officials

representing the various Governments, the peoples of the world would not be sure that some of the mistakes which preoccupied officials had admittedly made might not be repeated. It was impossible to conceive a method or an assembly so large and various as to be really representative of the great body of the peoples of the world, because, as I roughly reckon it, we represent as we sit around this table more than twelve hundred million people.

You cannot have a representative assembly of twelve hundred million people, but if you leave it to each Government to have, if it pleased, one or two or three representatives, though only a single vote, it may vary its representation from time to time, not only, but it may originate the choice of its several representatives, if it should have several, in different ways. Therefore, we thought that this was a proper and a very prudent concession to the practically universal opinion of plain men everywhere that they wanted the door left open to a variety of representation instead of being confined to a single official body with which they might or might not find themselves in sympathy.

And you will notice that this body has unlimited rights of discussion — I mean of discussion of anything that falls within the field of international relationship — and that it is specially agreed that war or international misunderstandings or anything that may lead to friction and trouble is everybody's business, because it may affect the peace of the world.

And in order to safeguard the popular power so far as we could of this representative body it is provided that when a subject is submitted, not to arbitration, but to discussion by the executive council, it can upon the initiative of either one of the parties to the dispute be drawn out of the executive council into the larger forum of the general body of delegates, because throughout this instrument we are depending primarily and chiefly upon one great force, *and that is the moral force of the public opinion of the world* — the cleansing and clarifying and compelling influences of publicity — so that intrigues can no longer have their coverts, so that designs that are sinister can at any time be drawn into the open, so that those things that are destroyed by the light may be properly destroyed by the over-whelming light of the universal expression of the condemnation of the world.

Armed force is in the background in this program, but it *is* in the background, and if the moral force of the world will not suffice, the physical force of the world shall. But that is the last resort, because this is intended as a constitution of peace, not as a league of war.

The simplicity of the document seems to me to be one of its chief virtues, because, speaking for myself, I was unable to foresee the variety of circumstances with which this League would have to deal. I was unable, therefore, to plan all the machinery that might be necessary to meet differing and unexpected contingencies.

Therefore, I should say of this document that it is not a strait-jacket, *but a vehicle of life.* A living thing is born, and we must see to it that the clothes we put upon it do not hamper it — a vehicle of power, but a vehicle in which power may be varied at the discretion of those who exercise it and in accordance with the changing cir-cumstances of the time. And yet, while it is elastic, while it is gen-eral in its terms, it is definite in the one thing that we were called upon to make definite. It is a definite guarantee of peace. It is a definite guarantee by word against aggression. It is a definite guaran-tee against the things which have just come near bringing the whole structure of civilization into ruin. Its purposes do not for a moment lie vague. Its purposes are declared and its powers made unmis-takable.

It is not in contemplation that this should be merely a League to secure the peace of the world. It is a League which can be used for cooperation in any international matter.

That is the significance of the provision introduced concerning labor. There are many ameliorations of labor conditions which can be effected by conference and discussion. I anticipate that there will be a very great usefulness in the bureau of labor which it is contem-plated shall be set up by the League.

While men and women and children who work have been in the background through long ages, and sometimes seemed to be forgotten, while Governments have had their watchful and suspicious eyes upon the maneuvers of one another, while the thought of statesmen has been about structural action and the large transactions of commerce and of finance, now, if I may believe the picture which I see, there comes into the foreground the great body of the laboring people of the world, the men and women and children upon whom the great burden of sustaining the world must from day to day fall, whether we wish it to do so or not; people who go to bed tired and wake up without the stimulation of lively hope.

These people will be drawn into the field of international consultation and help, and will be among the wards of the combined Governments of the world. There is, I take leave to say, a very great step in advance in the mere conception of that.

Then there is an imperative article concerning the publicity of all international agreements. Henceforth no member of the League can claim any agreement valid which it has not registered with the secretary general, in whose office, of course, it will be subject to the examination of anybody representing a member of the League. And the duty is laid upon the secretary general to publish every document of that sort at the earliest possible time.

Then there is a feature about this covenant which to my mind is one of the greatest and most satisfactory advances that has been made. We are done with annexations of helpless people, meant in some instances by some powers to be used merely for exploitation. We recognize in the most solemn manner that the helpless and undeveloped peoples of the world, being in that condition, put an obligation upon us to look after their interests primarily before we use them for our interest; and that in all cases of this sort hereafter it shall be the duty of the League to see that the nations who are assigned as the tutors, advisers and directors of those peoples shall look to their interest and to their development before they look to the interests and material desires of the mandatory nation itself.

There has been no greater advance than this. If you look back upon the history of the world you will see how helpless peoples have too often been a prey to powers that had no conscience in the matter. It has been one of the many distressing revelations of recent years that the great power which has just been happily defeated put intolerable burdens and injustices upon the helpless people of some of the colonies which it annexed to itself; that its interest was rather their extermination than their development; that the desire was to possess their land for European purposes, and not to enjoy their confidence in order that mankind might be lifted in those places to the next higher level. Now, the world, expressing its conscience in law, says there is an end of that. Our consciences shall be applied to this thing. States will be picked out which have already shown that they can exercise a conscience in this matter, and under their tutelage the helpless peoples of the world will come into a new light and into a new hope.

So I think I can say of this document that *it is at one and the same time a practical document and a humane document.* There is a pulse of sympathy in it. There is a compulsion of conscience throughout it. It is practical, and yet it is intended to purify, to rectify, to elevate.

And I want to say that, so far as my observation instructs me, this is in one sense a belated document. I believe that the conscience of the world has long been prepared to express itself in some such way. We are not just now discovering our sympathy for these people and our interest in them. We are simply expressing it, for it has long been felt, and in the administration of the affairs of more than one of the great States represented here — so far as I know, of all the great States that are represented here — that humane impulse has already expressed itself in their dealings with their colonies whose peoples were yet at a low stage of civilization.

We have had many instances of colonies lifted into the sphere of complete self-government. This is not the discovery of a principle. It is the universal application of a principle. It is the agreement of the great nations which have tried to live by these standards in their separate administrations to unite in seeing that their common force and their common thought and intelligence are lent to this great and humane enterprise.

CHAPTER TWENTY-THREE

The People or the "Rulers" in the United States

→⟫⟪←→⟫⟪←→⟫⟪←→⟫⟪←→⟫⟪←→⟫⟪←→⟫⟪←→⟫⟪←→⟫⟪←→⟫⟪←→⟫⟪←→⟫⟪←

Woodrow Wilson returned to the United States on **February 24,** *1919, via the port of Boston, Massachusetts. He was greeted by Governor Calvin Coolidge in these words:*

"We welcome him with a reception more marked than even that which was accorded General George Washington, more united than could have been given at any time during his life to Abraham Lincoln. We welcome him as the representative of a great people, as a great statesman, as one whom we assure we will support in the future in the working out of that destiny as Massachusetts has supported him in the past."

Wilson replied:

I wonder if you are half as glad to see me as I am to see you. It warms my heart to see a great body of my fellow citizens again because in some respects during recent months I have been very lonely, indeed, without your comradeship and counsel, and I tried at every step of the work which fell to me to recall what I was sure would be your counsel with regard to the great matters which were under consideration.

I do not want you to think that I have not been appreciative of the extraordinarily generous reception which was given me on the other side. I cannot tell you the inspiration that came from the sentiments that came out of these simple voices of the crowd. And the proudest thing I have to report to you is that this great country of ours is trusted throughout the world.

The nations of Europe have again and again clashed with one another in competitive interest. It is impossible for men to forget these sharp issues that were drawn between them in times past. They resort to that Nation which has won enviable distinction, being regarded as the friend of mankind. Whenever it is desired to send a small force of soldiers to occupy a piece of territory where it is thought nobody else will be welcome, they ask for American soldiers. And where other soldiers would be looked upon with suspicion and perhaps met with resistance, the American soldier is welcomed with acclaim.

Before this war Europe did not believe in us as she does now. She did not believe in us throughout the first three years of the war. She seems really to have believed that we were holding off because we thought we could make more by staying out than by going in. And all of a sudden, in eighteen short months, the whole verdict is reversed.

There can be but one explanation for it. They saw what we did, that without making a single claim we put all our men and all our means at the disposal of those who were fighting for their homes in the first instance, but for the cause — the cause of human right and justice — and that we went in, not to support their national claims, but to support the great cause which they held in common. And when they saw that America not only held the ideals but acted the ideals, they were converted to America and became firm partisans of those ideals.

And now do you realize that this confidence we have established throughout the world imposes a burden upon us — if you choose to call it a burden. It is one of those burdens which any nation ought to be proud to carry. Any man who resists the present tides that run in the world will find himself thrown upon a shore so high and barren that it will seem as if he had been separated from his human kind forever.

America is the hope of the world. And if she does not justify that hope results are unthinkable. Men will be thrown back upon bitterness of disappointment not only but bitterness of despair. All nations will be set up as hostile camps again.

Think of the picture, think of the utter blackness that would fall on the world. America has failed. America made a little essay at generosity and then withdrew. America said, "We are your friends," but it was only for to-day, not for to-morrow. America said, "Here is our power to vindicate right," and then next day said, "Let right take care of itself and we will take care of ourselves." America said, "We set up light to lead men along the paths of liberty, but we have lowered it — it is intended only to light our own path."

Arrangements of the present peace cannot stand a generation unless they are guaranteed by the united forces of the civilized world.

Wilson was quickly to learn that the new "rulers" — the Republicans in control of Congress with the help of reactionary Democrats — did not, perhaps could not, either understand what he was talking about or go along with his program. With domestic support crumbling — which the leaders of England, France and Italy well knew was happening — the League was being pushed out of the treaty back in Versailles. Wilson hurried back to save it.

When he got there he found that Colonel House and Secretary Lansing, yielding to the pressure, had gone over to the side of those believing that the time was not ready for the League. For one thing, Lloyd George had returned to England and had sent Winston Churchill to Paris to see that that "nonsense," the League, got what it deserved. Wilson took instant action. He sent out this release:

The President said today that the decision made at the Peace Conference at its plenary session, January 25, 1919, to the effect that the establishment of a League of Nations should be made an integral part of the Treaty of Peace, is of final force and that there is no basis whatever for the reports that a change in this decision was contemplated.

The resolution of the League of Nations, adopted January 25, at the plenary session of the Peace Conference, was as follows:

1. It is essential to the maintenance of the world settlement, which the associated nations are now met to establish, that a League of Nations be created to promote international cooperation,

to insure the fulfillment of accepted international obligations, and to provide safeguards against war.

2. This League should be treated as an integral part of the general Treaty of Peace, and should be open to every civilized nation which can be relied upon to promote its objects.

3. The members of the League should periodically meet in international conference, and should have a permanent organization and secretariat to carry on the business of the League in the intervals between the conferences.

APRIL 19, 1919

What President Wilson said about "secret treaties and other subjects at the conference is in the third person (as protocol called for). Yet the words are his.

He did not know and did not feel at liberty to ask whether France and Great Britain considered the treaty (the secret Treaty of London) as consistent with the principles on which the Peace Treaty was being based. He was at liberty to say, however, that he himself did not. To discuss the matter on the basis of the Pact of London would be to adopt as a basis a secret treaty. Yet he would be bound to say to the world that we were establishing a new order in which secret treaties were precluded. The Pact of London was inconsistent with the general principles of the settlement. He knew perfectly well that the Pact of London had been entered into in quite different circumstances, and he did not wish to criticise what had been done. But to suggest that the decision should be taken on the basis of the Treaty of London would draw the United States of America into an impossible situation.

APRIL 22, 1919 [THE SHANTUNG QUESTION]

Japan's claims to Shantung, under a secret treaty with England, disturbed Wilson profoundly. "The central idea of the League of Nations," his statement pointed out, "was that states must support each other even when their interests were not involved. The position in which he would like to see Japan, already the most advanced

*nation in the Far East with the leadership in enterprise and policy,
was that of the leader in the Far East standing out for these new
ideas. There could be no finer nor more politic role for her." Then
he went on:*

What he was after was to attain a more detailed definition as to
how Japan was going to help China as well as to afford an opportunity for investment in railways, etc. He had hoped that by pooling
their interest the several nations that had gained a foothold in China
(a foothold that was to the detriment of China's position in the
World) might forego the special position they had acquired and
that China might be put on the same footing as other nations, as
sooner or later she must certainly be. He believed this to be to the
interest of everyone concerned.

There was a lot of combustible material in China and if flames
were put to it the fire could not be quenched, for China had a population of four hundred million people. It was symptoms of that which
filled him with anxiety.

Baron Makino and Viscount Chinda knew how deep-seated was
the feeling of reverence of China towards Shantung which was the
most sacred Chinese Province and he dreaded starting a flame there
because this reverence was based upon the very best motives and
owing to the traditions of Confucius and the foundations of intellectual development. He did not wish to interfere with treaties.
The war had been undertaken partly in order to establish the sanc-
tity of treaties. Although he yielded to no one in this sentiment
there were cases he felt where treaties ought not to have been
entered into.

*Baron Makino's answer was vague and evasive. The trouble in the
end was the maze of treaties — imposed though they were — in
which China was involved. When the Chinese asked that Shantung
be returned to them, instead of being given to Japan, Wilson then
appealed for the true internationalist point of view — that the
League of Nations take over the problem and settle it.*

If this had been a lone struggle, Wilson might have been able to get justice for China. But there were countless other struggles. It was finally determined to let Japan have certain rights as a mandatory power.

In the United States Wilson had seen the powerful opposition that was building up against him. Ex-President William Howard Taft (whose support of the League is one of the great acts of his life) suggested certain revisions in the League. He now wired Wilson that if these revisions were made, in his opinion the League would get the approval of the Senate. These were: (1) specific recognition of the Monroe Doctrine; (2) provision for withdrawal of America from the League should she wish to later; (3) specific exclusion of domestic questions, such as the tariff and immigration, from the field of disputes open to international jurisdiction; and (4) stipulation that the acceptance of mandates was optional with the designated mandatory. The last one was to enable America to refuse to take a mandate if she wished to avoid the responsibility.

APRIL 23, 1919 [ON THE ADRIATIC QUESTION]

When Italy entered the war she entered upon the basis of a definite, but private, understanding with Great Britain and France, now known as the Pact of London. Since that time the whole face of circumstance has been altered. Many other powers, great and small, have entered the struggle, with no knowledge of that private understanding. The Austro-Hungarian Empire, then the enemy of Europe, and at whose expense the Pact of London was to be kept in the event of victory, has gone to pieces and no longer exists. Not only that. The several parts of that Empire, it is now agreed by Italy and all her associates, are to be erected into independent states and associated in a League of Nations, not with those who were recently our enemies, but with Italy herself and the powers that stood with Italy in the great war for liberty. We are to establish their liberty as well as our own. They are to be among the smaller states whose interests are henceforth to be as scrupulously safeguarded as the interests of the most powerful states.

The war was ended, moreover, by proposing to Germany an armistice and peace which should be founded on certain clearly defined principles which should set up a new order of right and justice. Upon those principles the peace with Germany has been conceived, not only, but formulated. Upon those principles it will be executed. We cannot ask the great body of power to propose and effect peace with Austria and establish a new basis of independence and right in the states which originally constituted the Austro-Hungarian Empire and in the states of the Balkan group on principles of another kind. We must apply the same principles to the settlement of Europe in those quarters that we have applied in the peace with Germany. It was upon the explicit avowal of those principles that the initiative for peace was taken. It is upon them that the whole structure of the peace must rest.

APRIL 28, 1919

The final Covenant, with the revisions suggested by Taft, was unanimously adopted and became a part of the treaty.

APRIL 30, 1919 [ON THE SHANTUNG SETTLEMENT]

The Japanese–Chinese matter has been settled in a way which seems to me as satisfactory as could be got out of the tangle of treaties in which China herself was involved, and it is important that the exact facts should be known.

In the treaty all the rights of Kiao-Chau and in Shantung Province belonging to Germany are to be transferred without reservation to Japan, but Japan voluntarily engages, in answer to questions put in conference, that it will be her immediate policy "to hand back the Shantung Peninsula in full sovereignty to China, retaining only the economic privileges granted to Germany and the right to establish a settlement under the usual conditions at Tsingtao. Owners of the railway will use special police only to insure security for traffic. They will be used for no other purpose. The police force will be composed of Chinese, and such Japanese instructors as the directors of the railway may select will be appointed by the Chinese government." It was understood in addition that inasmuch as the sovereign rights re-ceded to China were to be unqualified, all Japanese troops remaining on the peninsula should be withdrawn at the earliest possible time. Japan thus gets only such rights as an economic concessionaire as are possessed by one or two other great powers and are only too common in China, and the whole future relationship between the two countries falls at once under the Guarantee of the League of Nations of territorial integrity and political independence.

I find a general disposition to look with favor upon the proposal that at an early date through the mediation of the League of Nations all extraordinary foreign rights in China and all spheres of influence should be abrogated by the common consent of all the nations concerned. I regard the assurances given by Japan as very satisfactory in view of the complicated circumstances.

MAY 5, 1919

The Peace Conference at first was political but, inevitably, it became economic. With the world literally falling apart, with starvation spreading everywhere through Germany, Russia, Austria, Poland, with undemobilized armies and staggering debts, the leaders there wrangled for days and weeks over distant coral islands, for colonies in Africa, or over the tearing apart of the Turkish empire.

Wilson saw that this wasn't enough. He wanted something done about the starving peoples (and did it); he wanted to grapple on a sensible basis with the problems of Russia, but he could do little about it. The two present dangers hanging over civilization were militarism and complete disorganization. Instead of grappling with these and doing something about it, the old leaders, blind and totally incapable of seeing new forces arising in the world, went about creating their methods for insuring that the thing would soon fall apart again.

A letter from Wilson to Lloyd George indicates the manner in which economic problems were approached by the Allies:

It would not be possible for me to secure from the Congress of the United States authority to place a Federal guarantee upon Bonds of European origin. Whatever aid the Congress may see fit to authorize should, in my judgment, be rendered along independent lines. By that I do not mean in ways that would not involve close and cordial cooperation with European governments, for such harmony and cooperation I consider indispensable. I mean merely that such cooperation should not, so far as America is concerned, take the form of a guarantee upon bonds. Our Treasury also holds the view (and in this again I concur) that to the very limit of what is practicable such credits as may be wise to grant should be extended through the medium of the usual private channels rather than through the several Governments. Your Treasury, I understand, and certainly ours, believes it wise to retire at the earliest possible moment from "the banking business."

Meantime, may I not call to your attention the following facts and considerations with regard to Germany's present and prospective financial situation?

a) Germany requires working capital. Without that, she will be unable to start her industrial life again, and therefore unable to make any substantial progress in the way of reparations, but

b) The provisions of the reparation clauses of the proposed treaty demand that Germany shall deliver over at once all her working capital, that is, practically the whole of her liquid assets.

c) Simultaneously the suggestion is in effect made that America should in a large measure make good this deficiency, providing in one form or another credit, and thus working capital, to Germany.

Throughout the reparation discussions the American delegation has steadily pointed out to the other delegations that the plans proposed would surely deprive Germany of the means of making any appreciable reparation payments. I myself, as you know, have frequently made the same observation. But whenever any of us was urgent on this point, he was accused of being Pro-German. Our delegation finally gave assent to the reparation clauses as drawn, only because the reparation problem was one that chiefly concerned France, Great Britain, Belgium, and the other European countries, and not America.

America has, in my judgment, always been ready and will always stand ready to do her full share financially to assist the general situation. But America has grave difficulties of her own. She has been obliged within two years to raise by means of war loans and taxes the sum of forty billion dollars. This has been a very heavy burden, even for our well-to-do commonwealth, especially in view of the fact of the short period during which such sums of money had to be raised; and our Treasury informs me that our investing public have reached, and perhaps passed, the point of complete saturation in respect of investments. Such is our situation.

You have suggested that we all address ourselves to the problem of helping to put Germany on her feet, but how can your experts or ours be expected to work out a *new* plan to furnish working capital to Germany when we deliberately start out by taking away all Germany's *present* capital? How can anyone expect America to turn over to Germany in any considerable measure new working capital to take the place of that which the European nations have determined to take from her?

MAY 9, 1919 [ON THE TREATY]

One of the things that has disturbed me in recent months is the unqualified hope that men have entertained everywhere of immediate emancipation from the things that have hampered them and oppressed them.

You cannot in human experience rush into the light. You have to go through the twilight into the broadening day before the noon comes and the full sun is upon the landscape; and we see to it that those who hope are not disappointed by showing them the processes by which hope must be realized, processes of law, processes of slow disentanglement from the many things that have bound us in the past. You cannot throw off the habits of society immediately any more than you can throw off the habits of the individual immediately.

In the new League of Nations we are starting out upon uncharted seas, and therefore we must have, I will not say the audacity, but the steadiness of purpose which is necessary in such novel circumstances. And we must not be afraid of new things at the same time that we must not be intolerant of old things. We must weave out of the old material the new garments which it is necessary that men should wear.

On June 28, 1919, Wilson announced that the treaty had been signed. He said:

It is more than a treaty of peace with Germany. It liberates great peoples who have never before been able to find the way to liberty. It ends once for all, an old and intolerable order under which small groups of selfish men could use the peoples of great empires to serve their own ambition for power and dominion. It associates the free governments of the world in a permanent league in which they are pledged to use their united power to maintain peace by maintaining right and justice. It makes international law a reality supported by imperative sanctions. It does away with the right of conquest and rejects the policy of annexation and substitutes a new order under which backward nations . . . shall no more be subjected to the domination and exploitation of a stronger nation, but shall be put under the friendly direction and afforded the helpful assistance of governments which undertake to be responsible to the opinion of mankind in the execution of their task by accepting the direction of the League of Nations.

Here is an early germ of the "Point Four" program.

On July 10, 1919, Wilson presented the treaty to the Senate for its ratification. Then on August 19, 1919, he went before the Senate Committee on Foreign Relations and explained the treaty in detail.

When the Senate, under the leadership of Senators Lodge, Johnson and Borah, refused to ratify the treaty, Wilson started a swing around the country to get the force of public opinion behind him. As he swung westward, through Kansas City, up through Des Moines, into South and North Dakota, on to Montana, Idaho and the Pacific Northwest, then down the West Coast to San Diego, back through Nevada, Utah, Wyoming and, finally, to Pueblo,

Colorado, where he collapsed, he was winning his fight with the people. With the radio he might have won it.

What he said in several of his speeches indicates what he said in all of them.

SEPTEMBER 6, 1919 [AN AMERICAN DOCUMENT]

I came back from Paris bringing one of the greatest documents of human history, and one of the things that made it great was that it was penetrated throughout with the principles to which America has devoted her life. Principles are written into that treaty which were never written into any great international understanding before, and they had their natural birth and origin in this dear country to which we have devoted our life and service.

I have no hesitation in saying that in spirit and essence it is an American document.

It provides for the destruction of autocratic power as an instrument of international control, admitting only self-governing nations to the League of Nations. No nation is admitted whose people do not control its Government. The League of Nations sends autocratic governments to Coventry. That is the first point.

It provides for the substitution of publicity, discussion and arbitration for war. That is the supreme thing that it does. Every member of the League promises not to go to war until there has been a discussion and a cooling off of nine months, and if Germany had submitted to discussion for nine days she never would have dared go to war.

Instead of using force after this period of discussion, something very much more effective than force is proposed, namely, an absolute boycott of the nation that does not keep its covenant. There cannot be any kind of intercourse with that nation. It cannot sell or buy goods. It cannot receive or send messages or letters. It cannot have any transactions with the citizens of any member of the League, and when you consider that the League is going to consist of every considerable nation in the world, except Germany, you can see what that boycott will mean.

There is not a nation in the world, except this one, that can live without importing goods for nine months, and it does not make any difference to us whether we can or not, because we always fulfill our obligations, and there will never be a boycott for us.

It provides for placing the peace of the world under constant international oversight, in recognition of the principle that the peace of the world is the legitimate and immediate interest of every nation. Why, as it stands at present, if there is likely to be trouble between two nations other than the United States it is considered an unfriendly and hostile act for the United States to intervene.

This Covenant makes it the right of the United States, and not the right of the United States merely, but the right of the weakest nation in the world, to bring anything that the most powerful nation in the world is doing that is likely to disturb the peace of the world under the scrutiny of mankind. Yet this is the first document that ever recognized that principle.

It provides for disarmament on the part of the great fighting nations of the world.

It provides in detail for the rehabilitation of oppressed peoples, and that will remove most of the causes of war.

It provides that there shall be no more annexations of territory anywhere, but that those territories whose people are not ready to govern themselves shall be intrusted to the trusteeship of the nations that can take care of them, the trustee nation to be responsible in annual reports to the League of Nations; that is to say, to mankind in general, subject to removal and restricted in respect to anything that might be done to that population which would be to the detriment of the population itself.

So that you cannot go into darkest Africa and make slaves of those poor people, as some Governments at times have done.

It abolishes enforced labor. It takes the same care of the women and children of those unschooled races that we try to take of the women and children of ours. Why this is the great humane document of all time.

It provides that every secret treaty shall be invalid. It sweeps the table of all private understandings and enforces the principle that there shall be no private understandings of any kind that anybody is bound to respect.

It provides for the protection of dependent peoples.

It provides that high standards of labor, such as are observed in the United States, shall be extended to the workingman everywhere in the world.

It provides that all the great humane instrumentalities, like the Red Cross, like the conventions against the opium trade, like the regulation of the liquor traffic with debased and ignorant people, like the prohibition of the selling of arms and ammunition to people who can use them only to their own detriment, shall be under the common direction and control of the League of Nations.

I say without hesitation that no international agreement has ever before been drawn up along those lines — of the universal consideration of right and the interest of humanity.

SEPTEMBER 6, 1919 [THE FIRST COLD WAR]

The world is not at peace. We speak of the tragedy of this war, but the tragedy that lay back of it was greater than the war itself, because back of it lay long ages in which the legitimate freedom of men was suppressed. Back of it lay long ages of recurrent war in which little groups of men, closeted in capitals, determined whether the sons of the lands over which they ruled should go out upon the field and shed their blood.

For what? For liberty?

No; not for liberty, but for the aggrandizement of those who ruled them. And this had been slumbering in the hearts of men. They had felt the suppression of it. They had felt the mastery of those whom they had not chosen as their masters. They had felt the oppression of laws which did not admit them to the equal exercise of human rights. Now, all of this is released and uncovered and men glare at one another and say, "Now we are free and what shall we do with our freedom?"

What happened in Russia was not a sudden and accidental thing.

The people of Russia were maddened with the suppression of Czarism. When at last the chance came to throw off those chains, they threw them off, at first with hearts full of confidence and hope, and then they found out that they had been again deceived. There was no assembly chosen to frame a constitution for them, or, rather, there was an assembly chosen to choose a constitution for them and it was suppressed and dispersed, and a little group of men just as selfish, just as ruthless, just as pitiless, as the agents of the Czar himself, assumed control and exercised their power by terror and not by right.

And in other parts of Europe the poison spread — the poison of disorder, the poison of revolt, the poison of chaos.

And do you honestly think that none of that poison has got in the veins of this free people? Do you not know that the world is all now one single whispering gallery? Those antennae of the wireless telegraph are the symbols of our age. All the impulses of mankind are thrown out upon the air and reach to the ends of the earth; quietly upon steamships, silently under the cover of the Postal Service, with the tongue of the wireless and the tongue of the telegraph, all the suggestions of disorder are spread through the world.

Money coming from nobody knows where is deposited by the millions in capitals like Stockholm, to be used for the propaganda of disorder and discontent and dissolution throughout the world, and men look you calmly in the face in America and say they are for that sort of revolution, when that sort of revolution means government by terror, government by force, not government by vote. It is the negation of everything that is American; but it is spreading, and so long as disorder continues, so long as the world is kept waiting for the answer to the question, What kind of peace are we going to have and what kind of guarantees are there to be behind that peace? that poison will steadily spread more and more rapidly, spread until it may be that even this beloved land of ours will be distracted and distorted by it.

You know what the necessity of peace is. Political liberty can exist only when there is peace. Social reform can take place only when there is peace. The settlement of every question that concerns our daily life waits for peace.

The isolation of the United States is at an end, not because we chose to go into the politics of the world, but because by the sheer genius of this people and the growth of our power we have become a determining factor in the history of mankind, and after you have become a determining factor you cannot remain isolated, whether you want to or not. Isolation ended by the processes of history, not by the processes of our independent choice, and the processes of history merely fulfilled the prediction of the men who founded our Republic.

The thing is going to be done whether we are in it or not. If we are in it, then we are going to be the determining factor in the development of civilization. If we are out of it, we ourselves are going to watch every other nation with suspicion, and we will be justified, too; and we are going to be watched with suspicion.

America can stay out, but I want to call you to witness that the peace of the world cannot be established without America. America is necessary to the peace of the world, and the peace and good will of the world are necessary to America.

I do not say it because I am an American and my heart is full of the same pride that fills yours with regard to the power and spirit of this great Nation, but merely because it is a fact the organization contemplated by the League of Nations without the United States would merely be an alliance and not a league of nations.

There can be no league of nations in the true sense without the partnership of this great people.

You have the alternative, armed isolation or peaceful partnership.

SEPTEMBER 6, 1919 [AUTOCRACY IN RUSSIA]

There was something else we wanted that is accomplished by this treaty. We wanted to destroy autocratic authority everywhere in the world. We wanted to see to it that there was no place in the world where a small group of men could use their fellow citizens as pawns in a game; that there was no place in the world where a small group of men, without consulting their fellow citizens, could send their fellow citizens to the battlefields and to death in order to accomplish some dynastic ambition, some political plan that had been conceived in private, some object that had been prepared for by universal, world-wide intrigue.

The most startling thing that developed itself at the opening of our participation in this war was, not the military preparation of Germany — we were familiar with that, though we had been dreaming that she would not use it — but her political preparation — to find every community in the civilized world was penetrated by her intrigue.

It does not make any difference what kind of a minority governs you if it is a minority, and the thing we must see to is that no minority anywhere masters the majority.

That is at the heart of the tragical things that are happening in that great country which we long to help and can find no way that is effective to help. I mean the great realm of Russia.

The men who are now measurably in control of the affairs of Russia represent nobody but themselves. They have again and again been challenged to call a constitutional convention. They have again and again been challenged to prove that they had some kind of a mandate, even from a single class of their fellow citizens, and they dare not attempt it. They have no mandate from anybody.

There are only thirty-four of them, I am told, and there were more than thirty-four men who used to control the destinies of Europe from the Wilhelmstrasse. There is a closer monopoly of power in Petrograd and Moscow than there ever was in Berlin, and the thing that is intolerable is, not that the Russian people are having their way, but that another group of men more cruel than the Czar himself is controlling the destinies of that great people.

I want to say here and now that I am against the control of any minority anywhere. If we do not want minority government in Russia, we must see that we do not have it in the United States. If you do not want little groups of selfish men to plot the future of

Europe, we must not allow little groups of selfish men to plot the future of America.

Any man that speaks for a class must prove that he also speaks for all his fellow citizens and for mankind, and then we will listen to him. The most difficult thing in a democracy is to get classes, where they unfortunately exist, to understand one another and unite, and you have not got a great democracy until they do understand one another and unite.

It is the first great international agreement in the history of mankind where the principle adopted has been, not the power of the strong but the right of the weak.

To reject that treaty, to alter that treaty, is to impair one of the first charters of mankind. Yet there are men who approach the question with passion, with private passion, with party passion, who think only of some immediate advantage to themselves or to a group of their fellow countrymen, and who look at the thing with the jaundiced eyes of those who have some private purpose of their own.

If anybody dares to defeat this great experiment, then they must gather together the counsellors of the world and do something better.

Negation will not serve the world. Opposition constructs nothing. Opposition is the specialty of those who are Bolshevistically inclined — and again I assure you I am not comparing any of my respected colleagues to Bolshevists; I am merely pointing out that the Bolshevist spirit lacks every element of constructiveness.

They have destroyed everything and they propose nothing, and while there is a common abhorrence for political Bolshevism, I hope there will not be such a thing growing up in our country as international Bolshevism, the Bolshevism which destroys the constructive work of men who have conscientiously tried to cement the good feeling of the great peoples of the world.

SEPTEMBER 11, 1919

We fought Germany in order that there should be a world fit to live in. The world is not fit to live in if any great government is in a position to do what the German Government did — secretly plot a war and begin it with the whole strength of its people, without so much as consulting its own people. A great war cannot begin with public deliberation.

The next war would have to be paid for in American blood and American money. The nation of all nations that is most interested to prevent the recurrence of what has already happened is the nation which would assuredly have to bear the brunt of that great catastrophe.

America is going to grow more and more powerful; and the more powerful she is the more inevitable it is that she should be trustee for the peace of the world.

It happened that America laid down the specifications for the peace. It happened that America proposed the principles upon which the peace with Germany should be built.

Where did the suggestion first come from? Where did the idea first spread that there should be a society of nations?

It was first suggested and it first spread in the United States, *and some gentlemen were the chief proponents of it who are now objecting to the adoption of the Covenant of the League of Nations.* They went further, some of them, than any principle of that Covenant goes, and now for some reason which I must admit is inscrutable to me they are opposing the very thing into which they put their heart and their genius.

SEPTEMBER 11, 1919

One of the noblest sentences ever uttered was uttered by Mr. Garfield before he became President. He was a Member of Congress, as I remember it, at the time of Mr. Lincoln's assassination. He happened to be in New York City, and Madison Square was filled with a surging mass of deeply excited people when the news of the murder came. Mr. Garfield was at the old Fifth Avenue Hotel, which had a balcony out over the entrance, and they begged him to go out and say something to the people. He went out and, after he had attracted their attention, he said this beautiful thing: "My fellow citizens, the President is dead, but the Government lives and God Omnipotent reigns."

America is the place where you cannot kill your Government by killing the men who conduct it. The only way you can kill government in America is by making the men and women of America forget how to govern, and nobody can do that.

SEPTEMBER 13, 1919

In order to let you remember what the thing cost, just let me read you a few figures. If I did not have them on official authority I would deem them incredible. Here is what the war cost. These figures do not include what the different powers loaned each other; they are direct war costs:

It cost Great Britain and her dominions $38,000,000,000; France, $26,000,000,000; the United States, $22,000,000,000; Russia, $18,-000,000,000; Italy, $13,000,000,000; a total, including Japan, Belgium, and other countries, of $123,000,000,000. It cost the Central Powers: Germany, $39,000,000,000; Austria-Hungary, $21,000,000-000; Turkey and Bulgaria, $3,000,000,000; a total of $63,000,000,-000. A grand total of direct war costs of $186,000,000,000 — an incredible sum — to save civilization. Now, the question is, Are we going to keep it saved? The expenditures of the United States were at the rate of $1,000,000 an hour, including the night time, for two years.

The battle deaths — and this is the cost that touches our hearts — were: Russia, 1,700,000; Germany, 1,600,000; France, 1,380,000; Great Britain, 900,000; Austria, 800,000; Italy, 364,000; the United States, 50,300 dead. A total for all belligerents of 7,450,200 men dead on the field of battle! Seven and a half million! The totals for the wounded are not obtainable at present, but the number of torn and wounded for the United States Army was 230,000, excluding, of course, those who were killed.

The total of all battle deaths in all the wars of the world from the year 1793 to 1914 was something under 6,000,000; in all the wars of the world for more than 100 years fewer men died than have been killed upon the field of battle in the last five years. These are terrible facts, and we ought never to forget them.

SEPTEMBER 15, 1919

The whole trouble about our civilization as it looks to me, is that it has grown complex faster than we have adjusted the simpler ideas to the existing conditions. There was a time when men would do in their business what they would not do as individuals. There was a time when they submerged their individual consciences in a corporation and persuaded themselves that it was legitimate for a corporation to do what they individually never would have dreamed of doing. That is what I mean by saying that the organization becomes complex faster than our adjustment of the simpler ideas of justice and right to the developing circumstances of our civilization.

SEPTEMBER 15, 1919

If we want a league of nations, we must take this League of Nations, because there is no conceivable way in which any other league of nations is obtainable. We must leave it or take it.

I should be very sorry to have the United States indirectly defeat this great enterprise by asking for something, some position of privilege, which other nations in their pride cannot grant. I would a great deal rather say flatly, "She will not go into the enterprise at all."

And that is exactly what Germany is hoping and beginning to dare to expect. I am not uttering a conjecture; I am speaking of knowledge, knowledge of the things that are said in the German newspapers and by German public men.

They are taking heart because the United States, they hope, is not going to stand with the other free nations of the world to guarantee the peace that has been forced upon them. They see the hope that there will be two nations standing outside the League — Germany and the United States.

Germany because she must; the United States because she will. She knows that that will turn the hostility and enmity of all the

other nations of the world against the United States, as their hostil
is already directed against her. They do not expect that now
United States will in any way align themselves with Germany. Th
do not expect the sympathy of the United States to go out to th
now, but they do expect the isolation of the United States to br
about an alienation between the United States and the other f
nations of the world, which will make it impossible for the wo
ever to combine again against such enterprises as she was defea
in attempting.

All over this country pro-German propaganda is beginning to
active again, beginning to try to add to the force of the argume
against the League in particular and against the treaty and
several items of the treaty. And the poison of failure is being
jected into the whole fine body politic of the united world, a s
of paralysis, a sort of fear. Germany desires that we should s
"What have we created? A great power which will bring peace,
will that power be amiable to us? Can we control that power?"

We cannot control it for any but its proper purpose — the purp
of righteousness and peace — but for that purpose we are invi
to control it by the opinion of mankind, for all over the wo
peoples are looking to us with confidence, our rivals along w
the weaker nations. They believe in the honesty of purpose and
indomitable rectitude of purpose of the United States, and they
willing to have us lead.

George Sylvester Viereck promised 8,000,000 German-Ameri
votes to the Republicans if they would defeat the League of Nati
— and delivered 6,000,000.

SEPTEMBER 19, 1919

If anybody discusses this question on the basis of party adv
tage, I repudiate him as a fellow American. And in order to v
date what I have said, I want to make one or two quotations fr
representatives of a party to which I do not belong. The firs
shall make from a man who has for a long time been a member
the United States Senate.

In May, 1916, just about two years after the Great War began, this Senator [*Henry Cabot Lodge*], at a banquet at which I was myself present, uttered the following sentences:

"I know, and no one I think can know better than one who has served long in the Senate, which is charged with an important share of the ratification and confirmation of all treaties, no one can, I think, feel more deeply than I do the difficulties which confront us in the work which this League [*the League to Enforce Peace*] undertakes. But the difficulties cannot be overcome unless we try to overcome them. I believe much can be done. Probably it will be impossible to stop all wars, but it certainly will be possible to stop some wars, and thus diminish their number. The way in which this problem is to be worked out must be left to this League and to those who are giving this great question the study which it deserves. I know the obstacles. I know how quickly we shall be met with the statement that this is a dangerous question which you are putting into your agreement, that no nation can submit to the judgment of other nations, and we must be careful at the beginning not to attempt too much. I know the difficulties which arise when we speak of anything which seems to involve an alliance.

"But I do not believe that when Washington warned us against entangling alliances he meant for one moment that we should not join with the other civilized nations of the world if a method could be found to diminish war and encourage peace.

"It was a year ago," he continues, "that in delivering the chancellor's address at Union College I made an argument on this theory: that if we were to promote international peace at the close of the present terrible war, if we were to restore international law as it must be restored, we must find some way in which the united forces of the nations could be put behind the cause of peace and law. I said then that my hearers might think that I was picturing a Utopia, but it is in the search for Utopias that great discoveries have been made. Not failure, but low aim, is the crime.

"This League certainly has the highest of all aims for the benefit of humanity, and because the pathway is sown with difficulties is no reason that we should turn from it."

The quotation is from the Honorable Henry Cabot Lodge. I read another quotation from one of the most energetic, practical, and distinguished leaders of the Republican party, uttered in an article published in the New York "Times" in October, 1914:

"The one permanent move for obtaining peace which has yet been suggested with any reasonable chance of attaining its object is by an agreement among the great powers, in which each should pledge itself not only to abide by the decisions of a common tribunal, but to back with force the decision of that common tribunal. The great civilized nations of the world which do possess force, actual or immediately potential, should combine by solemn agreement in a great world league for the peace of righteousness." A very worthy utterance by Theodore Roosevelt. I am glad to align myself with such utterances as those. I subscribe to every word of them.

CHAPTER TWENTY-FOUR

Making Democracy Unsafe for the World

❯❯❯❮❮❮❯❯❯❮❮❮❯❯❯❮❮❮❯❯❯❮❮❮❯❯❯❮❮❮❯❯❯❮❮❮❯❯❯❮❮❮❯❯❯❮❮❮❯❯❯❮❮❮❯❯❯❮❮❮❯❯❯❮❮❮

*In his "State of the Union Message," December 2, 1919, Wilson
pointed out things that needed to be done on the domestic scene to
keep this country both efficient and democratic. He asked, among
other things, for the establishment of a budget system, tax simplification so that industry would not be stifled, yet a tax system that
would take into consideration that America was now a creditor and
not a debtor nation, and a quick consideration that would end what
he had called "armed isolation." He also asked for better laws dealing with labor, particularly child labor, so that the country might
have "a genuine democratization of industry based upon the full
recognition of the right of those who work to participate in some
organic way in every decision which directly affects their welfare."*

*In a Jackson Day message, January 8, 1920, he again warned
that we were still at war with Germany and that none of the old
wrongs we had fought to eliminate were eliminated. He also
pointed out that we could not rewrite the treaty and that without
our backing it would not be an effective treaty. Then he solemnly
warned:*

The world has been made safe for democracy, but democracy has
not been finally vindicated.

All sorts of crimes are being committed in its name, all sorts of
preposterous perversions of its doctrines and practices are being
attempted.

This, in my judgment, is to be the great privilege of the democracy of the United States, to show that it can lead the way in the solution of the great social and industrial problems of our time, and lead the way to a happy, settled order of life as well as to political liberty. The program for this achievement we must attempt to formulate, and in carrying it out we shall do more than can be done in any other way to sweep out of existence the tyrannous and arbitrary forms of power which are now masquerading under the name of popular government.

On January 13, 1920, Woodrow Wilson called the first meeting of the League of Nations — without the United States being present. On May 20, 1920, he vetoed a resolution to make a separate peace with the Central Powers. Then on October 3, 1920, with Governor James Cox of Ohio as the Presidential and Franklin D. Roosevelt as the Vice-Presidential candidates of the Democratic Party, he called upon the country to make the election an expression of the nation's opinion on the League of Nations. "The whole world will await the verdict," he said.

The Republican Party, with Senator Warren G. Harding as its Presidential candidate and Governor Calvin Coolidge as its Vice-Presidential candidate, was swept into power on their slogan of "Back to normalcy," which meant a sharp, quick return to isolationism and pre-1912 Republicanism.

DECEMBER 7, 1920
In his "State of the Union Message," Wilson pointed out:

Democracy is an assertion of the right of the individual to live and to be treated justly as against any attempt on the part of any combination of individuals to make laws which will overburden him or which will destroy his equality among his fellows in the matter of right or privilege, and I think we all realize that the day has come when democracy is being put upon its final test.

The old world is just now suffering from a wanton rejection of the principle of democracy and a substitution of the principle of autocracy as asserted in the name but without the authority and sanction of the multitude. This is the time of all others when democracy should prove its purity and its spiritual power to prevail. It is surely the manifest destiny of the United States to lead in the attempt to make this spirit prevail.

There are two ways in which the United States can assist to accomplish this great object: First, by offering the example within her own borders of the will and power of democracy to make and enforce laws which are unquestionably just and which are equal in their administration — laws which secure its full right to labor and yet at the same time safeguard the integrity of property, and particularly of that property which is devoted to the development of industry and the increase of the necessary wealth of the world. Second, by standing for right and justice as towards individual nations.

The law of democracy is for the protection of the weak, and the influence of every democracy in the world should be for the protection of the weak nation, the nation which is struggling towards its right and towards its proper recognition and privilege in the family of nations.

The United States is of necessity the sample democracy of the world, and the triumph of democracy depends upon its success.

One of Wilson's last official acts, March 3, 1921, was to veto a tariff bill aimed at giving relief to farmers. As he pointed out, the bill would give no relief — all it would do would be to move in the direction of giving protection again to industry. He then stated:

I imagine there is little doubt that while this measure is temporary, it is intended as *a foundation for action of a similar nature of a very general and permanent character.*

It would seem to be designed to pave the way for such action. If there ever was a time when America had anything to fear from foreign competition, that time has passed. I cannot believe that American producers who in most respects are the most effective in the world can have any dread of competition when they view the fact that their country has come through the great struggle of the last few years, relatively speaking, untouched, while their principal competitors are in varying degrees sadly stricken and laboring under adverse conditions from which they will not recover for many years.

If we wish to have Europe settle her debts, governmental or commercial, we must be prepared to buy from her, and if we wish to assist Europe and ourselves by the export either of food, of raw materials, or finished products, we must be prepared to welcome commodities which we need and which Europe will be prepared, with no little pain, to send us.

Clearly, this is no time for the erection here of high trade barriers. It would strike a blow at the large and successful efforts which have been made by many of our great industries to place themselves on an export basis. It would stand in the way of the normal readjustment of business conditions throughout the world, which is as vital to the welfare of this country as to that of all the other nations. The United States has a duty to itself as well as to the world, and it can discharge this duty by widening, not by contracting, its world markets.

As indicated by the tariff, the road was clearly back to an outworn and outmoded isolationism. On March 4, 1921, the Republican Administration came in to combine with a Republican Congress in attempting to return to a government by trusteeship. The United States was headed through that famous statement, "They hired the money, didn't they?" to the fantastic conclusion that hard times were forever licked and that there would be "a chicken in every plot and two cars in every garage" regardless of what happened to the rest of the world.

Then, when the ostrich got its head out of the sand, the sight that met its gaze was the Great Depression and war clouds all over the world.

E P I L O G U E

How the World May Come to Itself

⇢⟫⟪⇠⇢⟫⟪⇠⇢⟫⟪⇠⇢⟫⟪⇠⇢⟫⟪⇠⇢⟫⟪⇠⇢⟫⟪⇠⇢⟫⟪⇠⇢⟫⟪⇠⇢⟫⟪⇠⇢⟫⟪⇠⇢⟫⟪⇠

AUGUST, 1923

In an article in the Atlantic Monthly, *written just a few months before his death on February 3, 1924, Woodrow Wilson pointed out "the road away from revolution."*

In these doubtful and anxious days, when all the world is at unrest and, look which way you will, the road ahead seems darkened by shadows which portend dangers of many kinds, it is only common prudence that we should look about us and attempt to assess the causes of distress and the most likely means of removing them.

There must be some real ground for the universal unrest and perturbation. It is not to be found in superficial politics or in mere economic blunders. It probably lies deep at the sources of the spiritual life of our time. It leads to revolution; and perhaps if we take the case of the Russian Revolution, the outstanding event of its kind in our age, we may find a good deal of instruction for our judgment of present critical situations and circumstances.

What gave rise to the Russian Revolution? The answer can only be that it was the product of a whole social system. It was not in fact a sudden thing. It had been gathering head for several generations.

It was due to the systematic denial to the great body of Russians of the rights and privileges which all normal men desire and must have if they are to be contented and within reach of happiness. The lives of the great mass of the Russian people contained no opportunities, but were hemmed in by barriers against which they were constantly flinging their spirits, only to fall back bruised and dispirited. Only the powerful were suffered to secure their rights or even to gain access to the means of material success.

It is to be noted as a leading fact of our time that it was against "capitalism" that the Russian leaders directed their attack. It was capitalism that made them see red; and it is against capitalism under one name or another that the discontented classes everywhere draw their indictment.

There are thoughtful and well-informed men all over the world who believe, with much apparently sound reason, that the abstract thing, the system, which we call capitalism, is indispensable to the industrial support and development of modern civilization. And yet everyone who has an intelligent knowledge of social forces must know that great and widespread reactions like that which is now unquestionably manifesting itself against capitalism *do not occur without cause or provocation;* and before we commit ourselves irreconcilably to an attitude of hostility to this movement of the time, we ought frankly to put to ourselves the question, Is the capitalistic system unimpeachable? which is another way of asking, *Have capitalists generally used their power for the benefit of the countries in which their capital is employed and for the benefit of their fellow men?*

Is it not, on the contrary, too true that capitalists have often seemed to regard the men whom they used as mere instruments of profit, whose physical and mental powers it was legitimate to exploit with as slight cost to themselves as possible, either of money or of sympathy? Have not many fine men who were actuated by the highest principles in every other relationship of life seemed to hold that generosity and humane feeling were not among the imperative mandates of conscience in the conduct of a banking business, or in the development of an industrial or commercial enterprise?

And, if these offenses against high morality and true citizenship have been frequently observable, are we to say that the blame for the present discontent and turbulence is wholly on the side of those who are in revolt against them? Ought we not, rather, to seek a way to remove such offenses and make life itself clean for those who will share honorably and cleanly in it?

The world has been made safe for democracy. But democracy has not yet made the world safe against irrational revolution. That supreme task, which is nothing less than the salvation of civilization, now faces democracy, insistent, imperative. There is no escaping it, unless everything we have built up is presently to fall in ruin about us; and the United States, as the greatest of democracies, must undertake it.

The road that leads away from revolution is clearly marked, for it is defined by the nature of men and of organized society.

The nature of men and of organized society dictates the maintenance in every field of action of the highest and purest standards of justice and of right dealing; and it is essential to efficacious thinking in this critical matter that we should not entertain a narrow or technical conception of justice.

By justice the lawyer generally means the prompt, fair, and open application of impartial rules; but we call ours a Christian civilization, and a Christian conception of justice must be much higher. *It must include sympathy and helpfulness and a willingness to forego self-interest in order to promote the welfare, happiness, and contentment of others and of the community as a whole.* This is what our age is blindly feeling after in its reaction against what it deems the too great selfishness of the capitalistic system.

The sum of the whole matter is this, that our civilization cannot survive materially unless it be redeemed spiritually. It can be saved only by becoming permeated with the spirit of Christ and being made free and happy by the practices which spring out of that spirit. Only thus can discontent be driven out and all the shadows lifted from the road ahead.

Here is the final challenge to our churches, to our political organizations, and to our capitalists — to everyone who fears God or loves his country. Shall we not all earnestly cooperate to bring in the new day?

Thank You

Thank you, Edith Bolling Wilson, for your kind encouragement, and for your wonderful letter in which you state that this is really *Woodrow Wilson's Own Story,* and that, in your opinion, he would like it. You realized so completely that I was not trying to do a factual biography.

Thank you, Katherine E. Brand, for your indispensable advice and suggestions. You helped me more than you know.

Thank you, Ray Stannard Baker, for doing a "heart" rather than a factual biography of Woodrow Wilson. It took your sort of insight and sensitivity to give us the real man whom factual biographers and "scientific" historians will never comprehend.

And to the staff of the Manuscript Division of the Library of Congress, to its director, David C. Mearns, and especially to Dr. C. Percy Powell and his assistants, who saw to it that any material which I needed was promptly at my disposal.

Thank you, Clara Kent Pearce, for much more than a typing job. Your help spilled over into editing suggestions and encouragement that are deeply appreciated.

And, finally, thank you, Beth Day, for listening to me through many hours of talking about Woodrow Wilson and also for doing the final job of proofreading.

Sources and Acknowledgments

The six-volume Ray Stannard Baker and William E. Dodd edition of *The Public Papers of Woodrow Wilson,* Harper & Brothers, New York, 1925–1927, gives in a handy form many of the finest things that Wilson wrote and said.

In addition to the other sources as indicated in the datelines, excerpts from addresses and writings as indicated by the following dates may be read in their entirety in this collection:

March, 1880; April, 1880; June, 1887; April 30, 1889; September, 1894; October 21, 1896; December 22, 1900; March, 1901; October 25, 1902; October 13, 1904; June 10, 1907; April 13, September 30, 1908; January 19, February 12, November 2, 1909; April 16, August 31, 1910; June 15, 1911; February 1, February 12, April 13, 1912; March 4, April 8, May 26, August 27, October 3, October 27, December 2, 1913; March 20, May 16, December 8, 1914; January 28, February 3, May 10, July 21, November 4, December 7, 1915; January 27, January 29, January 31, February 1, February 26, April 18, May 27, June 2, June 13, August 11, August 29, September 2, 1916; January 22, March 4, April 2, May 15, May 18, May 22, July 12, August 11, August, November 12, December 4, 1917; January 8, March 4, March 12, July 4, September 27, October 14, October 23, October 25, November 11, November 28, December 2, December 29, December 30, 1918; January 3, January 13, January 25, February 14, February 24, May 9, September 6, September 11, September 13, September 15, September 19, 1919; January 8, December 7, 1920; August, 1923.

I have drawn heavily on Wilson's letters to Ellen Axson Wilson and Mary A. Hulbert. In them he told what was on his mind without the restriction imposed by speeches or writings or official statements. The complete file of these letters is not open. However, many of them have been published in Ray Stannard Baker's *Woodrow Wilson, Life and Letters,* and I have been given permission to use these. Since Mr. Baker had access to all of the letters the ones used are no doubt the most revealing.

With the exception of these letters, the collection of Wilson papers in the Manuscript Division of the Library of Congress was open to me. Much of the material in this book before his election to the Presidency, and all of it afterwards, unless indicated otherwise in the datelines, may be found in this collection.

An extremely handy guide to the collection is given by the Ray Stannard Baker papers. Here is a record — kept daily after Wilson became a prominent political figure — of his activities, together with abstracts from the most important letters written by and to him.

Wilson's letters to Charles Talcott, made available to Mr. Baker by his family, and to R. Heath Dabney, in the Library of the University of Virginia, have been splendid sources for understanding what was going on in Wilson's mind.

Where material was originally published in magazines I have given credit in datelines.

Index

Index

ADAMS, HERBERT B., 21, 27
Adams, John, 141
"Administration, The Study of," 36–37
Adriatic question, 330–331
Africa, 332, 337
Agriculture, Department of, 223
Alexander, Joshua, 216
Allied Armies, Marshal Foch, Supreme Commander of, 274
Allied Supreme War Council, 266
Alsace-Lorraine, 270
Alumni Weekly (Princeton), 78, 80–84
American Federation of Labor, 289
American Mining Congress, 168
American Statesmen series, 17
Americanism, 264–265
Annapolis, Maryland, 213
Appeasement, 205–207
Archangel, Russia, 278
Armaments problem, Peace Conference, 318
Armistice, first German note, 289–291; acceptance of terms, 298
Army, United States, 262–263
Asia, 315, 318
Atlanta, Georgia, 17, 18
Atlantic Monthly, Wilson articles, 43, 51–59, 85, 353–355
Augusta, Georgia, 7, 11
Austria-Hungary, 270, 330, 331, 332; food relief, 312; war costs, 344
Axson, Ellen, letters to, 20–31; marriage of Woodrow Wilson to, 31. See also Wilson, Ellen Axson

Axson, Reverend Samuel (Mrs. Wilson's father), 20
Axson, Stockton, 85, 98

"BACK TO NORMALCY," 350
Bagehot, Walter, 11, 24
Baker, Newton D., 258, 272, 274, 275, 291, 293, 295
Baker, Ray Stannard, 313
Balfour Declaration, 281
Balkan states, 270, 311, 312, 331
Baltimore, Maryland, 19
"Banker and the Nation, The," 86–88
Bar Association, Wilson speech to, 97–98
Baruch, Bernard M., 272, 303
Bass, Mrs. George, 252
"Battle Hymn of the Republic," 306
Belgium, 270; relief, 299; reparations, 333; war costs, 344
Bernstorff, Count von, 196, 198
Bertron, S. R., 274
Bible, quoted, 3
Bibles for servicemen, 263
Bismarck, 10
Bok, Edward W., 251
Bolshevists, 264, 307, 312, 314, 342
Borah, William E., 335
Boston, Massachusetts, 325
Brandeis, Louis D., 274
Breckinridge, Henry, 198
Brest-Litovsk, Treaty of, 264, 279
Bridges, Robert, 17, 18, 156
Bright, John, 10, 11, 13, 14
Brisbane, Arthur, 250
British Admiralty, 255–256, 260–261

Bryan, William Jennings, 46, 86, 124, 165, 301–302; Wilson meets, 112; Wilson letters to, 130, 168, 195–196, 268; resignation as Secretary of State, 196, 199

Bryn Mawr College, 27–28, 31

Bulgaria, 344

Burke, Edmund, 11

Burleson, Albert S., 274–275, 282

Business, Wilson appeal for co-operation of, 183–186

CAPITAL, 86–88, 255

Capitalism, 354–355

Catholicism, 277

"Cautious men," Wilson quoted, 89–90

Censorship, 250–251, 254–255, 282–283, 301, 304, 313

Central America, 200–202

Central Powers, 235, 268, 284, 289, 299, 311; undersea warfare, 206; Russia and, 264, 279; war costs, 344; separate peace with United States proposal, 350. See also Austria-Hunga.,' Bulgaria, Germany, Italy

Century Magazine, Wilson article, 60–66

Chambers of Commerce, 182

Chaucer, Geoffrey, 10

"Chicken in every pot," 352

Child Labor Law, 252, 274–275

China, 173–174, 329, 330; Shantung settlement, 331–332

Chinda, Viscount Sutemi, 329

Christianity, Wilson on, 7–8, 65–66, 263, 355

Churchill, Winston, 307–308, 327

Civil Service Commission, 156

Clark, Frank, 265

Clarke, John H., 274

Clayton bill, 170, 171

Clemenceau, Georges, 277, 301, 308, 318

Clemens, Samuel, 119

Cleveland, Grover, 25, 26, 124

Congress, United States, 11, 30, 105, 141; Wilson speeches and messages to, 141–142, 147, 155, 175–177, 179–180, 196–197, 200–202, 204–205, 208–210, 216–217, 243–247, 248, 266–268, 268–271, 289, 298–300, 303, 304, 312; Wilson's relations with, 148, 149, 169, 178, 242–243, 259, 293–295, 327; membership of, 231, 242, 291, 297, 327. See also Representatives, House of; Senate, United States

Congressional Government (Woodrow Wilson), 25, 27, 30, 177–178

Congressional Library, 160

Conscientious objectors, 282

Constitution, 29, 52–53

Convoy system, 256

Coolidge, Calvin, 325, 350

Corwin, Edward S., 280

County agent system, 215

Cox, James M., 350

Crane, Charles R., 275

Creel, George, 266, 279

Crosby, Oscar T., 277

Crowell, Benedict, 281, 282

Currency bill, 150–152, 171

Czar of Russia (Nicholas II), 339, 341

Czecho-Slovak peoples, 278, 282

DABNEY, R. HEATH, 17, 19, 40

Daniels, Josephus, 140, 166, 196

Dardanelles, 270

Democracy, Wilson quoted on, 39–40, 199, 349–350; in education, 80–84; "Make the world safe for," 247, 249

"Democracy and Efficiency" (Atlantic Monthly), 51–59

"Democracy's Opportunity," 120–123

Democrat, Wilson's definition, 127–128

Democratic Congress, Wilson's appeal for, 291, 292–295, 297

Democratic Convention (1912), 132–133

Democratic education, 71–75

Democratic National Committee, 123–124

Democratic Party, 46, 86, 350; Wilson's relations with, 101, 102, 105–107, 116, 133–134, 220, 291, 327; Wilson's credo, 120–123, 221–224

Depression, 352
Des Moines, Iowa, 335
Detective stories, 177
Disabled soldiers, rehabilitation of, 274
District of Columbia, 189
Dodge, Cleveland H., 84
Draft act, 250, 252, 253
Droppers, Garrett, 231

EASTERN FRONT, 283
Eating clubs (Princeton), 79
Elections (1918), 291–295
Eliot, Charles W., 147, 164
Encyclopedists, 47
England, 24, 40, 157, 199; Wilson on king of, 178. *See also* Great Britain
English Citizen series, 17
English tutorial system, 74
"Entangling alliances," Wilson on, 287
Entente Powers, 235, 295
"Epochs in American History" (Albert Bushnell Hart), 40
Europe, Colonel House's mission to, 180–182; Wilson positions on, 209–210, 227–228, 237, 315–316, 326; attitude of toward League of Nations, 277
Expediency, 94–95

FAIRBANKS, DOUGLAS, 266
Farmers, 155, 351–352
Federal Labor Building (Washington, D.C.), 214
Federal Reserve Act, 88, 155–156, 222, 224
Federalist Papers, 11, 24
Federalists, 40, 80
Fifth Avenue Hotel, New York, 343
Finance Corporation, 272
Flanders, fields of, 218, 263, 290
Foch, Marshal, 274, 295, 298, 305, 314
Food administration, 253–254, 275, 280
Food relief, 312
Foreign Affairs Committee, House of Representatives, 320
Foreign competition, 351–352

Foreign Relations Committee, United States Senate, 320, 335
Forum, Wilson articles, 41, 43–45, 46, 47–50
"Four Point" speech, 275–277
Four Points, Wilson on plans for his administration, 137–138
Fourteen Points, Wilson's, 268–271, 289, 295, 318
Fowler, H. Robert, 150
France, 57, 266, 275, 283, 304; attitude toward Wilson and Peace Conference, 258–259, 296, 300–301, 308, 313, 314, 317–320, 330, 333; Wilson on, 270, 290, 301, 318; secret treaty of London, 328; war costs, 344
Franklin, Benjamin, 41

GALLBREATH, J. F., 168
Galt, Mrs. Norman, 199, 200; marriage to Woodrow Wilson, 202. *See also* Wilson, Edith Galt
Garfield, James A., 343
Garrison, Lindley M., 164, 198
Gentleman's Magazine, 10
George, David Lloyd. *See* Lloyd George, David
George Washington, S.S., 305
Georgia state senate, 18
German-American votes, 346
German greatness, Wilson on, 271
German opera, 249
German people, Wilson on, 267–268
Germany, 218, 274, 311, 345–346; Wilson quoted on, 186, 196, 198, 199, 244–247, 258, 261, 301, 336, 342–343; warning to travelers, 190; Wilson notes on *Lusitania*, 196, 197–198; spy activities, 199; submarine activities, 208–210, 235; United States diplomatic relations severed, 242; Russian relations with, 264, 278; objects and terms of Allies for, 285, 288, 308, 316, 318–319; armistice notes, 289; Wilson on armistice, 289–291, 292, 295, 296; acceptance of terms by, 298, 330–331; Wilson's influence on people,

305; food relief, 312, 332; Shantung settlement, 331; financial situation, 333–334; peace treaty negotiations, 335, 349–350; war costs, 344

Gettysburg, fiftieth anniversary of battle of, 144

Gibson, Braxton D., 252

Gladstone, William E., 10, 11, 13, 15–16

Glass, Carter, 156

Glass, Frank P., 162, 281

Gompers, Samuel, 217, 263, 289

"Good neighbor policy," Wilson speech at Mobile, 152

Government, crux of Wilson's ideas on, 86

"Government of the Union, The," Wilson's projected essays on, 24

Graves, General William S., 283

Great Britain, 24, 40, 157, 199, 266, 275, 281; Wilson on policies of, 56, 58–59, 186, 215, 255–256, 258–259, 260–261, 281, 283, 295, 296–297, 301, 328; canal tolls, 157; German warnings on waters surrounding, 190, 208; attitude toward Wilson and Peace Conference, 296, 300–301, 304, 314, 317, 319–320, 330, 333; secret treaty of London, 328; war costs, 344

Green, J. R., *Short History of the English People*, 11

Grey, Sir Edward, 173

Gridiron Club, Wilson at, 142; speeches before, 158–161, 207–208

Griswold, Miss Florence, 147

Hague Court, 165

Haig, Field Marshal Douglas, 295

Hamilton, Alexander, 16, 80

"Happy Warrior," 11

Harding, Warren G., 350

Hardwick, Thomas W., 187–188

Harper's (Colonel George Harvey, editor), 79

Harrison, Russell B., 279

Hart, Albert Bushnell, 40

Harvard University, 84–85

Harvey, Colonel George, 79

Hay-Pauncefote Treaty, 157

Hebrew University, Jerusalem, 281

History of the American People (Woodrow Wilson), 43

Hitchcock, G. M., 291–292

Hitlerism, 307

Hoboken (New Jersey) Board of Trade, 111

Holmes, Oliver Wendell, Jr., 274

Hoover, Herbert, 253–254, 258, 275, 296, 312

House, Colonel E. M., 327; letters to, 173, 174, 196, 198, 215, 258, 263, 265, 266, 295, 296, 297, 300; instructions to 180–182, 266

Hoyt, Mary W., 199

Huerta, Victoriano, 146

Hughes, Charles Evans, 79, 220, 229–230, 231

Hulbert, Mary A., letters to, 107, 108, 109, 110, 112, 113, 115, 118, 123, 124, 129, 133, 134, 141, 142, 144, 145, 146, 148, 149, 151, 167, 174, 175, 179, 186, 187

Ibsen, Henrik, 45

Idaho, 335

Immigration bill, 179–180

Imperial German Government. *See* Germany

Inaugural address, first (Woodrow Wilson), 140–141

Income tax law, 142, 223

"Individual, The Ministry and the," 94–96

International relations, open, 273

International Review, 11

Interstate Commerce Commission, 216, 222

Ireland, 209

Isolationism, 58, 202–203, 340, 352

Italy, 266, 319; peace terms for, 259, 270, 296; food situation, 275; Adriatic question, 330; war costs, 344

Jackson Day messages, 123–124, 349–350

Jacobus, M. W., 197

Japan, 266, 278, 314; World War II terms, 307; Shantung settlement, 328–332; war costs, 344

Jefferson, Thomas, 3, 57, 80, 86; influence on Wilson, 16, 80; "What Jefferson Would Do," 130–132
Jerusalem, Hebrew University, 281
Jews, rights of, 281
Johns Hopkins University, 19, 21, 39
Johnson, Hiram, 293, 335
"Joint Committee in Congress on Expenditures in the Conduct of the War," 259
Jones, David B., 102, 103
Jusserand, Jean Jules, 215

KAHN, OTTO H., 249
Kansas City, Missouri, 335
Kerenski, Aleksandr, 264
Kiao-Chau, China, 331
Kola, military stores at, 278

LABOR, 216–219, 223, 229, 252–253, 255, 302
Labor, United States Department of, 223
Lamb, Charles, 215
Lane, Franklin K., 143–144
Lansing, Robert, 199, 283, 327; letters to, 173, 229, 301
Latin-American policy, 152–155
Lausanne, Switzerland, 295
League for Peace, proposal, 236
League of Nations, 4, 36–37, 293, 330; Wilson statements for, 211–213, 285, 286, 296, 305, 306, 314–324, 327–329, 334–338, 340; European attitude on, 277, 307–308, 327; adoption of Covenant, 331; Shantung settlement and, 332; opposition in the United States, 342–346; first meeting of, 350
League to Enforce Peace, 252, 347
Lee, Robert E., 89
Lenin, Nikolai, 264
Lenin–Trotsky government of Russia, 279
Lincoln, Abraham, 3, 7, 41–42, 90–93, 96, 259, 306, 325, 343
"Lincoln, Abraham, A Man of the People," 90–93
Lincoln's Birthday speech (Woodrow Wilson), 128–129

"Little group of willful men," 242–243
Lloyd George, David, 277, 301, 307, 327, 332
Lobbyists, 143
Lodge, Henry Cabot, 11, 289, 293, 296, 308, 335; Wilson attack on, 347–348
London, Treaty of (Pact of), 328, 330
London, Wilson address at, 308–311
Lotos Club (New York), 79
Lusitania, sinking of, 190, 195–198

McADOO, WILLIAM GIBBS, 157, 199, 272, 302
McCormick, Cyrus H., 266, 271
McKenna, Joseph, 274
McKinley, William, 46
Madero, Francisco I. (President of Mexico), 146
Madison Square (New York), 343
Madison Square Garden, 134
Makino, Baron Nobuaki, 329
Mandates, 316–317
Marbury, W. L., 157
March, General Peyton C., 283
Marcus Aurelius, 65
Martin, Chalmers, 152
Masaryk, Thomas G., 275, 282
Mason, Jeremiah, 23
Massachusetts, 325
Meeker, Royal, 280
Merchant marine, 222
Merchant ships, arming of, 242
Metropolitan Opera Company, 249
Mexico, 146; United States relations and crisis, 146, 161–163, 165, 168, 193–195, 208, 226–227
Middle West, Wilson trip through, 202
Middletown, Connecticut, 37
Militarism, 213–214
Mill, John Stuart, 22
Milner, Alfred, 295
"Ministry and the Individual, The," 94–96
Mobile, Alabama, 152
Monroe Doctrine, 163, 201, 241, 330
Montana, 335
Montenegro, 270

Moral force, Wilson on, 308
Morgan, J. P., 94, 167
Morley, Christopher, 251–252
Morrison, Frank W., 302
Moscow, monopoly of power, 341
Mount Vernon, Wilson address at, 290–291
"Muckrakers," the, 79
Murmansk, Russia, 278
Myers, Henry L., 301–302

NASHVILLE POST OFFICE (Tennessee), 142–143
National Guard, 250
National Museum, 160
National War Savings Committee, 279
Naval armaments, limitation of, 240
Navy, United States, 196–197
Navy officers, Wilson address to, 259–263
Neutrality, 197–199
Nevada, 335
"New Freedom," 120, 165
New Jersey, political activities of Wilson in, 101–117, 128
New Princeton Review, Wilson articles, 33–35, 37–39
New York, 284, 343; Wilson on bankers in, 94; politics in, 132–133, 277
New York Times, 164, 348
Newlands, Francis G., 158
Newspapermen, 274
Nicholas II, Czar of Russia, 243
North Dakota, 335
Norway, exports of, 266

OHIO, 40, 152
"One World," 210–211
Open Diplomacy, 273
Oratory, Wilson on, 23–24
Orient, frontage toward, 55–56
Ottoman Empire, 270

PACIFIC NORTHWEST, Wilson trip to, 335
Pacifism, 204
Page, Walter Hines, 164, 172, 173
Palestine, 281
Palmer, A. Mitchell, 138
Panama Canal, 157

Pan-Americanism, 200–202
Paris, 295; Wilson at, 284, 304, 306. See also Peace Conference
Party politics, 53, 187–188, 346–348
Patriotism, 257
Peace, Wilson on, 192–194, 205, 264, 268–271, 284–289, 314; European views, 258–259
Peace Commission (United States), 302
Peace Conference, 251, 307, 312, 313–314, 318, 332; Wilson at, 300–301, 305, 314–316; mandates, 316–317; League of Nations problems, 320–324, 327–328
Peace terms, 264, 268–271, 292, 295–296, 303, 304
Peace Treaty, 327–328, 334–335; Senate refusal to ratify, 335–336; Wilson speeches for, 336–348
"Peace without Victory" speech, 235–242
Pennypacker, Samuel W., 119
Pershing, John J., 208, 265
Pétain, Henri Philippe, 295
Petrograd, Russia, 255, 264, 272, 341
Phi Kappa Psi, 161
Philadelphia, Pennsylvania, 190
Philadelphia Public Ledger, 297
Philippines, 55–56
Philosophy, doctorate of, 26
Physiocrats, 38
Pindell, Henry M., 189–190
Pittsburgh, Pennsylvania, 96
Point Four program, early germ of, 335
Poindexter, Joseph B., 293
Poland, 271, 312, 314, 318, 332
Political Science Quarterly, Wilson article, 35–37
"Politics, Of the Study of" (New Princeton Review), 33–35
Preceptoral system (Princeton), 75, 78, 80–81
"Preceptoral System, The" (Alumni Weekly), 78
Preparedness, 175–177, 194, 199, 215–216
President of the United States, Wilson on, 118, 138–140, 141, 158–161, 177–178, 230

Price, I. Reese, 161
"Princeton for the Nation's Service," 46–47, 71–75
Princeton Inn, 108, 112
Princeton Theological Seminary, 112
Princeton University, 9, 11, 12, 20, 40, 46, 282; Wilson president of, 47, 66; his policies, 71–75, 78, 79, 80–84; opposition from alumni, 85, 86, 90, 96–98; his resignation, 108; attitude toward Wilson as President of United States, 124, 134, 156–157
Profiteering, 274
Profits, 256–258
Progressive Party, 224
Prohibition, wartime, 119, 273
Propaganda by War Department, 281–282
Protestant churches, 96
Prussia, 270
Public Ledger (Philadelphia), 297
Public Printing Office, 156
Pueblo, Colorado, Wilson collapse at, 335
Pulitzer, Ralph, 151
"Puritan, The," 51

RAILROADS, 217
Reading, Marquis of, 301
Red Cross, 338
Reichstag, 271
Reid, Mrs. Edith G., 66, 79, 132, 200
Religion, 46
Reparations, 308
Representatives, House of (United States), 242
Republican, Wilson definition of, 127
Republican Party, 86, 216, 220, 293, 346; Wilson on, 104, 107, 113–114, 116, 220–221, 224–225, 231, 291–292, 294, 347–348; opposition to Wilson on peace treaty, 291, 294, 296; victories, 297, 327, 350, 352
Rhine River, 318
Rice, Spring, 215
Richardson, Owen W., 84
Richmond, Virginia, 125
Riis, Jacob, 79
Ritz-Carlton Hotel, New York, 111

Rome, Georgia, 20, 164
Roosevelt, Franklin D., 101, 274, 275, 277, 350
Roosevelt, Theodore, 79, 231, 296; Wilson on, 129–130, 133, 348; attitude toward peace terms, 289, 293
Root, Elihu, 251, 255, 302
Rumania, 270
Rural Credits Act, 222
Russia, 279, 283, 307; abdication of czar, 243; United States Commission to, 249, 251, 255; revolution, 249, 264, 266, 283, 353–354; Wilson comments on, 265, 267–268, 270, 272, 275, 278–279, 299, 338–339, 340–342; France and, 314, 318; starvation, 332; war costs, 344

SAN DIEGO, California, 335
Saturday Evening Post, Wilson article in, 162–163
Savannah, Georgia, 31
Sayre, Mrs. Francis B., 188, 200. See also Wilson, Jessie Woodrow
Sayre, Nevin, 282
Scientific method, 47–50, 315
Scudder, Horace, 43
Seas, freedom of the, 239, 296–297
Secret treaties, 307, 313, 328
Selective Service, 250
Self-determination of peoples, 305–306, 319
Senate, United States, 289, 291; Wilson on, 188, 242–243; speech before, 235–242; refusal to ratify Peace Treaty, 335
Senate Foreign Relations Committee, 335
Serbia, 270
Shakespeare, William, 45
Shannon, Reverend Thomas B., 119
Shantung settlement, 328–332
Shaw, Dr. Albert, 157–158
Shaw, George Bernard, 3
Sheppard, Morris, 273
Shipping bill, 183, 186–187, 215–216
Siberia, 278–279, 283
Sims, William S., 255–256
Smith, Adam, 37–38
Smith, Alfred E., 277

Smith, James, Jr., 101, 105–107, 109, 113
Smith, Lucy M., 199
Smithsonian Institution, 160
"Social Co-ordination of the University, Report on the" (*Alumni Weekly*, Princeton), 80–84
South, Wilson on the, 40
South America, 158, 201–202
South Dakota, 335
Southwick, Mrs. Jessie Eldridge, 279–280
Soviet regime, 266. *See also* Russia
Spanish-American War, 51
Springfield (Massachusetts) *Republican*, 174
State of the Union messages, 349, 350–351
Staunton, Virginia, 7
Steffens, Lincoln, 79
Sterling, Hotel, Trenton, 116
Stockholm, Sweden, 339
Stone, W. J., 205–207
Submarines, 209–210
Sunday School Times, Wilson article, 76–78
Supreme Court, United States, 274
Supreme War Council, Allied, 278, 298, 299
Sussex, S.S., sinking of, 208–210

Taft, William Howard, 86, 105, 146, 165, 231, 297, 330, 331
Talcott, Charles, 12, 16, 17, 30, 32
Tarbell, Ida M., 79
Tariff bill, 143, 149–150, 351–352
Tariff Board, 216, 221
Textile and clothing price controls, 280
Thomas, Miss Carey, 27
Thomas, Norman (*The World Tomorrow*), 282–283
Thornton, J. R., 144
Tocqueville, Count Alexis de, 11
"Too proud to fight," 190–193
Toy, Mrs. Nancy, 174, 177, 182
Trade Commission, 170, 222
Treasury, United States, 333, 334
Trenton, New Jersey, 108, 109, 116, 146

Trotsky, Leon, 266
Trusts, 150
Tsingtao, China, 331
Tumulty, Joseph P., 108, 156
Turkey, 270, 332, 344
Turner, Frederick J., 66
Twain, Mark, 119

Unconditional surrender, 289
Undersea warfare, 206
Underwood, Oscar W., 142, 169
Union College, 347
United States, Wilson on the people of, 110, 192; relations with Mexico, 161–163, 208; effects of war on, 165–166; Wilson's blueprint for, 220–229; relations with Germany, 242; participation in World War, 243–247, 266; relations with Allies, 315–316, 319, 337, 340, 350; war costs, 344
Universal military service, 271–272
University of Virginia. *See* Virginia, University of
University of Virginia Magazine, 13, 15
"University Training and Citizenship," 43–45
Untermyer, Samuel, 150
Utah, 335

Vera Cruz, Mexico, 168
Versailles, France, Allied Supreme War Council at, 266, 299
Versailles, Treaty of, 4, 327. *See also* Peace Treaty
Viereck, George Sylvester, 346
Villa, Francisco (Pancho), 208
Villard, Oswald Garrison, 107, 145
Virginia, University of, 12, 13, 16, 161
Viviani, René Raphaël, 258
Vladivostok, Russia, 278

Waldorf-Astoria, New York, 137
Wall Street, 155, 279–280
War, message to Congress for declaration of, 243–247
War costs and dead, 344

War Department, United States, 281–282

War Industries Board, 258, 272–273

Warehouse Act, 222

Washington, George, 39, 43, 51, 287, 325, 347

Washington Post, 150

Webster, Daniel, 11, 23

Weizmann Commission (Zionist), 281

Wesleyan University, 37, 40

West, Andrew F., 90, 98

West Coast, Wilson's trip to, 335

West Hudson (New Jersey) Board of Trade, 111

West Point, Wilson address to graduates of, 213–214

White, William Allen, 11

White House, 118, 320

Wilhelmstrasse, 341

Williams, John Sharp, 151, 272

Wilmington, North Carolina, 16–17

Wilson, Edith Galt, 279–280, 292–293. *See also* Galt, Mrs. Norman

Wilson, Ellen Axson, 39, 46, 67, 98, 112, 200; death of, 164. *See also* Axson, Ellen

Wilson, Helen, 112, 199

Wilson, Jessie Woodrow, 112. *See also* Sayre, Mrs. Francis B.

Wilson, J. R. (brother), 142–143

Wilson, Reverend Joseph R. (father), 7

Wilson, Woodrow, birth and early life, 7; education, 9, 11–12, 16–18; articles on Bright and Gladstone, 13; *Congressional Government,* 25, 27, 30, 177–178; marriage, 31; teaching, 31, 37, 39–40; at Princeton University, 40, 46–47, 66, 71–80, 85–88, 90, 94, 96, 98; *History of the American People,* 43; New Jersey politics, 101–117; Presidential candidate, 133–134; first inaugural address, 140–141; Mexican crisis, 146, 161–163, 165, 194, 208; domestic reforms, 149, 155, 183–186, 187, 349; death of Mrs. Wilson, 164, 167–168; *Lusitania,* 190, 197–198; "Too proud to fight," 190–193; preparedness, 199; second marriage, 199–200, 202; speeches to counteract isolationism, 202–205; League of Nations, 211–213, 320–324, 327, 345–346, 350; second Presidential campaign, 220–229, 231; "Peace without Victory," 235–242; break with Germany, 242; "Little group of willful men," 242–243; war, 243–248; Fourteen Points, 268–271; "Four Point" speech, 275–277; Russian revolution, 283, 314, 332–334, 340–342, 353–354; peace terms, 284–289, 289–291, 292, 295–296, 303, 318–319; appeal for Democratic Congress, 292–295, 297; armistice, 298–300; at Peace Conference, 300–301, 304, 305–307, 308–312, 313–316, 316–317, 318, 327–328; brief return to United States, 325–327; effort to overcome opposition in United States to League of Nations and Peace Treaty, 330, 335–336, 336–348, 349–350; on democracy, 349–350, 350–351; Presidential elections (1920), 350; death, 353; "The road away from revolution," 353–355

Wise, Rabbi Stephen S., 251, 281

Wiseman, Sir William, 256

Woman Suffrage, 264

World economics, 203

World peace, Wilson's appeal to people of the world (Fourteen Points), 268–271

World Tomorrow, The, 282–283

World War I, 164, 165, 169, 249. *See also* United States

World War II, way paved for, 296

Wright, Ridgeway, 31

Wyoming, 335

"Young People and the Church, The" (*Sunday School Times*), 76–78

Zionist movement, 281